Patrick White Beyond the Grave

Patrick White Beyond the Grave

New Critical Perspectives

Edited by Ian Henderson and
Anouk Lang

ANTHEM PRESS

Anthem Press
An imprint of Wimbledon Publishing Company
www.anthempress.com

This edition first published in UK and USA 2015
by ANTHEM PRESS
75–76 Blackfriars Road, London SE1 8HA, UK
or PO Box 9779, London SW19 7ZG, UK
and
244 Madison Ave #116, New York, NY 10016, USA

© 2015 Ian Henderson and Anouk Lang editorial matter and selection;
individual chapters © individual contributors

The moral right of the authors has been asserted.

All rights reserved. Without limiting the rights under copyright reserved above,
no part of this publication may be reproduced, stored or introduced into
a retrieval system, or transmitted, in any form or by any means
(electronic, mechanical, photocopying, recording or otherwise),
without the prior written permission of both the copyright
owner and the above publisher of this book.

British Library Cataloguing-in-Publication Data
A catalogue record for this book is available from the British Library.

Library of Congress Cataloging-in-Publication Data
Patrick White beyond the grave : new critical perspectives /
edited by Ian Henderson and Anouk Lang.
   pages cm
Includes index.
ISBN 978-1-78308-397-8 (hard back) – ISBN 978-1-78308-398-5 (paper back) –
ISBN 978-1-78308-399-2 (pdf ebook) – ISBN 978-1-78308-445-6 (epub ebook)
1. White, Patrick, 1912-1990–Criticism and interpretation. I. Henderson, Ian,
1969-editor. II. Lang, Anouk, 1976-editor.
   PR9619.3.W5Z83 2015
   823'.912–dc23
   2015015239

ISBN-13: 978 1 78308 397 8 (Hbk)
ISBN-10: 1 78308 397 2 (Hbk)

ISBN-13: 978 1 78308 398 5 (Pbk)
ISBN-10: 1 78308 398 0 (Pbk)

Cover image © William Yang

This title is also available as an ebook.

CONTENTS

Acknowledgements		vii
Introduction		1
Part I.	**RESURRECTED PAPERS**	
Chapter 1.	The Evidence of the Archive *Margaret Harris and Elizabeth Webby*	17
Chapter 2.	Leichhardt and *Voss* Revisited *Angus Nicholls*	35
Part II.	**MANY IN ONE**	
Chapter 3.	White's London *David Marr*	67
Chapter 4.	Elective Affinities: Manning Clark, Patrick White and Sidney Nolan *Mark McKenna*	81
Chapter 5.	'Dismantled and Re-Constructed': *Flaws in the Glass* Re-Visioned *Georgina Loveridge*	101
Chapter 6.	Patrick White's Late Style *Andrew McCann*	117
Part III.	**THE PERFORMANCE OF READING**	
Chapter 7.	Patrick White's Expressionism *Ivor Indyk*	131

Chapter 8.	The Doubling of Reality in Patrick White's *The Aunt's Story* and Paul Schreber's *Memoirs of My Nervous Illness* Aruna Wittmann	141
Chapter 9.	Desperate, Marvellous Shuttling: White's Ambivalent Modernism Gail Jones	155
Chapter 10.	'Time and Its Fellow Conspirator Space': Patrick White's *A Fringe of Leaves* Brigid Rooney	163
Part IV.	**QUEER WHITE**	
Chapter 11.	Knockabout World: Patrick White, Kenneth Williams and the Queer Word Ian Henderson	181
Chapter 12.	Queering Sarsaparilla: Patrick White's Deviant Modernism Anouk Lang	193

Contributors	205
Index	209

ACKNOWLEDGEMENTS

The majority of chapters in this volume originated at the 'Patrick White: Modernist Impact, Critical Futures' conference held at the University of London in 2010. The editors would like to thank the institutions that supported the conference: the Menzies Centre for Australian Studies, King's College London, the British Australian Studies Association, the Institute of English Studies, School of Advanced Study, University of London, and the Lincoln Britain-Australia Trust. Particular thanks go to Professors Carl Bridge (KCL) and Warwick Gould (IES).

INTRODUCTION

Ian Henderson

There are moments when the critical revival of Patrick White seems rather a sustained defence of practising literary criticism at all in the twenty-first century; and in twenty-first-century Australia in particular. Even Simon During who, in *Patrick White* (1996), denounced his subject's relevance and, more recently, unfavourably compared White's talents with Saul Bellow's, did so principally to reassert the 'crucial social importance' of 'literary judgement' to contemporary culture.[1] But the situation can be put far more positively, and democratically. The 'revival' is nothing less than a celebration of reading itself. In the hands of the revivalists, reading White becomes – for all of us – an act which is at once personal and social, individualistic and political, devotional and subversive, sacred and profane.

Here, then, is reading as fundamentally relativistic, forged at the interface of print (or screen) and skin, of mind (even soul) and body, of one's own and other bodies (individuated or clumped as clans and societies of various hues), of individual desire and social politics, of art and the world and of the human and its horizons. This is not to say that such testing of the potentialities of human communication cannot occur elsewhere, including in board rooms, across suburban dining tables, on TV screens, in sports grounds across Australia and in numerous other sites of ritual Australian life. It is rather to station this specific contest in, through, and about the performance of literary reading. Hence to enter the realm of Patrick White's writing is quite distinct from closeted solipsism, but rather to test momentarily in apparent silence the capacities of the Australian word.

Whether or not one believes in the epic myth of White's personal artistic odyssey, for so many readers his words (consciously arranged and/or intuitively assembled) occasion new ambitions for their own. Over the years, many critics have registered the moment they became 'hooked' on White for this very reason. It seems to matter little whether this is a surrender to prevailing intellectual fashion or 'purely' for the stimulation it induced. What matters is the action it occasioned: not only the further provocation of reading itself but also *writing*, and thereby the perpetual invocation of challenging ideas.

Not least among these are the ones to which During refers: about how literature combats the insidious aggressions practised by 'our contemporary political and political-economic modes of government'.[2] And as often as not they are ideas seeded in a space – Australia – which is itself an entanglement of political, social, aesthetic and sacred practices, dynamically indigenous and/or warped in the crossing from every other part of the globe. But whatever the case, it is as the 'common' transfiguration of difficult reading into responsive writing (or provocative conversation) that we interpret During's literary judgement; rather, that is, than siting it exclusively in the person of the professional critic. And in White's work – enhanced no doubt by the historical breadth, depth and internationalism of his critical reception – we find suitably challenging ground for elite-level play in this everyday sport of art.[3]

Broadly, this new collection contributes to the 'new' White scholarship that emerged since his death in 1990. As such it registers the structural difference between analysing developments in the ongoing work of a living writer and treating the *oeuvre* of a still recently dead author for its peculiar mix of contemporary relevance and historic artefact. The former proceeded from the eventual discovery of a canonisable author and the reviewing with increasing seriousness of each new production to the seeking in academic journals to 'fit' new productions within White's perceived aesthetic, devotional and social preoccupations (a T. S. Eliot-style jostling, as it were, of the White 'tradition').[4] It celebrated or railed against changes in his motivations and style: most notoriously with the apparent apostasy of *The Twyborn Affair* (1979), *Flaws in the Glass* (1981), *Memoirs of Many in One* (1986), the 'late crazy plays' and overt political activism.[5]

What has happened since? The impact of David Marr's magisterial yet witty biography, *Patrick White: A Life* (1991), can hardly be underestimated. Read, re-read and approved by White himself shortly before his death, it brought new attention to a writer's life which had traversed so much of Australia's political, social and artistic development in the course of his 78 years, evinced not least in White's various allegiances to Britain, America and cosmopolitan Europe. It found illuminating but not overbearing biographical details in White's plots, articulated the epic qualities of his own literary development and eclipsed in its currency the very literature it set out to celebrate. Marr's collection of White's letters followed, in 1994, revealing further both the searing personality behind the work and his significant place among so many other influential practitioners and promoters of twentieth-century arts in Australia and beyond.

But in the 1990s, contextualised by fierce debates in public culture over the realities and extent of colonial violence and contemporary oppression, Australian criticism was justifiably preoccupied with seeking to understand how the complex politics of race registered in the country's literature. It sought and tested critical methodologies drawn from postcolonial theory to approach historic and contemporary writing by Aboriginal Australians and their representation in non-Aboriginal culture. Work on White was comparatively thin on the ground as a result,[6] and indeed a sustained focus on indigenous representations arrived belatedly in White studies with Cynthia vanden Driesen's *Writing the Nation: Patrick White and the Indigene* (2009).[7]

Even so nascent postcolonialism merged with Jungian theory in David Tacey's landmark and still influential *Edge of the Sacred: Transformation in Australia* (1995), where *Voss* featured prominently.[8] The work of less metaphysically inclined psychoanalytic and semiotic theorists also began to creep into White scholarship,[9] though the contributors to John McLaren's *Prophet of the Desert* (1995), like others maintaining faith in the insights gained from straight (if theoretically aware) literary history, were more concerned with placing and illuminating White's novels in the context of European modernist thought.[10]

During's monograph (1996) drew together historical and theoretical approaches to literature, psychoanalysing the author as the product equally of an ambitious mother and a nation desperate for artistic credibility, in the process denigrating – in excessive terms – White's literary skill and declaring his work of doubtful future relevance. (His stance has since been itself historically contextualised and critiqued by writers of the right and left respectively.[11])

Among the many striking features of this rare example of Australian critical iconoclasm, what stands out particularly clearly is During's vision of Australia's future. For him, 'White's conceptions of suburbia, Aborigines, women and homosexuality, [did] not quite fit the Australia of the 1990s'; 'official Australian culture is characterised by a policy of tolerance and integration'.[12] More than anything else, this places During's book at the tail end of Australia's Hawke/Keating Labor governments, with 'reconciliation' seemingly realisable, recognition of the Stolen Generations imminent and a republic on the cards. In fact in 2015, if specifics have altered, White's conceptions seem as relevant as ever. Himmelfarb might be an asylum seeker imprisoned on Manus Island, Alf Dubbo the subject of racialist laws under the Northern Territory Emergency Intervention Act, Mrs Godbold a benefit scrounger and Mrs Hare a madwoman turned extremist. Meanwhile, Bluey is a buy-to-let investor who boasts membership of a Pentacostal megachurch and skill at 'plating up' to a restaurant standard at home. Though only half of his mates are white, none is divorced from the trajectory of White's vision of our capacity for ordinary Australian malice.[13]

Criticism did not fall completely silent after During's attack. Michael Giffin's monograph *Arthur's Dream: Patrick White and the Religious Imagination* was published in the same year.[14] Tipping into the twenty-first century, James Bulman-May's *Patrick White and Alchemy* conjured medievalist alchemical lore as the basis of the 'spiritual' White.[15] But a more enduring thread in the exploration of the sacred and White's writing has come from Bill Ashcroft and Lyn McCredden, notably in their contributions to *Intimate Horizons: The Post-Colonial Sacred in Australian Literature* which was published in 2009,[16] and in scholarly journals and edited collections since. It is with their 'super-enriched' vein of twenty-first-century 'sacred' White literary studies that Andrew McCann engages in this volume.[17]

McCann has been at the forefront of theorising White's queer relations with the Australian suburban milieu since the late-1990s. In one sense he shares Nathanael O'Reilly's later ambition in *Exploring Suburbia: The Suburbs in the Contemporary Australian Novel*, which demonstrates the ambivalence of White's representations of his fictional suburb Sarsaparilla.[18] In another, his work better resembles later work by Jennifer Rutherford, Elizabeth McMahon, Brigitta Olubas and Bridget Grogan in terms of his turn to complex theories of modernity, the psyche and the body to articulate the more finely grained complexities of White's representation of 'ordinary' Australians.[19] This is not least by seeking ground beyond the binaries ('cosmopolis good/suburbia bad') that usually structure approaches to White's social critique. In so doing he ventures into – and illuminates the links between – questions of the sacred, White's language and his sexuality, as explored more fully in his contribution to this volume.

If During's monograph represented a critical nadir in the reception of White's prose, the regular revival of White's plays – remarkable for any twentieth-century Australian drama – kept him current on the Australian stage, not least for their continuous reinvention through innovative direction and performance. Productions included the Playbox Theatre's *Big Toys* (1993), a string of Neil Armfield-directed revivals of *A Cheery Soul* (1992, 1994, 1996, 2000), Benedict Andrews' *The Season at Sarsaparilla* (2007, 2008), Michael Kantor's *The Ham Funeral* (2000, 2005) and Adam Cook's version of the same play at the Adelaide Festival of 2012 (the 50th anniversary of its original rejection); however, even this impressive list is not comprehensive.[20] Their success speaks not only to a continuing faith in White among Australian audiences but also to the value placed in his plays by Australian performers. As Armfield himself noted in 2012, White's plays are unlike anything else in the Australian theatre. They have their feet in vaudeville and their heads in the stars, in the vaulted air of the cathedral. They have a crystalline hardness tempered with earth and blood. And the plays will continue to be staged, because he created parts that actors love to play.[21]

The prominence of these productions, moreover, might be coupled to a series of sometimes unexpected events which brought White back into the headlines. The death of Manoly Lascaris, White's partner, on 13 November 2003 was a historical event in its own right, leading to obituaries in the press and moving recollections by Marr and, later, Vrasidas Karalis and Debra Adelaide.[22] Wrangling ensued about whether or not to transform the Centennial Park residence Lascaris had shared with White into a museum or artist's retreat; the home was eventually sold into private ownership.[23] In July 2006, the *Australian* newspaper's Jennifer Sexton revealed 10 publishers had rejected chapter 3 of *The Eye of the Storm* (1973) sent as a sample by an 'unknown' author. But in November of the same year came the great *coup de théâtre* of White studies: literary agent Barbara Mobbs' revelation that she had not, as commanded by White, burned a stash of papers and manuscripts, but withheld them from the public until after Lascaris' death. Sold to the National Library of Australia, the papers have become an extraordinary and revitalising resource, prompting new studies and collections – like this one – their story told within these pages by Margaret Harris and Elizabeth Webby.[24]

The excitement of the White manuscript discoveries contextualised one of the most significant White-focused symposiums of the last decade, 'Remembering Patrick White', which took place in Sydney in late May 2007. The subsequent volume, *Remembering Patrick White: Contemporary Critical Essays* (2010), edited by co-convenors Elizabeth McMahon and Brigitta Olubas, has become in turn a landmark in White studies whose influence is readily seen in these pages.

As well as contributions by Brennan, Olubas and Rutherford already mentioned above, it was notable for developments in interpretations of the White 'sacred' by Veronica Brady, McCredden and Ashcroft. There was also attention to those later plays of White's which have not been revived, but which, John McCallum has it, anticipated and pushed Australian dramaturgy forward.[25] And *Remembering*'s 1994–2009 bibliography of critical work on White complemented Brian Hubber and Vivian Smith's of 2004.[26] But of keener significance for our purposes was Brigid Rooney's re-articulation of White's political activism and his literature as interwoven via a concept of 'irritation': on the 'real' skin as the motivation to speak and write; on the 'surface' of his writing. 'White's prose yields irritable energies directed towards the carving out of depths, so that surfaces paradoxically become sites of intensity of feeling, and this does the work of affective and social excavation.'[27] This speaks not only to the carnality of language discussed by Ian Henderson in the present collection but also to the shuttlings and jitterings which characterise the performance of reading White for Ivor Indyk and Gail Jones in this volume, the starting place for their own 'excavations' of his meaning. Rooney's approach to White was more broadly contextualised in a monograph on Australian public intellectuals;[28] and in the current volume her focus is also on literary structures – here the 'chronotrope' – which open out socialised experiences of reading.

But perhaps most influential for this volume has been Elizabeth McMahon's essay on *The Twyborn Affair*, discussed by several contributors to the present volume. In bringing conceptions of 'late style' and queer epistemologies into dialogue, McMahon also punctured traditional teleologies of a writer's development. Queer readings, then, range across the work, seeking later explicit features of White's writing that were 'always already' there. It is, in a manner, analogous to the effects of reading the work of a dead author, and to the shift from locating the sacred in climactic epiphanies to discovering its immanence in material reality,[29] but here related to the sexual politics of White's life history, and the not infrequently homophobic nature of his critical reception. Hence McMahon's chapter in *Remembering Patrick White* speaks to a rich conversation regarding White's queerness which continues in these pages.[30]

The rediscovery of White's papers also energised the lead-up to the centenary of his birth in 2012. This included the re-issue of *The Vivisector* as a 'Penguin Classic' in 2009 with an introduction by J. M. Coetzee, and its shortlisting for the 'Lost Man Booker Prize' of 2010,[31] as well as the appearance of a great rarity, a film-adaptation of a White novel, Fred Schepisi's *The Eye of the Storm* (2011) starring Judy Davis, Charlotte Rampling and Geoffrey Rush. It also saw the Adelaide Festival's 'apology' production of *The Ham Funeral* (later adapted and broadcast on ABC Radio National), the National Library of Australia exhibition *The Life of Patrick White* (2012) and the publication by Random House Australia of one of the prize discoveries among the Mobbs papers, an unfinished yet publishable novel, *The Hanging Garden* (2012).

In the lead-up to the centenary, Sydney University Press also released *Patrick White within the Western Literary Tradition* (2010) celebrating the rich comparative critical work in White studies of John Beston over the last thirty-five years.[32] In 2012 itself a special edition of *Cercles*, the University of Rouen's journal of Anglophone culture, was devoted to White, under the editorship of David Coad.[33] Among other contributions it included a stand-out chapter by Charles Lock whose attention to grammatical detail for understanding the 'conduct' of White's writing joins the many critics, like McCann, Rooney and Olubas above, who illuminate White through interest in the relationship between the 'surface' detail of his words and their social, devotional or in Ashcroft's terms, horizonal – beyond the edge of their material – meanings.[34]

Two major conferences occurred in the lead-up to 2012, both outside Australia. 'Patrick White: Modernist Impact, Critical Futures (2010)' was hosted by King's College London and the Institute of English Studies, University of London, and is the original source of this volume. The other took place in 2012 at the University of Hyderabad, India, under the auspices of the Association for the Study of Australia in Asia. This has led to the publication in 2014 of a new and splendidly inclusive collection of work on White, *Patrick White Centenary: The Legacy of a Prodigal Son*, edited by Cynthia vanden Driesen and Bill Ashcroft.[35] This has been published too recently for the contributors to this volume to engage with it in detail; however, it offers a rich dialogue with the work published here. It presents a magnificent range of contributions, including further work on White and the sacred, his drama,[36] White and film,[37] the latter both adding to twenty-first-century scholarly interest in White and music,[38] and the visual arts.[39] The volume is noteworthy also for its comparative work by and about Asian writers among others, and importantly, contributions from Indigenous Australian scholars.[40] It is worth mentioning, though, that the principal turns in Australian literary research which it neglects are also neglected here: towards interactions between Australian and American literary networks and readerships; and broader understandings of Australian literary culture made possible by digital research.[41]

The chapters in this volume dismantle and reconstruct established ways of approaching White's life and work, demanding moreover yet newer ways of understanding its significance. So if all of the chapters give a sense nonetheless of the rich critical history of White's reception, they are lodged in forward-oriented methodologies of the critical present. And as much as they account for White's importance today, they are designed to inspire new work from a rising generation of scholars.

In their chapter, Harris and Webby give an overview of the newly discovered notebooks and manuscripts enhanced by their long experience researching White's writing, and their thorough examination of the 'new' collection's breadth and scope. And if Harris and Webby's chapter throws down the gauntlet to young scholars of twentieth-century literary studies the world over, Angus Nicholls's remarkable new reading of the German romanticism in *Voss* (1957) provides an inspiring example of what practised hands can do with the hoard.

In 'White's London', David Marr reveals in tone and content White's queer history in London: his connections to the city's homosexual subculture, the impact of the Blitz on his art, his regular returns to London, now a famous writer, and his continued identification as a Londoner living in Australia. Mark McKenna traces the ups and downs of another queer relationship, the oftentimes unreciprocated love of Australia's 'great' historian Manning Clark for the visionary he saw in White. He shows how Clark's monumental multi-volume *History of Australia* expresses greater allegiance to the preoccupations of Australia's 'elite' mid-century writers and artists, notably White and Sidney Nolan, than to the work of Clark's contemporaries in the academic discipline of history. McKenna's comparative biography is suggestive also of how this approach can add to the more familiar comparative literary criticism of White studies.

With '"Dismantled and Re-Constructed": *Flaws in the Glass* Re-Visioned', Georgina Loveridge begins a more overt dismantling of our understanding of White in the wake of his own late re-envisioning of his work. The chapter, then, zeroes in on the potential for critical collapse threatened (or perhaps promised) in the preoccupation with jitters, tremblings, contradictory times, ambivalences, madnesses, revisions and disconcerting revelations in nearly all our chapters. She reads *Flaws* as a treatise on the nature of truth with White extending a continuous dismantling of his own symbolic apparatus and offering a blueprint for re-reading his entire work.

In 'Patrick White's Late Style', Andrew McCann shows how White's, and our, minor quakes find full expression in *Memoirs of Many in One* (1986): in hilarity not tragedy. He argues that over the course of his career, White's impulse is towards the farcical collapse of signification which in itself can be figured as a revelatory path to non-revelatory non-understanding. The postcolonial 'sacred' turn in White scholarship is turned on its head; or rather it disintegrates alongside White's apparent faith in language's ability to carry universal themes. Hence *things* as idio-psychic projections of sacred feeling in White's work, a subtle process like those explored in Indyk's and Jones's chapters, for McCann are finally destroyed in White's late style by the very thing-ness those projections celebrated. From McCann's chapter, too, Henderson has drawn his attention to the abjectness of language itself in White's work. But it is here for McCann where the sacred becomes 'impossible' that White's indicates new possibilities for its cognizance.

In 'The Performance of Reading', contributors dwell upon the experience of reading Patrick White's prose, tracing the effects and development of White's language, how it works. In 'Patrick White's Expressionism', Ivor Indyk identifies White's exaggeration of small, complex emotional jitters, placing this in the context of both an expressive mode of Australian literature and modernism at large, describing (with eloquent self-reflexivity) 'the *experience* of reading a Patrick White novel', affording insight thereby also into the significance of material objects in White's writing. He articulates what White's language can *do* to the living body, while widening the remit to consider also White's work as 'operatic' and/or 'epic' in that its account of dynamic emotions passing between characters, and between text and reader, describe 'not individuals' but 'a people', a people defined 'by their nervousness'. Aruna Wittman's chapter, which follows, compares *The Aunt's Story* (1948) with Paul Schreber's *Memoirs of My Nervous Illness* (1903), confirming not only the precision of White's description of such ways of being-in-the-world but also enabling her to illuminate the specificities of that 'madness' which so many artists and critics sense 'behind' modernist aesthetics.

Gail Jones, in 'Desperate, Marvellous Shuttling: White's Ambivalent Modernism', brings Theodor Adorno's characterisation of the post-war era, T. J. Clark's thoughts on modernist visual imagery and Walter Benjamin's *Arcades Project* into dialogue with White's post-war novel, *The Aunt's Story*, providing a deeply insightful meditation on its infamous middle section, the 'Jardin Exotique', to reassess the controversial spiritualism of White's work. This she revises through an exposition of 'faithless belief' lodged in 'an assertive vulgar materialism' in ways which have spurred Henderson's thoughts on the incarnation of Whitean language, dwelling also upon the possibilities of a non-idealist form of resurrection. Her attention to 'textual agitation and indeterminacy' resonates also with Indyk's reading of Whitean affect (and opens, incidentally, new critical pathways for engagement with her own work as a novelist). In effect, moreover, with their sensitive readings of White's style, both Jones and Indyk offer a rejoinder to During's recently restated dismissal of his literary skills.

In 'Time and Its Fellow Conspirator Space', Brigid Rooney explores what she refers to as the 'chronotopic system' of the narrative in White's *A Fringe of Leaves* (1976). She illuminates metaphors of movement within the novel, principally those enclosed spaces in which characters travel (ships and carriages, for example), demonstrating their significance not only to the formulation of readerly experience within the novel (picturing, as they do, our own travelling with the narrative) but also to the ways in which the overlaying of asynchronous conceptions and experiences of time inform and problematize the novel's postcolonialism. Without shying away from the novel's possible re-inscription of white-settler claims on Aboriginal territory, she shows how readers, in working and being worked by the narrative, enact multiple and difficult claims on and exclusions from country.

Opening 'Queer White' with 'Knockabout World: Patrick White, Kenneth Williams and the Queer Word', Henderson builds on McKenna's comparative biography and on queer theoretical approaches to White's writing, venturing a new interpretation of White's linguistic experimentation via a historical approach. He compares White's language with that of *Carry On* star Kenneth Williams (1924–1988), who read and commented on White's *The Living and the Dead* in 1982. This enables White's writing (and modernism per se) to be brought into dialogue with Polari, 'the lost language of gay men', which is in tune with other scholarly theories of the 'incarnation' of language in White's work. Meanwhile, in 'Queering Sarsaparilla' Anouk Lang demonstrates how, now a more overt scholarly exploration is 'out', it can contribute to understandings of modernism's global reach.

All these chapters represent recent returns to White by the contributing authors, or work from emerging scholars. They deploy methodologies of the critical present by writers working on opposite sides of the globe. But they also point new ways forward for scholarship on White, on global modernism and on queer literature and theory, with a view to the extraordinary gift we have been given in White's papers delivered beyond the grave.

Notes

1 Simon During, *Patrick White* (Oxford: Oxford University Press, 1996); Simon During, 'Patrick White, Saul Bellow and the Problem of Literary Value', *Australian Literary Studies* 27, no. 2 (2012): 1–17 (16). The latter was drawn from a keynote paper at the conference from which the contributions to this volume are drawn. For During, while White's rise had been sustained by the peculiarities of the mid-twentieth century academy, and while the academy itself was funded by a liberal hegemony, the techniques professional literary criticism instils allow us to see how 'great literature of the modern period is always wary of our contemporary political and political – economic modes of government'. Hence the necessity that critics eschew 'liberalism' and practise 'literary judgement': which in During's case means abhorring White for his inability to express the inner lives of his characters in a language appropriate to their condition.
2 During, 'Problem', 16.
3 This, in accord with During, entails quite a different vision of literature and/or culture from that 'viewed from the state's point of view as a national resource to be administered and taught'; During, *White*, 100.
4 See During, *White*, 9–10.
5 Regarding the apostasy, see David J. Tacey, 'Patrick White: The End of Genius', *Meridian: La Trobe University English Review* 5 (May 1986): 89–91; repr. in *Critical Essays on Patrick White*, ed. Peter Wolfe (Boston: G. K. Hall, 1990), 60–64 (63): 'In a sense White's last two novels, as well as his own *Self-Portrait*, have attempted to smear dirt and shit upon his own religious edifice, his literary *oeuvre* and his past. He seems to delight in his own self-levelling, to relish his own collapse and to enjoy the stench of his own decay.' Note also John McCallum, 'The Late, Crazy Plays', in *Remembering Patrick White: Contemporary Critical Essays*, eds Elizabeth McMahon and Brigitta Olubas (Amsterdam: Rodopi, 2010), 139–48.
6 An exception was Mark Williams, *Patrick White*, Macmillan Modern Novelists (London: Macmillan, 1993), which took a comparative approach placing White's early work in the context of 1930s England and later in terms of twentieth-century white-settler writing.
7 Cynthia vanden Driesen, *Writing the Nation: Patrick White and the Indigene* (Amsterdam: Rodopi, 2009).
8 David Tacey, *Edge of the Sacred: Transformation in Australia* (Melbourne: HarperCollins, 1995). See also David Tacey, *Patrick White: Fiction and the Unconscious* (Oxford: Oxford University Press, 1988).
9 See, for example, Joan Kirkby, 'The Lure of Abjection: Kristeva's Borderliner and Australian Masculinity in Hal Porter, A. D. Hope, Patrick White', in *Representation,*

Discourse and Desire: Contemporary Australian Culture and Critical Theory, ed. Patrick Fuery (South Melbourne: Longman Cheshire, 1994), 138–62; and David Coad, 'Intertextuality in Patrick White's *The Solid Mandala*', *Commonwealth: Essays and Studies* 17, no. 2 (Spring 1995): 111–16.

10 John McLaren and Mary-Ellen Ryan, ed., *Prophet from the Desert: Critical Essays on Patrick White* (Melbourne: Red Hill, 1995).

11 Michael Giffin, 'Four Approaches to Patrick White', *Quadrant* 50, no. 12 (December 2006): 70–75; Jennifer Rutherford, 'Homo Nullius: The Politics of Pessimism in *The Tree of Man*' in McMahon and Olubas, *Remembering*, 47–64.

12 During, *White*, 99; 100.

13 Bernadette Brennan has written in a more sustained and serious manner on the ongoing relevance of *Riders in the Chariot*, from which these characters are drawn. Bernadette Brennan, '*Riders in the Chariot*: A Tale of Our Times', in McMahon and Olubas, *Remembering*, 19–34.

14 Michael Giffin, *Arthur's Dream: Patrick White and the Religious Imagination* (Sydney: Spaniel, 1996).

15 James Bulman-May, *Patrick White and Alchemy* (Melbourne: Australian Scholarly Publishing, 2001).

16 Bill Ashcroft, Frances Devlin-Glass and Lyn McCredden, *Intimate Horizons: The Post-Colonial Sacred in Australian Literature* (Hindmarsh: AFT Press, 2009).

17 Building on earlier work: see Andrew McCann, 'The Obstinacy of the Sacred', *Antipodes* 19, no. 2 (2005): 152–57.

18 Nathanael O'Reilly *Exploring Suburbia: The Suburbs in the Contemporary Australian Novel* (Amherst: Teneo Press, 2012). See also Garry Kinnane, 'Shopping at Last! History, Fiction and the Anti-Suburban Tradition', *Australian Literary Studies* 18 (1998): 41–55.

19 Jennifer Rutherford, *The Gauche Intruder: Freud, Lacan and the White Australian Fantasy* (Melbourne: Melbourne University Press, 2000); on McMahon see below. From Bridget Grogan see 'The Decorative Voice of Hidden, Secret Flesh: Corporeal Dynamics in Patrick White's Fiction', *Journal of Literary Studies* 30, no. 2 (2014): 1–19; 'Ladies and Gentlemen? Language, Body and Identity in *The Aunt's Story* and *The Twyborn Affair*', *Australian Literary Studies* 28, no. 3 (2013): 59–71; 'Resuscitating the Body: Corporeality in the Fiction of Patrick White', *JASAL* 12, no. 3 (2012), accessed 21 January 2015 online: http://www.nla.gov.au/openpublish/index.php/jasal/article/view/2547/3319; and 'Abjection and Compassion: Affective Corporeality in Patrick White's Fiction', *Journal of Literary Studies* 28, no. 3(2012): 93–115. In her study of White's early plays, Olubas not only reiterates 'Andrew McCann's argument that White's social purchase, his satire, is primarily aesthetic but also extends this insight to argue that these plays stage a meeting of poetic and civil worlds. In this way, in White's drama we see, literally, the aesthetic as the domain in which the self meets the state, where interiority unfolds'. Brigitta Olubas, '"Some of the Doors of the House Have Never Been Seen Open": Poetic Habitation and Social Space in Patrick White's Early Drama', in McMahon and Olubas, *Remembering*, 149–62 (161).

20 For a more comprehensive listing, see the AusStage database, accessed 15 January 2015 online: http://www.ausstage.edu.au/pages/work/2130/.

21 Neil Armfield, *Meanjin* 71, no. 2 (2012): 18–28 (28).

22 David Marr, 'Gentle Foil to Patrick White's Fury', *Sydney Morning Herald*, 22 November 2003, accessed 20 January 2015 online: http://www.smh.com.au/articles/2003/11/21/1069027331090.html?from=storyrhs; Vrasidas Karalis, *Recollections of Manoly Lascaris* (Blackheath, NSW: Brandl & Schlesinger, 2008); Debra Adelaide, 'No One Comes to See

Me Now: Manoly Lascaris and Patrick White's Ghost', *The Monthly*, December 2011 – January 2012): 68–71, accessed 15 January 2015 online: http://www.themonthly.com.au/issue/2011/december/1327012684/debra–adelaide/no–one–comes–see–me–now.
23. See Emma-Kate Symons, 'The Eclipse of a Cultural Icon', *Weekend Australian*, 30–31 October 2004, 21; Sharon Verghis, 'Eye of the Sale Storm', *Sydney Morning Herald*,15 November 2004, 15, accessed 15 January 2015 online: http://www.smh.com.au/articles/2004/11/14/1100384418827.html?from=storyrhs; 'The Patrick White House', NSW Government Environment and Heritage register, accessed 15 January 2015 online: http://www.environment.nsw.gov.au'/heritageapp/ViewHeritageItemDetails.aspx?ID=5001213.
24. Harris and Webby's work was funded by an Australian Research Council project 'Patrick White in the Twenty-First Century' centred on the NLA's new archive.
25. John McCallum in McMahon and Olubas, *Remembering*, 139–48.
26. Brian Hubber and Vivian Smith, ed., *Patrick White: A Bibliography* (Newcastle, NSW: Oak Knoll Press, 2004).
27. Brigid Rooney, 'Public Recluse: Patrick White's Literary – Political Returns', in McMahon and Olubas, *Remembering*, 3–18 (15).
28. Brigid Rooney, *Literary Activists: Writer-Intellectuals and Australian Public Life* (St Lucia: University of Queensland Press, 2009).
29. See Danny Anwar, 'The Island Called Utopia in Patrick White's *The Tree of Man*', *Southerly*, 74, no. 1 (2014): 217–34 (219).
30. The influence of McMahon's sophisticated renderings of White's significance can also be seen in White scholarship that appears in *Southerly*, of which she is a co-editor. See, for example, Anwar, 'Island': 217–34; and W. D. Aschroft, 'The Horizon of the Future', 74, no. 1 (2014):12–35.
31. 'The Lost Man Booker Prize', accessed 21 January 2015 online: http://www.themanbookerprize.com/lost–man–booker–prize.
32. John Beston, *Patrick White Within the Western Literary Tradition* (Sydney: Sydney University Press, 2010).
33. David Coad, 'Introduction: Patrick White Centenary: A Tribute', *Cercles* 26 (2012), accessed 16 January 2015 online: http://www.cercles.com/n26/coad.pdf.
34. Charles Lock, 'And Stood Breathing: Patrick White and the Novelistic Discourse of Modernism', *Cercles* 26 (2012), accessed 16 January 2015 online: http://www.cercles.com/n26/lock.pdf. Ashcroft, 'Horizon', 22–23. See also Bill Ashcroft, '*A Fringe of Leaves*: The Edge of the Sacred', *Cercles* 26 (2012), accessed 16 January 2015 online: http://www.cercles.com/n26/ashcroft.pdf.
35. Cynthia vanden Driesen and Bill Ashcroft, *Patrick White Centenary: The Legacy of a Prodigal Son* (Cambridge: Cambridge Scholars Press, 2014).
36. May-Brit Ackerholt, '"A Glorious Terrible Life": The Dual Image in Patrick White's Dramatic Language', in vanden Driesen and Ashcroft, *Centenary*, 152–63. For other recent work on White's drama, see John McCallum, *Belonging: The Story of 20th-Century Australian Drama* (Sydney: Currency, 2009), 91–112; Elizabeth Schafer, 'A Ham Funeral: Patrick White, Collaboration and Neil Armfield', *Australian Studies* 3 (2011), accessed 21 January 2015 online: http://www.nla.gov.au/openpublish/index.php/australian–studies/article/view/2227/2641, a paper which began life as a keynote at the London conference; John Arnold, 'The True History of the Publication of Patrick White's "Peter Plover's Party"', *Script and Print* 37, no. 1 (2013): 40–44; and Denise Varney, 'Australian Theatrical Modernism and Modernity: Patrick White's

Season at Sarsaparilla', *Australasian Drama Studies* 62 (2013): 25–40, 224. Varney holds an Australian Research Council Discovery Grant (2014–16) for *Patrick White and Australian Theatrical Modernism: From Modern Drama to Contemporary Performance.*

37 Sissy Helf, 'Patrick White-lite: Fred Schepisi's Filmic Adaptation of *The Eye of the Storm*', in vanden Driesen and Ashcroft, *Centenary*, 181–95; for other recent work on White and film, see Elizabeth Webby and Margaret Harris, 'Patrick White and Film', *JASAL* 13, no. 2 (2013), accessed 21 January 2015 online: http://www.nla.gov.au/openpublish/index.php/jasal/article/view/2728/3733; and Jonathan Rayner, 'Meditative Tangents: Fred Schepisi's *The Eye of the Storm* (2011)', *Australian Studies* 4 (2012): 1–15, accessed 16 January 2015 online: http://www.nla.gov.au/openpublish/index.php/australian-studies/article/viewFile/3056/3589.

38 See Fiona Richards, '"Rubbed by the Warming Violins": Music and Patrick White', *Cercles* 26 (2012), accessed 21 January 2015 online: http://www.cercles.com/n26/richards.pdf.

39 Notably the much-cited Helen Hewitt, *Patrick White, Painter Manqué: Paintings, Painters and Their Influence on His Writing* (Melbourne: Melbourne University Press, 2002).

40 Vicki Grieves, 'Patrick White, "Belltrees" and the "Station Complex": Some Reflections', in vanden Driesen and Ashcroft, *Centenary*, 429–42; and Jeanine Leane, 'White's Tribe: Patrick White's Representation of the Australian Aborigine in *A Fringe of Leaves*', in vanden Driesen and Ashcroft, *Centenary*, 257–68. See also Jeanine Leane, 'Tracking Our Country in Settler Literature' [Dorothy Green Memorial Lecture], *JASAL* 14, no. 3 (2014), accessed 21 January 2015 online: http://www.nla.gov.au/openpublish/index.php/jasal/article/viewFile/3294/4109.

41 See Roger Osborne, 'Patrick White and the American Middlebrow: Book-of-the-Month Chooses Voss', in *Telling Stories: Australian Life and Literature 1935–2012*, eds Tanya Dalziell and Paul Genoni (Melbourne: Monash University Publishing, 2013), 188–94; Robert Dixon and Nicholas Birns, eds, *Reading Across the Pacific: Australia – United States Intellectual Histories* (Sydney: Sydney University Press, 2010); Katherine Bode, *Reading by Numbers: Recalibrating the Literary Field* (London: Anthem Press, 2012. See also Robyn Holmes, 'Enhancing the Ebook: Patrick White and the Australian Cultural Landscape', *Humanities Australia* 3 (2012): 35–44, accessed 21 January 2015 online: http://www.humanities.org.au/Portals/0/documents/Publications/HumanitiesAustralia/Issue_3/HumAust3.pdf.pdf.

Part I
RESURRECTED PAPERS

Chapter 1

THE EVIDENCE OF THE ARCHIVE

Margaret Harris and Elizabeth Webby

Literature made front-page news in Australia on 3 November 2006: not a common occurrence. In Patrick White's home town, the lead story in the broadsheet *Sydney Morning Herald* was a report by his biographer David Marr about the National Library of Australia's purchase of a collection of Patrick White's papers, previously thought destroyed, from his agent and literary executor, Barbara Mobbs. 'The old bastard,' Marr began. 'Patrick White told the world over and over again that none of this existed. "Don't bother hunting for drafts and manuscripts," he snapped when I asked him years ago. "They've all gone into the pit." They hadn't.'[1] Other media, both in Australia and internationally, picked up the story. The *Times Literary Supplement* ran a major essay on White by novelist David Malouf, while the *Australian Book Review* carried a piece by Marie-Louise Ayres, then the Library's curator of manuscripts, in which she described the material and indicated some of the insights it provides.[2]

In preparation for the announcement of this extraordinary acquisition, Dr Ayres had led National Library of Australia (NLA) staff in an operation conducted in secrecy. They compiled a finding list of the 33 boxes of material found for release simultaneously with the announcement: an extremely valuable document describing the various items in the collection, which itself made history because of the way in which it was put together.[3] Such catalogues are usually the work of a single librarian over an extended period, whereas this team performed the task in a matter of weeks. A small exhibition accompanied the announcement: it included *realia* like White's trademark beret and beanie, a pair of his spectacles and a selection of manuscript material. The librarians involved were aware that they were part of a once-in-a-lifetime experience; scholars round the world were stirred (there were early enquiries from as far afield as Scandinavia and the United States); and there was considerable public interest.

Soon, it was apparent that this material constituted 'literary treasure' in Marr's phrase.[4] He was able to show, for example, that throughout the 10 working notebooks are scattered drafts for the openings of half a dozen of White's novels, including *The Aunt's Story* (1948). The richness of the treasure has become even more apparent as we have embarked on plumbing the depths of MS9982. In this chapter, we outline how the new material provides the occasion for a stocktaking of Patrick White and his legacy and what it shows about his writing life.[5]

In the first place, it needs to be understood that although Patrick White's critical reputation underwent the usual slump after his death in 1990, he has never ceased to attract scholarly attention. Year after year, the AustLit database tabulates more critical publication on White than on any other Australian author (Henry Lawson is the runner-up).[6] His work has stayed tenuously in print, with steady though small sales of his novels getting a boost in 2010, when *The Vivisector* (1970) was shortlisted for the Lost Man Booker Prize, and again in 2012, when the centenary of his birth was marked by the publication of an unfinished novel, *The Hanging Garden*, and the reissue of his first novel, *Happy Valley* (1939).[7] His plays have continued to be produced: there was a notable Sydney Theatre Company production of *The Season at Sarsaparilla* (1965), directed by Benedict Andrews, in 2007, while *The Ham Funeral* (1947) was directed by Adam Cook for the 2012 Adelaide Festival. In addition, a film of *The Eye of the Storm* (1973), directed by Fred Schepisi and starring Charlotte Rampling, Judy Davis and Geoffrey Rush, was released to critical acclaim in 2011, anticipating the 2012 centenary.

The National Library's acquisition of such a significant collection of manuscripts was marked by a symposium held there early in 2007, followed by a dinner based on some of White's very 1950s recipes, also preserved in his papers (the celebration was not a cerebral one only). Later in 2007, the jubilee of the publication of *Voss* in 1957 was the occasion for another symposium 'Remembering Patrick White', organized by colleagues from the Universities of New South Wales and Western Sydney in association with the Sydney Writers' Festival.[8]

Yet another event, 'The Voss Journey', held in Canberra in 2009, was exemplary of the way the opening of the archive NLA MS9982 can expand knowledge of White's work. Spearheaded by Vincent Plush of the National Film and Sound Archive and Robyn Holmes of the NLA, the occasion also involved 14 other agencies, including the Australian Broadcasting Corporation, Opera Australia and the Australian Institute for Aboriginal and Torres Strait Islander Studies. It was at once an event with public outreach and an extraordinary exercise in scholarly recuperation. The focus was on the novel *Voss* and its afterlife. There were presentations on various attempts to adapt *Voss*, still ongoing. At various times, Harry M. Miller; Joseph Losey, David Mercer and Maximilian Schell; and Sidney Nolan and Stuart Cooper (a British director who now holds the film rights) have been involved in negotiations about a possible film version. An adaptation that did eventually happen, the opera *Voss*, featured prominently. Many of those from the 1986 Opera Australia production participated: David Malouf, the librettist; Moffatt Oxenbould, then artistic director of Opera Australia; Jim Sharman, the director; and especially memorable, Geoffrey Chard (Voss) and Marilyn Richardson (Laura), who spoke and coached younger singers to recreate some scenes. The production was screened, and composer Richard Meale's 'Suite from Voss' was premiered. The convenors have prepared a record of the event, with extended commentary, as *Patrick White, Voss and the Australian Cultural Landscape*.[9]

Significantly, *The Voss Journey*, as the title indicates, located White in the context of the flowering of Australian performance culture in the 1970s. It foregrounded the importance of his relationships with key figures of that flowering such as Jim Sharman and Moffatt Oxenbould, many of whom are now depositing their papers at the NLA and elsewhere. Such a perspective situates White in an Australian and, specifically, Sydney context, in which he is no longer the sole colossus. It is exemplary of the way new material and the passage of time can identify unrecognized dimensions of his career.

It is important to realize that MS9982 is only one part of the White archive: the NLA already held considerable correspondence together with the curious and contentious manuscript of *Memoirs of Many in One* (1986), jointly owned with the State Library of New South Wales (SLNSW). Among the State Library's other White holdings are his portable typewriter, writing desk and chair, donated by his partner Manoly Lascaris after White's death. Typescripts of some early plays were deposited during the 1980s and 1990s in the Mitchell Library (SLNSW), the Fryer Library (University of Queensland) and the NLA. The manuscripts shown at the NLA in a white gloves event held as part of *The Voss Journey* included some from the papers of David Marr, Richard Meale, artist and set designer Desmond Digby and others.

What Material Is There?

The earliest material in the collection can be found in White's 10 working notebooks, which include entries made from the 1930s to 1980s. These notebooks were used by him in very different ways at various stages in his career, and contain entries ranging from student notes to confessional diary entries recorded during his war service, and extended drafts of fiction and plays. As a group, they are undoubtedly the richest items in the collection.[10]

Notebook 1, dating from White's time at Cambridge studying modern languages in the 1930s, is a commonplace book containing many transcriptions of poems by French authors, mainly from the nineteenth century. Notebook 2, dating from the later 1930s to the early 1950s, also begins as a commonplace book with quotations from a large number of authors White was presumably reading at the time, ranging all the way from Chaucer and Cervantes to contemporaries such as Mahatma Gandhi, D. H. Lawrence and Katherine Mansfield. But after some 10 pages of quotations and a larger number of blank pages, White begins to use the notebook to jot down ideas for his own work. There is material here relating to *Happy Valley*, *The Living and the Dead* (1941), *The Aunt's Story* and *Voss*, appearing in seemingly random order in the notebook rather than anticipating the chronology of publication. There are also brief snatches of dialogue and lists of characters from several different plays, deriving from White's attempts in the 1930s to establish himself as a London playwright. Notebook 3 is White's fascinating diary of his experiences on war service in Sudan in 1941; it also contains many drafts of sections of *The Aunt's Story*, some extending to several pages, as well as drafts of a few poems and stories. Notebook 4 appears to have been in use during the 1940s and '50s and includes historical research for both *Voss* and *A Fringe of Leaves* (1976), as well as drafts for sections of *Riders in the Chariot* (1961), *The Ham Funeral* and other plays. Notebook 5, which also dates from the 1940s to the '50s, may be earlier than Notebook 4 and contains notes on the extensive historical research White undertook for *Voss*, while Notebook 6 has material relating to *The Solid Mandala* (1966), *The Vivisector*, *The Eye of the Storm* and *Memoirs of Many in One*, as well as plays and stories. Notebook 7 includes further historical research for *A Fringe of Leaves* as well as drafts of material for *The Twyborn Affair* (1979) and the plays *Big Toys* (1977) and *Netherwood* (1983). The last three notebooks contain mainly drafts of three of the plays, entitled 'Four Love Songs', which White was working on toward the end of his life, though Notebook 8 also has extensive drafts of a story, 'The Last Long Week End', plus a short piece of autobiographical writing, 'My Memories of Last Palm Sunday March'.

Other drafts of the 'Four Love Songs' exist elsewhere in the collection, also dating from the 1970s to the 1980s. One of them, 'My Big American', is a partial play script in the version in Notebook 8. Evie ('a large, florid woman. Plenty of lipstick, rouge, though she is not a whore; at least she would not like to be taken for one [...] She is the type that surfaces with wars and Americans on leave') and Vanda ('skinnier than EVIE, less outgoing. Clothes black, a fashionable-frumpish style') meet in a park, and fall into a risqué discussion of their experiences with men, especially American servicemen.

> EVIE: Not for me. Though I gotta admit I caught the diarrhoea in Honnerloulou.
> VANDA: You can catch anything in Honoloulou.
> (SHE PRONOUNCES THE PLACE NAME IN HER MOST ELOCUTED STYLE)

Here, the 'Big American' is Evie's collective term for her American lovers. There are two complete versions elsewhere (box 13, folder 34), one written for radio, the other for stage performance. In the latter, again the two women discuss men and conquests, harking back to Americans in World War II but mentioning also Korea and Vietnam. Here, 'the Big American' appears to have only a phallic connotation, until the light fades to a rosy glow:

> 'It's happening'
> 'It's happened …'
> (BOTH) The Big American BOMB

Such multiple drafts allow unprecedented access to White's thinking about individual pieces as segments of a larger work, drawing on his repertoire of character types and narrative motifs. Here too his increasing preoccupation in his last years with contemporary issues like nuclear disarmament is apparent (evidenced in other ways in MS9982, such as the drafts of speeches delivered in the 1970s and 1980s in box 15, folders 1–2).

Another example of the richness of the notebooks for students of White is his 1941 war diary in Notebook 3. This was drawn on by White himself when he was writing *Flaws in the Glass* (1981), as Ayres noted, pointing to his use of a description of a ewe giving birth.[11] Many of the diary entries were also included by David Marr in his edition of White's *Letters* (1994), White having let him have 'a typescript of one gorgeous chunk of the notebooks'.[12] This plangent section of the notebook is the least mediated of any of White's self-writing, which is not to say that the reflections of the young man on war service are unselfconscious. Here is a characteristic passage from the diary, written at Khartoum in February 1941, with mordant musings alternating with comments on his surroundings:

> There is nothing like the state of superfluity in which I almost perpetually find myself in the RAF, for destroying faith, self-respect, everything else. All the morning I have been sitting in a room doing nothing. Round me the esoteric signs, acts, which nobody will take the trouble to explain. Either they are too

busy, or else they are jealous of their esotericism. Many more of these mornings and I shall start listening to the walls, the way you can sometimes *hear* blank walls when [you] are both miserable & unemployed.

M. I like. He is small, neat, has a kind of nonchalant elegance. None of the HQ constipation and self-importance that I detest. If it does nothing else, this trial by RAF administrative [sic] may teach me to be humble. And how I shall value my own existence afterwards [...]

Je m'ennuie lying on my bed. All this staleness, sameness, effeteness, of music, of dishes in the kitchen downstairs.

We are all to blame, we are all to blame ... and if only all were convinced of it! Dostoevsky *The Possessed* (box 4, folder 4)

The quotation from Dostoevsky is one of several at this stage in the notebook, the bleak despairing mood of *The Possessed* (1872) evidently congenial to Pilot Officer White.

What is most extraordinary is the way the diary is intercalated with drafts of *The Aunt's Story*. There are a number of passages several pages in length including a draft of the opening of the novel ('Theodora Goodman went into the room where the coffin lay. It was not now the bedroom of her mother.') and many more sections of a few lines or a couple of paragraphs. In 1958, White wrote in his essay 'The Prodigal Son' about the ambivalence he experienced as a returning expatriate, referring to his reading the *Journal* of the explorer Edward Eyre during air raids in London in 1940 as possibly the moment when *Voss* was conceived.[13] But until now, it has not been apparent quite how early both *The Aunt's Story* and *Voss* took shape, and how they are connected through the experience of vastation of the author and characters. So, in this notebook, we have at once new White text and material that requires revision of assumptions about the shape and trajectory his career took. This example shows how the archive offers new perspectives: its import is in the ways it enables fuller illumination by focussing, filling out and extending our understanding of White's writing life. Thus far, while any expectation that MS9982 would generate sensational revelations has been disappointed, at every turn this body of material surprises and rewards investigation, sometimes in ways that are completely unexpected.

The notebooks foreground fragments. There are many lists of characters and titles, quotations, observations from real life as well as data transcribed from White's reading. We are forced to look hard at short pieces – and are reminded, for instance, how sharp an 'ear' White had, how good he was at dialogue and the short snatch. While the notes from the 1930s tend to capture the idiom of English people of both upper and lower classes (as in the play drafts discussed later), White noted in an interview that 'When I came back from overseas I felt I had to learn the language again', and his rendition of Australian idiom and intonation is a feature of his mature writing.[14] In this connection, an unexpected treasure found elsewhere in White's papers is documentation relating to his service on the ABC's Standing Committee on Spoken English in 1983: 'I am sorry I took this on ... affectation is the worst sin. There is your man who talks about the "Ebbysee" [ABC] "jell" (gaol) [...] "reddio" (radio) [...] "stedge" (stage) [...] "Nevvy" (Navy)' (box 3, folder 65).

The challenge is to see what scrap gets worked up, where and how: as in the case of 'My Big American' there are connections among unpublished pieces as well as between published and unpublished material. We should bear in mind that White's published works are the tip of the iceberg: think for a start of the novels that he worked on in the 1930s of which there is no apparent trace – 'The Immigrants', 'Sullen Moon', 'Finding Heaven' and 'Nightside' – though parts of them may have found their way into other works.

MS9982 also includes a quantity of correspondence, with about a dozen letters from White himself. Most are letters sent to him, some from friends, many of them public figures, a number of them theatre people. These complement and extend existing holdings of the NLA and other libraries, which are being steadily augmented as more papers are acquired – of his fellow novelist Randolph Stow, for example. And despite the thoroughness of Marr's *Letters*, more of White's correspondence keeps turning up: in 2010, the State Library of NSW bought a previously unknown collection of letters and postcards from White to Ragnar Christopherson, professor of English at Oslo University and a friend from White's schooldays in England. One moving sequence in the NLA papers (boxes 30–31, folders 1–7) consists of condolence letters sent to his partner Manoly Lascaris, which show the mixture of affection and exasperation White the man aroused, together with admiration and respect for White the writer.

There are complete manuscript and typescript drafts of the memoir *Flaws in the Glass* as well as a good deal of material relating to *Memoirs of Many in One*. But there are no substantial manuscripts or typescripts of any of the published novels, with the exception of *Memoirs*, though there is a late carbon copy of a close to final typescript of *A Fringe of Leaves* with some handwritten corrections, and fragments of typescripts of *The Vivisector* totalling about sixty pages, no individual section being more than a few pages in length.

The collection also includes copious drafts of plays, some of them produced, like *Signal Driver* (1982), *Netherwood* and *Shepherd on the Rocks* (1987), and others not produced, like 'The White Goddess and the Firebird'. There are also a number of film scripts – for example, screenplays based on White's stories 'Willy Wagtails by Moonlight', 'Clay' and 'Down at the Dump'. Later screenplays reveal White's love of parody and his often unacknowledged flair for comedy, as seen especially in his send-up of literary pretensions in 'Monkey Puzzle' which even includes a parody of *Voss*.[15]

In addition, there are versions of a number of short stories, again both published and unpublished. And MS9982 also features big tranches of unpublished longer fiction, some of which is discussed in more detail later.

A rich miscellany of other items in the collection variously illuminates facets of White's life and work. There are many photographs of family and friends, places and events, the work of both amateurs and professionals including Cecil Beaton (boxes 24 and 25, and folio box 1). There are maps, including one of Alexandria that he used while on active service (box 29); theatre programmes and recipes (boxes 25 and 26), appointment diaries and address books (box 19) and an index to his collection of classical music recordings (box 19).

Most of MS9982, apart from the earlier notebooks, dates from the late 1970s. It is unclear why White started to keep material. In 1977, he famously told Dr George Chandler, NLA Director-General, 'I can't let you have my "papers" because I don't keep any.'[16] Yet demonstrably, he did. There were fires at 'Dogwoods' before he moved to Martin Road in 1964, and his literary agent Barbara Mobbs did a major cull with White in 1988.[17] What we have is substantial, but mostly from White's last fifteen years, and even with other material such as letters cannot be regarded as 'a complete record of his life or writing career'.[18]

What MS 9982 Tells Us

Biographical information

Clearly, a major possibility opened by the new material is biographical, and while there is not a great deal that is specifically biographical, some of it is of considerable consequence. For example, White's wealthy background and social standing has always been seen as an important aspect of his career. With documentation of his assets at his death, notably a large portfolio of shares in blue-chip Australian companies and other financial data, David Marr could spell out just how rich White was, and the relatively small proportion of his income derived from his writing.[19]

Marr's *Herald* piece was supplemented by an extended essay, 'Patrick White: The Final Chapter', which gave a fuller account of Marr's reactions to the discovery of these manuscripts and described the long widowerhood? of White's partner Manoly Lascaris. As the title indicates, Marr sketched out how he would now write the final chapter of the biography, among other things dilating on his earlier contention that White was concerned to manage his death so as not to replicate the ignominy of his mother (and Elizabeth Hunter), dying enthroned on a commode.

Life writing

With White, separation of the life and the work is perilous. What the archive offers is the opportunity to look more closely at his life writing, and to test further – for example – the kinds of proposition that Brigid Rooney, in dialogue with Simon During, has developed about 'White's theatrical staging of his life through fiction'.[20] The issue baldly stated has to do with the various ways White wrote about himself and the material relating to his memoir *Flaws in the Glass*, and his last novel *Memoirs of Many in One*, provides the basis for more grounded discussion of White's fascination with the construction of identity. There's a ready-made PhD thesis topic or two here, though any student would do well to bear in mind White's caution in a letter to Lord Parmoor of the London antiquarian bookseller Bernard Quaritch: 'If I had any manuscripts I should have to let Australia have them, but I always make a point of destroying them after the book is printed. I feel the final printed version is what matters, & should satisfy the dreadful race of thesis writers.'[21]

The extent of White's work across genres

A major illumination concerns the extent to which White experimented in different genres from early on. He knew he wanted to be a writer but of what? His earliest publications in the 1920s and '30s were poems, and while some unpublished poems appear in the notebooks (especially Notebook 3) and elsewhere in the manuscripts, a case for White as a neglected poet doesn't emerge. The same notebook, in addition to the material relating to the novels such as *The Aunt's Story*, has plans for a volume of short stories provisionally called 'The Sparrows' and includes one piece already published, 'The Twitching Colonel': the early thoughts of *The Cockatoos* (1974)?[22] White also noted: 'Perhaps a novel about a Squadron, if hokum can be avoided. But it is difficult to skirt the set pieces of the cinema. All the same, somebody must do all this dust and dirt, and coming and going of the Hurricanes.'

Dramatic material

The amount of dramatic material is of particular note. MS9982 includes a good deal of writing for the theatre, radio and film. It is well known that White wrote for the stage from early in his career (1930s) both in Sydney and in London, then again in the 1960s, turning to drama even more in the 1970s and 1980s. The copious drafts in the collection of plays from this later period, both published and performed and unperformed and unpublished, enable a revised account of the significance of White's dramatic works, especially in the last phase of his career. The working notebooks, moreover, also provide new insights into some of White's earliest work as a dramatist. Notebook 2, for example, contains brief snatches of dialogue and lists of characters relating to several different plays. Most of these appear to mock the pretensions of the London upper middle classes as does his successfully performed revue sketch 'Peter Plover's Party' (1937), a monologue originally written for Ronald Waters, a school friend turned actor.[23] In many, however, there is a strong focus on female rather than male characters, while some show early attempts at experimental staging.

Particularly interesting with respect to White's later work are the four pages of draft of a play entitled 'Marriages are Made in Hell'. White begins with an outline of its main theme:

> The *Bassetts* are, in their own opinion, happily married. *Brionne* and *Julian* are living in what they accept as satisfactory sin. But *Hochtenfel* awakens doubts. Why should *Mr Bassett* accept his wife's nagging? Has not *Mrs Bassett* always suppressed somewhat luxurious and ambitious thoughts? *Julian* has endured *Brionne's* tantrums for years because he has not the willpower to avoid them. *Brionne's* clinging to *Julian* is the consequence of ambition and vanity.
> Both the *Bassetts* and *Brionne & Julian* are the victims of their separate codes, on the one hand the conventional, on the other the unconventional. (Notebook 2)

As the following scraps of dialogue make it clear, Brionne is one of the bright young things who feature in several of White's dramatic attempts from this period, while Hochtenfel appears to be something of a chorus figure:

> *Brionne*: A sense of morality just happens. Some people are born with it, some aren't. I *wasn't*. So however hard you look at me, Mrs Bassett, you won't make me a good woman.
> *Hochtenfel*: Mrs Bassett once had a sense of morality. Now she's morality itself.
> *Brionne*: Oh, dear, how uneventful for her. Poor Mrs Bassett!

A later section of dialogue between the Bassetts reveals that they are clearly intended to come from the lower middle classes. Their relationship as sketched by White in the summary quoted above, and demonstrated in this dialogue, looks forward to that between Mr and Mrs Lusty in *The Ham Funeral*:

> *Mrs Bassett*: You know I could never abide dogs.
> *Mr Bassett*: I must say some dogs 'ave very takin' ways. There's Mr Edwards' Tinker now, 'e can stand on 'is hind legs like a Christian, and smoke a pipe of tobacco.
> *Mrs Bassett*: That brings me no closer to likin' dogs. Nasty little creatures … soilin' the carpets, and leavin' hair over everything. I've got no time for 'em.
> *Mr Bassett*: Nobody asked you to 'ave time.

> *Mrs Bassett*: That's a cheeky answer for a man to give his wife.
> *Mr Bassett*: A man 'as to say something.
> *Mrs Bassett*: There are ways *an'* ways of sayin', Henry. But evidently that's something you never learnt.
> *Mr Bassett*: All right, Flo. All right.
> *Mrs Bassett*: No, it isn't all right.
> *Mr Bassett*: All right then, it isn't. I wonder if tomatoes do down here?

The long-suffering husband and dissatisfied wife sketched here look forward not only to *The Ham Funeral* but also to Stan and Amy Parker in *The Tree of Man* (1955) and to many other married couples in White's later plays, stories and novels.

Notebook 4 contains material explicitly relating to *The Ham Funeral*. This probably dates from White's return to that play around 1958 rather than from the time of its initial composition in 1947. His renewed interest in *The Ham Funeral* would seem to have been provoked by his very negative reaction to seeing Ray Lawler's *Summer of the Seventeenth Doll* (1955). White's criticisms of Lawler's hit play are forthright:

> The night I went the line that got the biggest laugh was: 'These bloody mozzies!' That line & its reception seems to me to illuminate the very core of the work, & to explain why the author has succeeded. […] In *The Doll* Lawler merely *reproduces banality*. The reproduction has not the faintest tinge of great art. It remains a rather boring version of the real. (Notebook 4)

He modified his opinion after reading the play, while continuing to object to its realism. That objection is the basis of his addition of the prologue to *The Ham Funeral* where the Young Man warns the audience that this may not be their kind of play.

Immediately following White's criticisms of Lawler, there is a draft of the most controversial scene in *The Ham Funeral*, the one where the two knockabout ladies, rooting in the dustbin, find the dead foetus. The next eight pages contain drafts of most of this scene, in one case intercut by a section of draft for *Riders in the Chariot*. White later made some small but significant changes in the ladies' dialogue, not always for the better. For example, the Second Lady's reaction to the First Lady's scream on finding the foetus is, in the notebook version, as follows: 'Oh, 'ark at *'er!* She's remembered 'er own wedding night.' In the published version of the play, this has become the rather blander 'Oh, 'ark at 'er! She's remembered somethink she lost.'[24] Generally, however, the final version of their dialogue shows few changes from this draft. More changes were made in the Young Man's reflections after the two ladies depart, with some of the more pompous lines in the notebook version cut.

As a character who is part chorus, part individual, the Young Man's dialogue needs to reflect a certain level of pretension that is initially part of his characterization as Poet with capital P without alienating the audience's sympathies too much. The Young Man's comments on the foetus show his growing sympathy for others, anticipating his final coming to terms with the Landlady as representing desire and the body and his move away from his enclosed room into the wider world. It was, therefore, important that some of the over-writing seen in the notebook draft was removed in the final version.

> Poor little fellow! There was never any question of you making the decision. You died too soon ... or were not even born. No angel struck you on the mouth, to silence the infinite knowledge that you were still capable of expressing. Your love returned to love, without ever having experienced the thumbscrew & the rack. Tender, humorous foetus! Such a one the landlady might have carried, & dropped, almost without knowing, & tried bitterly to remember. Like almost everything of importance the face is difficult to remember. Dreams wear no faces when it is important to identify. (Notebook 4)

In the published version, while the Young Man's speech remains basically the same, significant changes were made. For example, the second sentence here, a rather pointless remark about suicide, was cut in favour of a more dramatic reaction by the Young Man: 'There was never such brutality.... *(On second thought)* Or was it ... so very brutal?' In the sentence beginning 'No angel struck you', 'the infinite knowledge that you were still capable of expressing' became the simpler and so much more effective 'what you already knew'. And the rather vague second last sentence here was also cut.[25] It is of course possible that these changes were made while the play was in production.

Methods of composition

The manuscripts give new insight into White's ways of working. He famously maintained that his usual practice was to do three drafts of each novel: 'The first is always agony and chaos; no one could understand it. With the second you get the shape, it's more or less all right. I write both of those in longhand. The third draft I type out with two fingers: it's for refining of meaning, additions, and subtractions.' There is the possibility now of fine-grained demonstration of the basis for his famous claim that 'I rewrite endlessly, sentence by sentence; it's more like oxywelding than writing'.[26]

Here is an example of oxywelding from a partial typescript of *The Vivisector* (box 7, folder 4), showing the kind of revision that is likely to have occurred many more times than can be documented. On the back of a discarded typed page which refers to the Duffield family ring and the grandfather dying of a seizure in Parramatta Road, there are some handwritten sentences about Mrs Courtney and the boy Hurtle:

> She smiled at him so sweetly
> She cocked her head, and smiled at him so sweetly
> She cocked her head and smiled so sweetly [illegible]: he might have been a man

We see here progressive elaboration of the basic action, with the interpretation and development of Hurtle's point of view finally consolidated. Later in the typescript, the sentence has evolved further, almost to the form of words that appears in the published novel: 'She cocked her head, and smiled so sweetly *at him*, you wouldn't have thought she had the advantage: he might have been a man.' (The italicized words are added in the published version.)[27]

Research for the novels

White's use of historical material in his fiction has occasioned debate at least since *Voss*. In *Patrick White: A Life*, Marr repeatedly insists on White's concern for factual accuracy in his work. In the notebooks and other papers, we now can see in detail the extent of his research: thus, he studied much Jewish material for *Riders in the Chariot*, drawing on contemporary texts like Abraham Herschel's *God in Search of Man: A Philosophy of Judaism* (1955) and a number of titles by Martin Buber (in German) as well as older material. He quarried Australian sources mainly for *Voss*, *A Fringe of Leaves* and *The Eye of the Storm*. For *Voss*, he read copiously in both primary sources such as the journals and notebooks of the explorer Ludwig Leichhardt (mainly in English translation) and secondary ones such as Alec Chisholm's *Strange New World: The Adventures of John Gilbert and Ludwig Leichhardt* (1941). His many notes from Chisholm focus on factual detail about the terrain, vegetation and wildlife, though neither Chisholm's character assessments of the explorers nor his accounts of their interactions are reflected in *Voss*.

Similarly for *A Fringe of Leaves*, White ranged through nineteenth-century sources dealing with Eliza Fraser and early Queensland history as well as later secondary material. He looked at studies and translations of Virgil (so important to the fictional Austin Roxburgh), a dictionary of costume and A. L. Rowse's *Autobiography of a Cornishman: A Cornish Childhood* (1942). White's determination to be accurate and to avoid anachronism is everywhere evident. At the end of the manuscript of *The Hanging Garden*, he made a note: 'Foregoing passage on end of the war in Europe in need of revision as the news came through in the morning.'[28] He attributed a similar concern to the character of

Eirene in that work: 'hidden in the mangroves blacks are waiting to spear the landing parties of explorers. [Find out about these mangroves.]' (96–97)

Major Fiction Manuscripts

Of all the material in MS9982, the three major fiction manuscripts are in some respects the most substantial. They are certainly the most voluminous and present different opportunities for thinking about the ways White returned to and reworked themes and characters. He cannibalized 'Dolly Formosa and the Happy Few' (about 25,000 words) and 'The Binoculars and Helen Nell' (about 160,000 words), both dating from the late 1960s, for his last novel *Memoirs of Many in One*. 'The Hanging Garden', begun and put aside in 1981, is a different case. Although it is clear that White intended it to continue, this 45,000-word story has its own integrity, like the parts of *The Twyborn Affair* and *The Aunt's Story*. After reading the manuscript, Marr declared it 'a masterpiece in the making'.[29] Discussion ensued about possible publication, and we prepared a transcript for Barbara Mobbs, White's literary executor, to read. She took the decision to publish: 'I'm extremely nervous of posthumous publishing, which I usually don't admire. But this is up to a very high standard and even though it is only part one, it is complete in itself […] I have no doubt it deserves to see the light of day.'[30]

The Hanging Garden engages freshly with both personal experience set against contemporary history and satirical social commentary cut with lyrical romanticism. Set in Sydney in the later years of World War II, ending on VE Day, the story centres on an adolescent girl, Eirene, evacuated from Greece, where she was born to a Greek father, now dead, and an Australian mother. She is housed with the British widow of a warrant officer who had served in India with the father of another adolescent evacuee, the English Gilbert Horsfall. The house and garden are familiar from White's other works, though this time set on the north side of Sydney Harbour.

White is writing at the top of his form. Here is a cameo, describing Gilbert:

> Salt scales had replaced the scurf of his own skin on legs and arms, now the colour of Arnott's Milk Arrowroot. ('Most Australian kiddies love these biscuits, and I expect you will too Gilbert.' He agreed they were – beaut, carefully.) He licked the scales off his left forearm before pitching his last stone. (6)

The iconic fawn-coloured oval biscuit recurs when Gilbert builds a tree house – a retreat for him and Eirene – which features an Arnott's biscuit tin: he 'wants me to sit on the biscuit tin and let him hear I am peeing on our dunny' (114). White did not need to research Arnott's Milk Arrowroot biscuits with which he would have been familiar as a staple especially suitable for children and invalids, until the 1950s distributed in fourteen pound (six kilogram) tins and weighed out to order by the grocer. The rectangular tins were sometimes recycled for storage and as camp ovens, perhaps also, as in Gilbert's construction, as a chamber pot. This passage depicting the adolescent boy coming to terms with all aspects of his new environment, including its idiom, achieves part of its effect by imaginative deployment of telling period detail.

The central dynamic is an exercise in the chemistry of adolescent relationships reminiscent of 'Down at the Dump', the last story in *The Burnt Ones* (1964). In a way, it is the story of White and his partner Manoly Lascaris, the fair Anglo and the dark Greek, though Eirene and Gilbert do not end up together as far as we know. There are familiar motifs: cultural displacement, father figures who are sexual predators, a range of mothers (one may be a prostitute), a volcano, a cairngorm, fuchsias – together with a box containing a talisman (this time a shrunken head from the Amazon). Less familiar is a recognisable 'real-life' cameo of the exclusive Sydney girls' school Abbotsleigh (here Ambleside), under its legendary headmistress and one-time captain of the English women's cricket team, Betty Archdale.

Critics generally reiterated Marr's initial claim for the masterly qualities of *The Hanging Garden*. In a long review in the *Australian*, Geordie Williamson hailed its publication as bringing 'life stirring back to a long-dormant oeuvre', proposing that 'White's incessant questions – is there anything beyond the physical world? may there be loving human unions beyond the carnal? – are posed here in ways as profound and subtle as anywhere else in his work'.[31] Paul Dunn in the London *Times* described it as 'a fragment, but a glittering one', a conclusion similar to that reached by James Hopkin in a carping review in the *Times Literary Supplement*: 'it works as a self-sufficient novella, and a fine one at that.'[32] The *Sydney Morning Herald*'s chief reviewer, Andrew Riemer, dissented: 'In its present state, *The Hanging Garden* is an exploration, even perhaps an experiment […] My feeling is that the centenary of White's birth would have been more appropriately marked by the republication of *Happy Valley*, the remarkable early novel he never allowed to be reprinted.'[33]

Unknown to Riemer, negotiations were already in train. Conscious of White's repeated question, 'Will they read me when I'm dead?', and with an eye to a centennial symmetry, Barbara Mobbs made the decision to complement *The Hanging Garden* with a reissue of *Happy Valley*: 'two things that might revive White and introduce him to another audience.'[34] One consequence could not have been imagined. White's reason for refusing to allow *Happy Valley* to be reprinted was that he was apprehensive that the Yen family, on whom he had based the Quongs in the novel, might sue for libel. The *Sydney Morning Herald*'s announcement that *Happy Valley* was to be republished provoked a wonderful letter from Laurann Yen, granddaughter of Minnie and Frank. 'None of the Yens of Adaminaby took much notice of Patrick White's *Happy Valley* until David Marr's biography,' she wrote, and went on first to describe her generation's reading the novel in a photocopy from the State Library and then to a lapidary demonstration of the power of White's writing. She concluded, 'White starts to "sound" like White in *Happy Valley* [...] The revenge of the Yens is that hardly anyone knows that it is a really good read.'[35]

These are only some of the ways in which the National Library manuscripts provoke re-reading of White. At once they extend the canon of White's work and variously illuminate current perceptions of, and perspectives on, his achievement. The centenary of his birth provided an occasion for framing different questions about White's achievement, and recasting old ones. The contexts in which we read him have altered. In the multicultural Australia of the twenty-first century, his ambivalent relationship with Australia and Australianness, at once critical and celebratory, is no longer stigmatized as the attitude of an expatriate. The dimensions of his comedy and of his social satire can be freshly explored. We can reflect on how useful it is to consider White as a modernist writer, as David Malouf proposed, or whether it is more salient to consider him as a postmodernist on the strength of *Memoirs of Many in One* and his later plays at least. Like Voss's legacy, White's is a troubling and challenging one.

Notes

1 David Marr, 'Patrick White's Return from the Pit', *Sydney Morning Herald*, 3 November 2006, 1.
2 David Malouf, 'Castle Hill Lear: Patrick White Reappraised', *Times Literary Supplement*, 5 January 2007: 12–13; Marie-Louise Ayres, '"My Mss are Destroyed": The Patrick White Collection', *National Library of Australia News* 17, no. 6 (March 2007): 3–6; repr. *Australian Book Review* 290 (April 2007): 8–11.
3 National Library of Australia. 'Guide to the Papers of Patrick White', Collection No. 9982, accessed 8 April 2014, online: http://www.nla.gov.au/cdview/nla.ms-ms9982.
4 David Marr, 'White's Return', 1.
5 Research for this essay has been carried out with the support of an Australian Research Council Discovery grant to Margaret Harris and Elizabeth Webby for the project 'Patrick White in the Twenty-first Century'. An earlier version was published as 'Patrick White's Papers', *Australian Book Review* 327 (December 2010–January 2011): 62–64. We thank Barbara Mobbs, literary agent for Patrick White's estate, for permission to quote unpublished material.
6 AustLit Database. Accessed 8 April 2014, online: http://www.austlit.edu.au/.
7 Patrick White, *The Hanging Garden* (Sydney: Knopf, 2012); Patrick White, *Happy Valley* (Melbourne: Text Publishing, 2012).

8 Papers from the symposium have been published as *Remembering Patrick White: Contemporary Critical Essays*, ed. Elizabeth McMahon and Brigitta Olubas (Amsterdam: Rodopi, 2010).
9 See Robyn Holmes, 'Enhancing the Ebook: Patrick White and the Australian Cultural Landscape', *Humanities Australia* 3 (2012): 35–44; Robyn Holmes and Vincent Plush, *Patrick White, Voss and the Australian Cultural Landscape* (Canberra, ACT: National Library of Australia and Sound Archive of Australia, in press).
10 The literary notebooks are in NLA MS9982, boxes 4–5, folders 1–10. All further references to MS9982 will be incorporated parenthetically in the text.
11 Ayres, *NLA News*: 4–5.
12 David Marr, 'Patrick White: The Final Chapter', *The Monthly* (April 2008): 28–42 (36). White's war diary is now complemented by extracts from the diaries of a South African, H. C. Nicholas, who served with White in the Royal Air Force for a time in 1941, and encountered him again in 1942: see Janet Sanders, '"Long Hours of Nothing": A Portrait of Patrick White at War', *Times Literary Supplement*, 4 July 2014, 14–15. Nicholas's recollections of the recreational activities of the young men on active service give no hint of the melancholy White describes in Notebook 3.
13 First published in *Australian Letters* 1, no. 3 (April 1958): 37–40; repr. Peter Wolfe, ed., *Critical Essays on Patrick White* (Boston: G.K. Hall, 1990), 21–24 (23).
14 Craig McGregor, *In the Making* (Melbourne: Nelson, 1969), 218–22; repr. Wolfe, 25.
15 Elizabeth Webby and Margaret Harris, 'Patrick White and Film', JASAL 13:2 (2013), accessed 24 April 2014, online: http://www.nla.gov.au/openpublish/index.php/jasal/article/view/2728/3733.
16 Patrick White to George Chandler, 9 April 1977, in David Marr, ed., *Patrick White Letters* (Sydney: Random House, 1994), 492.
17 David Marr, *Patrick White: A Life* (Sydney: Random House, 1991), 638.
18 Ian Morrison, 'Paper Lives', *Australian Book Review*, May 2010, 44.
19 David Marr, 'A Secret Life of Love, Loss and Stroganoff', *Sydney Morning Herald*, 3 November 2006, 12.
20 Brigid Rooney, *Literary Activists: Writer-intellectuals and Australian Public Life* (St Lucia: University of Queensland Press, 2009), 37.
21 Patrick White to Bernard Quaritch, 29 October 1978, BL Misc. Letters and Papers Add79.532 KK, British Library.
22 Patrick White, 'The Twitching Colonel', *London Mercury* 35 (April 1937): 602–9, repr. Alan Lawson, ed., *Patrick White Selected Writings* (St Lucia, Queensland: University of Queensland Press, 1994), 3–10.
23 Published in Lawson, *Patrick*, 199–200.
24 *The Ham Funeral*, in Patrick White, *Four Plays* (London: Eyre & Spottiswoode, 1965), 11–75 (43).
25 Patrick White, *Four Plays*, 43.
26 McGregor, *Making*; repr. Wolfe, 25–26.
27 Patrick White, *The Vivisector* (London: Jonathan Cape, 1970), 32.
28 MS9982, Box 8, folder 10: *The Hanging Garden*, 224.
29 Marr, 'Final': 30.
30 David Marr, 'A Note on *The Hanging Garden*', in *The Hanging Garden*, 217–24 (224). Marr recounts what is known of the composition of this work and the steps taken to achieve its publication.

31 Geordie Williamson, 'Patrick White, the Outcast, Returns to the Fold with *The Hanging Garden*', *Australian*, 31 March 2012, quoted from the slightly revised version published as 'Patrick White 1912–1990' in Geordie Williamson, *The Burning Library: Our Great Novelists Lost and Found* (Melbourne: Text Publishing, 2012), 74–85 (80, 84).
32 Paul Dunn, 'A Jewel Left Hanging: A Tantalising Glimpse of a Story Reveals a Past Master at Work', *The Times*, 24 March 2012; James Hopkin, 'Accidental Families: A Haven of the Unorthodox in Patrick White's Unfinished Work', *Times Literary Supplement*, 15 June 2012: 19.
33 Andrew Riemer, 'The Last Word', *Sydney Morning Herald*, 24–25 March 2012: 32–33 (33).
34 David Marr, 'Patrick White's Rare First Novel Revived for a New Audience', *Sydney Morning Herald*, 26–27 May 2012, 3.
35 Laurann Yen, letter, *Sydney Morning Herald*, 30 May 2012, 8.

Chapter 2

LEICHHARDT AND *VOSS* REVISITED

Angus Nicholls[1]

For Darriel Jeffree on his 50th birthday

Introduction: An Overview of Patrick White's *Voss* Notebook

In 1958, the future translator and editor of Ludwig Leichhardt's correspondence – Marcel Aurousseau – was asked by the literary journal *Meanjin* to comment upon 'The Identity of *Voss*'. Taking into account a range of source material, Aurousseau reached the following, at that time speculative, conclusion:

> It seems most likely that Mr. White has read Leichhardt's letters to his relatives, I should say in the original German edition of 1881, and that he read them with most perceptive understanding.[2]

Following the recent discovery of a collection of White's letters, notebooks and manuscripts, sold to the National Library of Australia (NLA) in 2006, it has become possible to examine White's principal research notebook for *Voss* online via the NLA catalogue.[3] The *Voss* notebook now reveals Aurousseau's opinion of 1958 to be a statement of fact, albeit one subject to some significant qualifications. On the basis of the *Voss* notebook, we now know that White conducted research into all three of Leichhardt's expeditions, with probably the most detail being devoted to the first attempted east-west crossing of Australia of 1846–47 (Leichhardt's second major expedition overall).

White even includes a basic bibliography in which he lists a range of names (see Figures 2.1 and 2.2 below). Some of these refer to Leichhardt's early contacts: William Nicholson, Leichhardt's research companion in Germany and England; William Branwhite Clarke, the Sydney clergyman and geologist who had supported Leichhardt's career as an explorer; and

John Gould, the renowned zoologist who had employed John Gilbert, the researcher and ornithologist who would later die during Leichhardt's first expedition to Port Essington (all listed on Figure 2.1). Others are, like Gilbert, members of the first expedition: John Roper, William Phillips (both Figure 2.1) and Christopher Pemberton Hodgson (Figure 2.2). Another group consists of those who went in search of Leichhardt after his disappearance in 1848, such as Hovenden Hely (also a member of Leichhardt's failed second expedition of 1846–47, who embarked on a search for Leichhardt in 1852), Sir John Forrest (who commanded the 1869 expedition in search of Leichhardt's remains that was organised by Ferdinand Jakob Heinrich von Mueller) and even the dubious Andrew Hume, who made a scarcely plausible claim to have come across a survivor from Leichhardt's final expedition (August Classen) on his outback wanderings during 1862 (all on Figure 2.2).[4] Thomas Mitchell's *Three Expeditions into the Interior of Eastern Australia* (1838) is listed (Figure 2.1), and White may also have looked at Sir George Grey's *Journals of Two Explorations of Discovery in North West and Western Australia* (1841), since Grey's name also appears in the *Voss* notebook (also listed on Figure 2.1). Another interesting possible source on the social history of the Australian colonies is Caroline Chisholm, whose name suggestively appears (see Figure 2.2), but with no further information.

What is the significance of this information? In some respects, it merely amounts to a list of names, since in all of the cases so far mentioned there is no further evidence in the *Voss* notebook of White having actually researched their writings. White did, however, take down direct quotations from the following sources on the list (see the endnotes for the pages of the *Voss* notebook upon which they are cited): letters written during the 1830s by Elizabeth Gould, the ornithological illustrator and wife of John Gould (listed on Figure 2.1);[5] Lady Jane Franklin's *Overland Journey to Port Phillip and Sydney* undertaken in 1839 (Figure 2.2);[6] Edward John Eyre's *Journals of Expeditions of Discovery into Central Australia* (1845, Figure 2.1);[7] John Dunmore Lang's *Cooksland in North-Eastern Australia* (Figure 2.2, 1847, which included a detailed account of Leichhardt's first expedition);[8] and the report of Augustus Charles Gregory regarding his search for Leichhardt's remains in 1857–58 (Figure 2.2).[9]

It also turns out that some names *not* appearing on White's initial list are just as important as those that do. These include Charles Sturt's *Narrative of an Expedition into Central Australia* (1849),[10] John McDougall Stewart's *Explorations in Australia* (1865)[11] and especially Georgiana McCrae's *Journal* (published by her grandson, the poet Hugh McCrae in 1934), which is quoted extensively, presumably as a source on social mores of the period.[12] Indeed, the most crucial names of all – those of L. L. Politzer and Daniel Bunce – are not

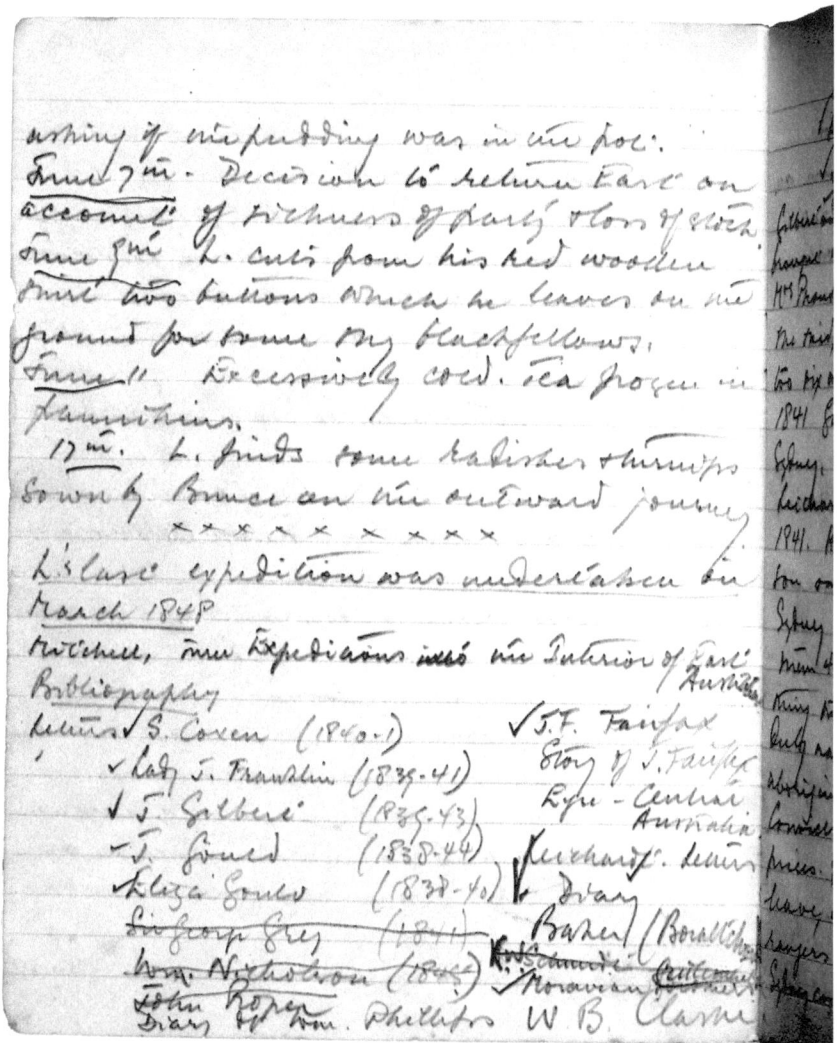

Figure 2.1 National Library of Australia, MS 9982 Papers of Patrick White, 1930–2002; series 2: literary notebooks, 1930s–1970s; item 5: notebook containing research for *Voss* (1957), c. 1955–57, part 20. Also available online via the NLA catalogue.

listed by White: it was Politzer who translated a small selection of Leichhardt's *Letters* that appeared in 1944, a volume from which White transcribed a series of important passages;[13] and nearly a quarter of the *Voss* notebook is comprised of notes taken from Daniel Bunce's account of Leichhardt's failed and controversial second expedition of 1846–47.[14] Leichhardt's own English-language account of the successful first expedition of 1844–46, titled *Journal*

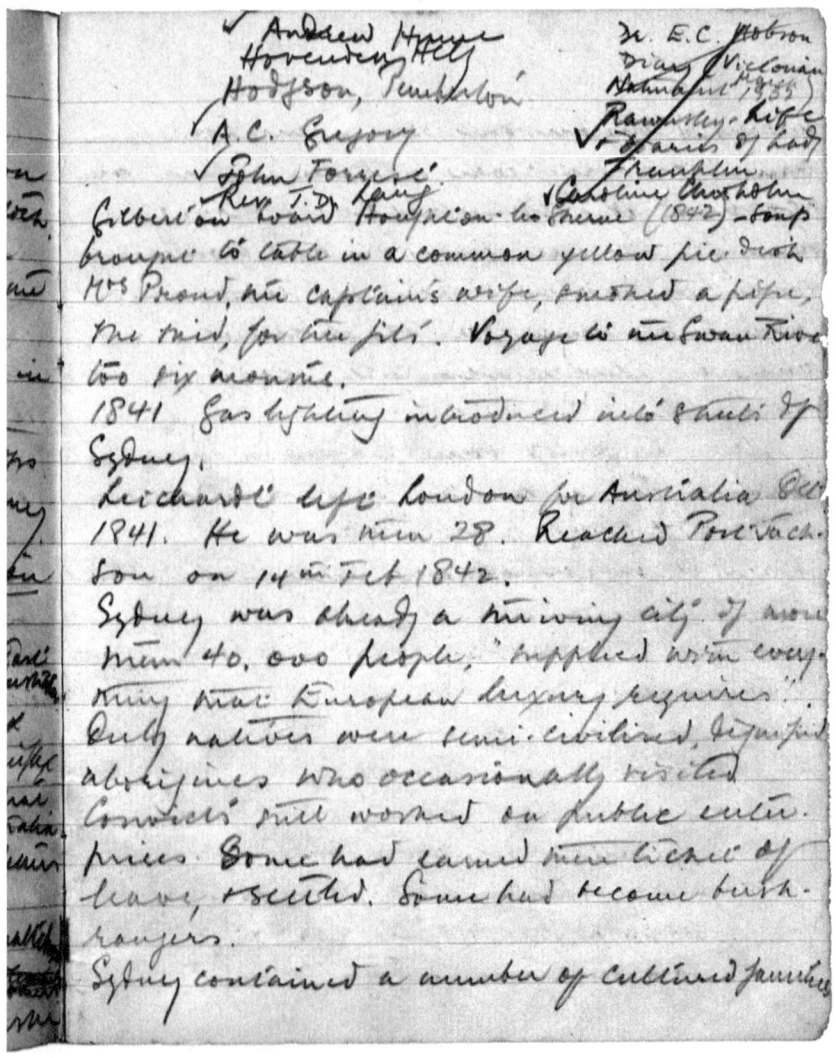

Figure 2.2 National Library of Australia, MS 9982 Papers of Patrick White, 1930–2002; series 2: literary notebooks, 1930s–1970s; item 5: notebook containing research for *Voss* (1957), c. 1955–57, part 21. Also available online via the NLA catalogue.

of an Overland Expedition in Australia from Moreton Bay to Port Essington (published in 1847),[15] does not seem to be mentioned in the *Voss* notebook, but passages found in parts 23 and 24 of the *Voss* notebook, which allude to the botanical and ornithological findings of Leichhardt and Gilbert, have apparently been transcribed from John Gilbert's diary of that expedition, which would have been available to White in the Mitchell Library.[16] Nevertheless, White's

Figure 2.3 The cover to L. L. Politzer's 1944 translation of *The Letters of Dr. Ludwig Leichhardt*, the edition quoted in White's *Voss* notebook.

obvious concentration in the *Voss* notebook on the second journey of 1846–57 would suggest – especially keeping in mind the plot of *Voss* – that when it came to Leichhardt, he was more interested in the pathos of failure than he was in success.

The *Voss* notebook, therefore, presents us with a complicated picture. It cannot, of course, be regarded as an exhaustive list of White's sources for the novel, and the question as to which of the sources listed in the notebook actually exerted an influence on the final version of *Voss* cannot systematically be answered here. But with respect to the relation between Ludwig Leichhardt and the character of Voss, the *Voss* notebook is significant: it presents conclusive evidence that White did read at least some of Leichhardt's writings about Australia, while at the same time not confirming Marcel Aurousseau's suggestion that White read Leichhardt in German. The *Voss* notebook now makes it incumbent upon scholars to take Leichhardt's writings seriously as primary literary sources that may have informed both the ideas and the language of *Voss*. Why should Leichhardt's writings be considered as *literary* as opposed to scientific or historical source material? The answer to this question is that Leichhardt did not only write as a scientist or as an explorer but also wrote letters to his relatives. White may well have avoided Leichhardt's *Journal of an Overland Expedition* precisely because it was written in a dry and neutral English befitting its scientific status. By contrast, Leichhardt's letters to his family – which, as will also be discussed here, were actually intended for publication – were first penned in his native language and show a stylistic awareness of a particular literary genre: that of German romantic travel writing.

The possibility that these letters may have provided literary source material for *Voss* may have been overlooked or underplayed for two possible reasons. The first reason is admittedly speculative: one might ask how many Australian literary scholars, apart from Aurousseau and Leichhardt's biographer Colin Roderick, have actually bothered to read Leichhardt's German correspondence in the original language and in its proper literary context, despite the fact that White himself (who had a solid command of the German language and a strong awareness of German cultural history) certainly could have. The second reason is a matter of public record: from the mid- to late nineteenth century up until at least the late 1970s, a more or less sustained public campaign was waged against Leichhardt in Australia, emerging initially from accounts by members of his own expeditions. White's significant reliance on the account of Daniel Bunce – who was, as we shall see, one of the main protagonists in this anti-Leichhardt campaign – means that his research for *Voss* should be seen in this context. Yet unlike the historians and biographers, White was probably not interested in what really happened on Leichhardt's expeditions. As a novelist, he may in fact have relished the fact that we will never definitely know if Leichhardt the explorer was an astute scientist who led his men admirably under extremely difficult conditions, or whether he was a misguided, Teutonic tyrant who was totally unprepared for those conditions, as much of his negative Australian reception suggests.

The focus of this chapter is, therefore, not so much the 'truth' concerning Leichhardt the explorer but rather 'Leichhardt' as a textual phenomenon: as a mythic figure in Australian culture and as a would-be contributor to the tradition of German romantic travel writing. When eighteenth- and nineteenth-century German travellers and explorers wrote letters to their relatives, many of them were not only engaging in private correspondence but also contributing to an existing literary genre. Many of Leichhardt's letters to his family are self-consciously literary documents in which Leichhardt puts on display some key elements of German romantic writing, especially concerning the relationship between the self and nature. Rather than the writings of Goethe and Nietzsche, which have often been mentioned as having been possible source material for *Voss*, I will propose that Leichhardt himself may have provided the primary romantic source material for White's novel. In order to make this argument, it is necessary not only to examine the correspondence by Leichhardt that was read by White but also to consider the entire context of Leichhardt's background and education, as well as the problematic Australian reception of his explorations.

Leichhardt's Background and Education

Friedrich Wilhelm Ludwig Leichhardt (1813–48) is without doubt the most important – and also in some accounts the most derided – German in nineteenth-century Australian history. Arriving in Sydney on 14 February 1842, Leichhardt completed one of his century's most astonishing journeys of Australian exploration. This journey began in the Darling Downs region to the west of Brisbane in 1844, extended through the Gulf of Carpentaria and concluded in the far north-western settlement of Port Essington in 1845–46, an overland trek through largely unmapped territory which covered some 4,800 kilometres. Upon returning to Sydney from this journey in 1846, Leichhardt was probably the most famous man in Australia.

Following the success of this first journey, Leichhardt's goal was to undertake the first east–west crossing of Australia. His first attempt in 1846–47 (recorded by Bunce) was abandoned due to difficult weather conditions, which led to hardship and squabbling amongst its members. But it is the tragic 1848 expedition in particular that has taken on a mythic status in Australian culture, since it led to

Leichhardt and his party disappearing altogether. A number of search parties attempted to provide explanations for Leichhardt's fate and their failure to do so conclusively has only fuelled the Leichhardt myth, which has been likened to that of the bushranger Ned Kelly.[17] Leichhardt's name is literally written into the Australian landscape: a suburb in Sydney's inner west carries his name, as does a major highway in Queensland and a river running through the Queensland town of Mount Isa.

Leichhardt has been both eulogized and condemned. According to some, he was a visionary explorer who brought the rigours of a European scientific training to the 'dark heart' of the Australian continent; yet for others, he represented the worst possible combination of Prussian inflexibility and German romantic monomania, being seen as a flawed Faust of the Australian bush, blundering towards his end in an unforgiving landscape which he allegedly underestimated and misunderstood. As Horst Priessnitz has shown, Leichhardt's Prussian – German identity has been viewed both positively and negatively by Australian commentators, depending upon their various ideological agendas and historical contexts.[18] In aesthetic terms, the significance of Leichhardt's legacy lies in his indirect contribution to Australian literary modernism. In having provided the inspiration and much of the source material for *Voss*, Leichhardt's journeys to the so-called 'primitive interior' of Australia and his encounters with Aborigines lie at the heart of Australian literature's definitive high-modernist epic. Looking beyond *Voss*, a recent study has also estimated that Leichhardt is the subject of more than forty works of poetry in the history of Australian literature.[19] Yet it may also be the case that the literary representations of Leichhardt, including the one found in *Voss*, have served to obscure much that is significant about his actual reactions to Australia.[20] And although there has been a range of both popular and scholarly biographies of Leichhardt in English[21] and in German,[22] as well as one comprehensive edition of his correspondence,[23] the original German versions of his letters from Australia have rarely been analysed in any great detail, while also being obscured by some problematic translations into English.[24] For this reason, all translations of Leichhardt's correspondence quoted in this chapter are my own.

Leichardt was born in 1813 in the town of Trebatsch (near Cottbus) in the state of Brandenburg, located in the Kingdom of Prussia. Upon finishing his secondary education, Leichhardt began his studies in 1831 at the Humboldt University in Berlin, where he read philology under Professor Franz Bopp (1791–1867), the leading German specialist on Sanksrit and Indo-European languages during the early to mid-nineteenth century. Leichhardt's other main focus at the Humboldt University was philosophy, where both Fichte and Hegel had recently been prominent professors, Hegel having died only a week after Leichhardt arrived in Berlin. Based on his analysis of Leichhardt's pre-Australian diaries, Colin Roderick has argued that Leichhardt became convinced during his time in Berlin of one of the key precepts of post-Kantian German idealism, that knowledge arises out of a dynamic interaction between subject and object and that 'to know one's self, one must seek an understanding of the phenomena of nature'.[25] In another more recent biography of Leichhardt, Dietmar Felden theorizes that Leichhardt may also have encountered the German romantic author and natural scientist Adelbert von Chamisso (1781–1838), who had been appointed as curator of the Botanic Gardens in Berlin in 1819.[26] Prior to taking up this post, Chamisso had been head scientist on the Russian Rurik Expedition (1815–18), a voyage which attempted to navigate the North-West Passage and which also explored the Pacific region around Polynesia and Hawaii. Leichhardt almost certainly visited these Botanic Gardens, and Chamisso's example may well have inspired him to undertake his own journeys of exploration.

In 1833, Leichhardt left Berlin in order to study at the University of Göttingen. During the second half of the eighteenth century, this institution was the leading German centre for the collection of travel literature from the European colonies, providing useful source material for the then nascent discipline of *Völkerkunde* (ethnology). The director of the University Library at Göttingen, Christian Gottlob Heyne (1724–1812), became preoccupied with contemporary travel literature dealing with indigenous populations in Africa and North America. Heyne's aim in collecting these sources was to found the discipline of comparative ethnology by providing it with a philological basis.[27] Heyne's students – who included August Wilhelm Schlegel and Friedrich Schlegel, Friedrich August Wolf, Friedrich Creuzer and Wilhelm von Humboldt, among others – were some of the central personalities in German comparative philology. The myths and folklore of Europe, the Orient and the so-called New World would later become important subjects for these writers, some of whom (the Schlegels in particular) belonged to the vanguard of German Romanticism.[28]

It was in this enlightened climate that Leichhardt continued his study of philology, while also branching out into the natural sciences. Leichhardt's teachers in Göttingen included the professor of comparative anatomy Johann Friedrich Blumenbach (1752–1840); Jakob Grimm (1785–1863), the philologist and (with his brother Wilhelm) famous collector of fairy tales; the Orientalist Georg Heinrich August Ewald (1803–75); and the philosopher Johann Friedrich Herbart (1776–1841). Herbart, who attempted to transform Kant's transcendental philosophy into a science by combining it with mathematics and physics, also reportedly persuaded Leichhardt to prioritise the natural sciences over the humanities.[29] Leichhardt spent the remainder of the 1830s on scientific and medical study in Berlin and on various research expeditions in Britain, France, Switzerland and the Mediterranean undertaken with William Nicholson. He then departed England for Australia on 26 October 1841. Despite the fact that some publications refer to Leichhardt using the title of 'Dr', he did not complete a university degree. And since he also embarked for Australia without having reported for his compulsory Prussian military service, which had only been deferred until October 1840, he was now at least legally speaking an exile from his homeland.[30]

From the very beginning of his time in Australia, Leichhardt's Prussian heritage seems to have been an obstacle to his progress in the young British colony. Leichhardt's early attempt to be appointed as superintendent of the Botanic Gardens in Sydney was unsuccessful because he lacked English qualifications.[31] Before Leichhardt's departure from England, the renowned English biologist Richard Owen had written a letter introducing Leichhardt to the Surveyor General of New South Wales, the explorer Sir Thomas Mitchell. Leichhardt's request for such a letter was strategic, since his aim seems to have been to accompany Mitchell on a proposed research journey from the coast of southern Queensland to Australia's northeast coast. When Mitchell's proposed undertaking was delayed because it had not yet been approved by the Home Office in London, Leichhardt organised his own expedition, funded by private resources.[32] The resounding success of this journey – completed at the beginning of 1846 – was the principal reason for Leichhardt becoming the most significant non-Anglophone explorer in Australian history.

Leichhardt's Australian Reception

Why, then, does Leichhardt have such an ambivalent status in Australian cultural history? Negative descriptions of Leichhardt, replete with overtones of anti-Prussian and anti-German prejudice, emerged from both the first and second of his expeditions. In 1938, the diaries of the naturalist and ornithologist John Gilbert (1810?–45) – who was killed by Aborigines near the Gulf of Carpentaria during Leichhardt's first expedition of 1844–46 – were discovered in England by the Australian historian Alec H. Chisholm. These diaries expressed criticisms of Leichhardt's conduct during this first expedition, and they were in turn highlighted by Chisholm in a study entitled *Strange New World: The Adventures of John Gilbert and Ludwig Leichhardt* (1941). Writing in the context of the Second World War, Chisholm alleges that Leichhardt was an 'unbalanced German' who was an 'unworthy leader' who merely 'blundered through' in this successful first expedition. Worse still, Leichhardt's conduct is said to have undermined the

Australian principle of 'mateship', and it is also claimed that he 'thrashed' his mules for no apparent reason and 'starved his dogs unnecessarily and foolishly'. Depicted as an unworldly German romantic with no grasp of real Australian bushcraft, Leichhardt's activities as an explorer are equated with the blind striving of 'the moth for the star'.[33] Chisholm seems to have been regarded as the main Australian authority on Leichhardt during the 1940s, since he also wrote the introduction to Politzer's 1944 translation of Leichhardt's letters, in which Leichhardt is again presented as a 'scatter-brained' army deserter who was 'weak of sight', 'unable to use a gun' and who was uniformly despised by his expedition companions.[34] Since we now know that White used Politzer's translation as a primary source for *Voss*, it is almost certain that he read and was influenced by Chisholm's caricature of Leichhardt.

The negative image of Leichhardt that arose from the second expedition of 1846–47 is the result of acrimony between Leichhardt and other members of that party, and the other main source from the *Voss* notebook emerged from this context: it was Daniel Bunce's *Travels with Dr Leichhardt* (1859) which first alleged that Leichhardt had stolen food from others in the expedition party.[35] For his part, Leichhardt had, in a letter to his German brother-in-law dated 20 October 1847, attributed the failure of that expedition to a lack of endurance and character among his companions. These men, claimed Leichhardt, were used to 'a cushy and comfortable city life' (*ein weichliches, behagliches Stadtleben*) and expected only to receive the rewards of success without undergoing the tribulations of the journey.[36] Following the publication of this letter (translated into English) in the *Adelaide Observer*, the *Geelong Advertiser* and the *Sydney Morning Herald* in January 1866, members of Leichhardt's party set out to defend their own conduct during the expedition while also castigating Leichhardt. One such example is John Frederick Mann's *Eight Months with Dr Leichhardt in the Years 1846–1847* (1888).[37] Even as late as 1979, when Bunce's memoirs were republished by Oxford University Press, the new foreword written by Russel Ward portrayed Leichhardt as having been 'greedy, tyrannical, pompous, unpredictably erratic in his behaviour and utterly lacking any faculty of self-criticism or sense of humour'.[38] While it is not our purpose here to analyse in detail the veracity of these accounts of Leichhardt's conduct – and regardless of the fact that the truth of what occurred on this second expedition cannot objectively be determined – the scholarly work of Marcel Aurousseau, E. M. Webster and Colin Roderick has pointed to a number of inconsistencies in the various condemnations of Leichhardt; all three scholars have convincingly argued that the Australian image of Leichhardt was distorted by anti-Prussian and later anti-German prejudices, with Chisholm's wartime account in particular being an exercise in damning caricature.[39]

As Irmtraud Petersson and Susan Martin have shown, the character that emerges from depictions of Leichhardt in Australian poetry and prose fiction published prior to *Voss* is also ambivalent.[40] Initially, Leichhardt's literary reception seems to have been positive. A poem entitled simply 'Leichhardt' (1880) written by the poet Henry Kendall (1839–82) depicts Leichhardt as a stoic figure who 'faced for Science thirsty tracts of bitter glow' and who found his spiritual home in the natural setting of Australian bush:

Thus he came to be a brother of the river and the wood –
Thus the leaf, the bird, the blossom, grew a gracious sisterhood!
Nature led him to her children in a space of light divine –
Kneeling down, he said – 'My Mother, let me be as one of thine!'[41]

But already with 'The Lost Leichhardt' – written by A. B. (Banjo) Paterson (1864–1941) and first published in the Australian weekly newspaper the *Bulletin* in 1899 – a certain jadedness with respect to the Leichhardt mystery sets in. Paterson's poem takes up a cynical attitude toward the search parties that had tried to find Leichhardt's remains since his disappearance in 1848: 'Another search for Leichhardt's tomb/Though fifty years have fled/Since Leichhardt vanished in the gloom,/Our one Illustrious Dead.' The poem recommends that these naïve and 'rash excursionists' should give up their quest for Leichhardt and it ends ironically: 'Ah, yes! Those British pioneers/ Had best at home abide,/For things have changed in fifty years/Since Ludwig Leichhardt died.'[42]

In the twentieth century, literary treatments of Leichhardt begin to see him more as a series of narratives than as a real historical human being. Here, the key example is Francis Webb (1925–73) who produced in 1947 a series of poems under the title of *Leichhardt Pantomime*, serialized in the *Bulletin*. These poems depict Leichhardt as a mythic figure in the landscape of Australian history and were later revised and published in Webb's collection *Leichhardt in Theatre* (1952). The fact that Webb chose to depict Leichhardt as a character within a stage drama, referring to him continually as 'The Doctor', brings to mind obvious parallels with Goethe's *Faust*. Webb's Leichhardt is the director of his own drama who 'summons the elements' of his stage setting, which is the southern land of Australia: 'Southward the new, the visionary!/This is a land where man becomes myth.' Webb's Leichhardt appears to be a series of myths or fictions to the extent that when reading this poem or play 'It's hard to judge from a front seat view/Whether he's Leichhardt or whether there are two'.[43] Webb's poem is divided into three acts corresponding with

Leichhardt's three expeditions. As the following passage from the 1947 version demonstrates, Webb's vision of Leichhardt appears to have been influenced by Chisholm's *Strange New World*, yet in the lines quoted below, it also shows an awareness that 'Leichhardt' is a mythic construct, assembled from a series of disparate and often contradictory sources:

> Come out, good Doctor,
> Misshapen maniac! Come out and blink
> With sad extravagance. Walk up and down!
> Mumble your specious part, rave into the night,
> With honour, courage, ambition – matted madness,
> While the wind plucks at your crazy hair, while the light
> Runs in and out of your head. You are bric-à-brac,
> A child's worn doll. Hollow. Falling to pieces.[44]

If, by the middle of the twentieth century, Leichhardt had indeed become an assemblage of images and conflicting (often tendentious) accounts, how did Patrick White's *Voss*, the definitive literary treatment of Leichhardt, contribute to this discourse?

Leichhardt, White and the Composition of *Voss*

On 11 September 1956, White wrote the following to his American editor Ben Huebsch:

> Some years ago I got the idea for a book about a megalomaniac explorer. As Australia is the only country I really know in my bones, it had to be set in Australia, and as there is practically nothing left to explore, I had to go back to the middle of last century. When I returned here after the War and began to look up old records, my idea seemed to fit the character of Leichhardt. But as I did not want to limit myself to a historical reconstruction (too difficult and too boring), I only based my explorer on Leichhardt. The latter was, besides, merely unusually unpleasant, whereas Voss is mad as well.[45]

A key issue in this letter is White's differentiation between Leichhardt and Voss; the former (presumably on account of White having read both Bunce's *Travels with Dr. Leichhardt* and Chisholm's introduction to the *Letters*) is described as 'unusually unpleasant', while the latter is seen simply as 'mad'. To further complicate matters, White would later write to the editor of Leichhardt's correspondence, Marcel Aurousseau, that the character of Voss was assembled from 'bits of Leichhardt' and also from Eyre's journals, a suggestion now borne out by the *Voss* notebook. To this White also cryptically added that there is more of his 'own character than anybody else's' in the figure of Voss.[46] Writing in the late 1980s and early 1990s and without the benefit of the NLA archive, White's biographer David Marr was of the opinion that White 'took little directly from Leichhardt's papers' but rather relied predominantly on 'Alec Chisholm's often mocking attitude to the explorer set out in *Strange New World*, the book in which White first discovered Leichhardt'.[47]

White's research notebook for *Voss* now reveals Marr to have been incorrect in his assumption that White took little from Leichhardt's papers, though it certainly remains likely that Chisholm's *Strange New World* was a significant source for *Voss*. The *Voss* notebook shows that White undertook extensive research into Leichhardt's letters, while its carefully dated chronological account of key events on the second expedition of 1846–47 matches, often word for word, the record found in Bunce's *Travels with Dr. Leichhardt*. Yet we should also not forget that White's bibliography in the *Voss* notebook also contains a reference not only to Leichhardt's 'Letters' but also to his 'Diary' (see Figure 2.1).[48] Here, White could be referring to Leichhardt's *Journal of an Overland Expedition* or to the large collection of Leichhardt's papers held in the Mitchell Library in Sydney.[49] In order to have understood the latter sources, White would have needed to read handwritten German. White's facility in the German language is, in fact, evidenced in other notebooks not directly related to *Voss*, in which he flawlessly has transcribed quotations from a number of German sources (though admittedly not handwritten ones from the nineteenth century) including the works of Martin Buber and Gershom Scholem, the result of his interest in Jewish mysticism.[50] This is hardly surprising, since White had studied German as an undergraduate at Cambridge, making regular visits to Germany during the 1930s and reading extensively in German literature.[51] David Marr notes that 'the only Germany White ever knew was Nazi', and this factor may also have influenced White's approach to Leichhardt and in turn to the character of Voss. In his autobiography, *Flaws in the Glass* (1981), White remarks that he conceived of the novel during his time serving as a soldier in Egypt, observing that 'the real Voss, as opposed to the actual Leichhardt, was a creature of the Egyptian desert, conceived by the perverse side of my nature at a time when all our lives were dominated by that greater German megalomaniac.'[52]

The continuities and discontinuities between White's novel and the actual events of Leichhardt's expeditions have generated a lively and complex secondary literature.[53] Already in 1958, the editor of the comprehensive edition of Leichhardt's letters, Marcel Aurousseau, had established a plausible framework for this relation: there is no doubt that Voss is based upon Leichhardt without being a historical portrait of him; the plot of *Voss* was assembled by

White from aspects of all three of Leichhardt's journeys, with a heavy emphasis on the drama of the second expedition of 1846–47: terrible weather conditions, extreme sickness, near starvation, low morale and a partial mutiny against the leader. The conclusion of White's narrative, in which a tribe of Aborigines murder Voss, represents fiction standing in for the total lack of any definitive explanation for Leichhardt's disappearance. Apart from the character of Voss, it is Palfreyman – the ornithologist who is also murdered by an Aboriginal – who is based upon a real historical individual in John Gilbert. There may be other similarities between fictional characters and real people, but these should not lead us to conclude that White's aim was to document history.[54] Crucially, in light of the recently discovered *Voss* notebook, we can now definitively answer two of the key questions first posed by Aurousseau in 1958: White did read Leichhardt's letters (though probably not in German), he may have read some of Leichhardt's journals and he definitely looked at Gilbert's journal of the first expedition.

What of the character of Voss as a representation of Leichhardt? Marr is correct in pointing out the influence of Chisholm's account on White; just as Chisholm, writing in the midst of World War II, sees Leichhardt through the prism of his German nationality, so too is the character of Voss repeatedly referred to simply as 'the German' throughout White's narrative and his speech is peppered with German exclamations and expressions – for example, *Ach!* and *wirklich* – which in White's post-war context had become more or less clichés of Anglophone representations of German people. But a closer examination of White's text soon reveals more complex processes of representation than those found in Chisholm's work, and these are suggestive of White's deep engagement with Leichhardt's own writings, including Leichhardt's letters to his relatives. In fact, White seems to have had a kind of empathetic awareness of how life in mid-nineteenth-century Australia might have been for an educated German given to high seriousness. This is because the stark anti-German prejudices like those found in Chisholm's account of Leichhardt are refracted by White through the views of other characters in the novel, while at the same time never receiving any unequivocal confirmation from the novel's third-person narrative voice.

When Voss appears on the first page of White's novel, arriving at the estate of Mr Bonner, the colonist who will finance his journey of exploration, he is described as 'a kind of foreign man' by Mr Bonner's servant. Lieutenant Radclyffe, the fiancé of Mr Bonner's daughter, then refers to Voss as 'a madman' who is engaged in a 'battle between German precision and German mysticism'. Later, we are afforded an insight into Voss's own view of how others perceive him: 'Some pitied him. Some despised him for his funny appearance as a foreigner. None, he realised with a tremor of anger, was conscious of his strength.'

Following Voss's disappearance in the Australian interior, his failed journey is referred to in polite society as 'the expedition led by that mad German', while in a conversation held by the niece of Colonel Hebden – the leader of a search party which attempts to find Voss's remains – one of her friends remarks that 'the German was eaten by blacks, and a good thing, too, if he was going to find land for a lot of other Germans'.[55] All of these quotations arguably demonstrate White's emphasis on the provinciality and parochialism of mid-nineteenth-century Australian life, and the difficulties that these cultural conditions would have presented to an educated European outsider like Leichhardt.

At the same time, the third-person narrative voice of White's novel *does* tend to posit a direct relation between the German background of Voss on the one hand and his high romantic tendencies on the other hand, to the extent that the reader is often presented with a version of German romanticism that verges on the burlesque. As we shall soon see, these high romantic features of *Voss* may, at least in part, have emerged from Leichhardt's own letters to his relatives. Voss's high romanticism is related to the novel's central narrative device, in which Voss the romantic hero forms a psychic connection with the niece of Mr Bonner, Laura Trevelyan, to whom White later referred in Jungian terms as being akin to Voss's *anima*.[56] Voss and Laura establish a relationship that remains unconsummated, but which is characterized by pantheistic and mystical overtones, lived out through a kind of telepathy connecting Laura in Sydney with Voss in the Australian interior. Laura is of the unorthodox opinion that the Australian landscape belongs to Voss 'by right of vision', an opinion which Voss had earlier confirmed with the melodramatic declaration that he is 'compelled into this country'. Voss seeks to know Australia with his 'heart' and believes himself to be pursued by a kind of 'necessity' which requires him to 'wrestle with his daemon'.[57] One of his many ultra-romantic moments then occurs in the following passage, in which he discusses his planned expedition with his fellow explorer Frank Le Mesurier:

> Every man has a genius, though it is not always discoverable. Least of all when choked by the trivialities of daily existence. But in this disturbing country [...] it is possible more easily to discard the inessential and to attempt the infinite. You will be burnt up most likely, you will have the flesh torn from your bones, you will be tortured probably in many horrible and primitive ways, but you will realise that genius of which you sometimes suspect you are possessed.[58]

As the novel unfolds, Voss's romantic quest becomes the stage upon which his subjectivity is confronted by, and attempts to unify itself with and eventually contain, the Australian landscape and its indigenous inhabitants. Voss is described as 'taking possession' of the Australian interior, and as being

> drawn closer to the landscape, the seldom motionless sea of grass, the twisted trees in grey and black, the sky ever increasing in its rage of blue; and of that landscape, always, he would become the centre.[59]

Although he has no grasp of Aboriginal languages, Voss is 'sustained by a belief that he must communicate intuitively with these black subjects, and finally rule them with a sympathy that is above words'. In this mystical belief, he is entirely mistaken, since his expedition ends with him being held prisoner by a tribe of Aborigines, starving and half conscious, with a shaky grasp on reality. The erstwhile romantic hero thus becomes a 'skull with a candle expiring inside', and later 'a frail god upon a rickety throne'. Voss is finally decapitated by Jackie, a young Aboriginal boy who had formerly been a member of his expedition, demonstrating that his attempts at intuitive intercultural communication have been foiled by a profound lack of understanding between European and Aboriginal cultures. The concluding statement on Voss emerges from his companion of the spirit, Laura Trevelyan, who opines that 'Voss did not die [...] He is there still, it is said, in the country, and always will be. His legend will be written down, eventually, by those who have been troubled by it.'[60]

As Irmtraud Petersson has shown in her excellent study on *German Images in Australian Literature*, commentators on White's novel have related the character of Voss to various figures and motifs in the history of German literature and thought.[61] One of the most common analogies drawn is between Voss and the figure of Faust, especially Goethe's version,[62] while Nietzsche's conception of the *Übermensch* has also frequently been suggested as a prototype for Voss, most notably by Vincent Buckley, who sees White's novel as nothing less than 'a case history of Nietzschean man'.[63] (The *Voss* notebook admittedly offers some support for this Nietzschean interpretation since it contains the following quote from Nietzsche's *Wille zur Macht* which White has transcribed in English: 'since there ceased to be a God, loneliness has become intolerable.')[64] Similarly, Noel Macainsh has argued that Voss is a representative 'German' who embodies the inwardness and extreme subjectivity of German romanticism and idealism. In more recent criticism on *Voss*, increasing emphasis has correctly been placed upon the elements of parody in White's treatment of his German sources. Carolyn Bliss has observed that White's perspective on the character of Voss is 'ironic to an extent unprecedented in his earlier fiction',[65] while Glenn Nicholls has shown the extent to which White, who by his own admission had undergone a *Sturm und Drang* phase during his adolescence and was 'obsessed' by German romantic literature during his time spent in Germany between 1932 and 1935,[66] is able in *Voss* to 'treat German culture with skepticism and irony'. Nicholls compares White's treatment of German romanticism to Thomas Mann's ironic take on Wagnerian motifs in texts like *Tristan*, arguing that *Voss* offers a modernist parody of German romanticism rather than a literal adoption of it.[67]

White himself was often bemused by scholarly attempts to find German romantic prototypes for the character of Voss, which he referred to with playful derision as a form of 'symbol-chasing'.[68] On the question of Nietzsche's influence on *Voss*, for example, he claims only to have read *Also Sprach Zarathustra* 'without being drawn to it'.[69] The *Voss* notebook with its quotation from Nietzsche's *Wille zur Macht* now proves this claim to be false, while also suggesting that White did have sources such as Nietzsche in mind when parodying the German romantic tradition. But the discovery of White's research notebook on *Voss* also raises the possibility that he may have found plentiful romantic source material in Leichhardt's own letters. How then did Leichhardt himself write in his native German about Australia?

Leichhardt's *Briefe an seine Angehörigen*

The selection of Leichhardt's *Letters* that White consulted was translated by Politzer from an earlier German edition entitled *Dr. Ludwig Leichhardt's Briefe an seine Angehörigen* (Dr Ludwig Leichhardt's Letters to his Relatives, 1881).[70] The English edition of Leichhardt's *Letters* used by White is shorter than the original German version, which was edited by the meteorologist Georg Balthasar von Neumayer and includes some of his pre-Australian correspondence. The lucid and informative overview of Leichhardt's background and his journeys of exploration provided by Neumayer, which is also translated by Politzer in the English edition, would have been an excellent source of information for White when he was conducting research for *Voss*.[71] These letters are quite different from Leichhardt's scientific writings such as the *Journal of an Overland Expedition*. Although, as Horst Priessnitz has noted, this journal does contain some romantic asides,[72] and it is mostly written in a dull but competent English, fulfilling the requirements of an objective scientific report tabled primarily for the benefit of an Anglophone audience. By contrast, Leichhardt's letters to his family are written in his native language and their aim is to relate the author's subjective impressions of Australian life to a German audience.[73]

Through his education in Berlin and Göttingen during the later stages of the German romantic period, Leichhardt seems to have become aware of stylistic elements of published letters and travel journals. Such writings had, following the examples of scientific writers such as Alexander von Humboldt and also more literary authors such as Johann Gottfried Herder, become a recognisable genre of German literature during the late eighteenth and early nineteenth centuries.[74] The fact that Leichhardt's personal letters display a self-consciously literary sensibility can be attributed to his knowledge of such authors, especially Alexander von Humboldt, whose account of his Latin American explorations functioned as a model for Leichhardt's own endeavours in Australia.[75] Like many educated Germans of this period, Leichhardt also pays ostentatious tributes to the writings of Goethe and Friedrich Schiller,[76] the two leading authors of German classicism, and his own personal letters need to be seen within this rich literary context. Indeed, as the following passage from a letter sent by Leichhardt to his mother on 6 September 1842 demonstrates, it was Leichhardt's aim to publish his correspondence:

> For the whole time I have ceaselessly been working and collecting; gradually, as my materials become more ordered, I will send you some things to be printed at home; and if Schmalfuß [Leichhardt's brother-in-law, AN] could inquire with a reputable publisher such as Reimer in Berlin, I could perhaps be of use to you from here, in that I would give the proceeds of the royalties to you. It would seem to me most advantageous to arrange such a publication in the form of letters, like for example Raumer's letters about England or Italy.[77]

Leichhardt refers here to the writings of the historian Friedrich Ludwig Georg von Raumer (1781–73),[78] and his clearly expressed desire to publish a similar volume of his own means that his 'private' letters were also intended as public literary documents. It is this eminently literary Leichhardt who may have offered a rich literary resource for White when he was undertaking his background research for *Voss*.

Indeed, there exists at least one clear case in which Leichhardt's reflections on the Australian landscape in the *Letters* make their way not only into White's research notebook for *Voss* but also onto the pages of *Voss* itself. On 6 September 1842, Leichhardt, after recently arriving in Australia, writes to his mother:

> I do not feel unhappy! Since after all this time I have gotten used to living with nature and to finding joy through observing and researching her. Sydney is surrounded by outcrops of sandstone and by sand hills, which often remind me of the sandy Mark Brandenburg.[79]

The following page from White's research notebook for *Voss* lists a series of direct quotes from what White refers to as 'Leichhardt's Letters' and they match Politzer's translation word for word. About two-thirds of the way down this page, one can find a direct transcription of Leichhardt's comparison between the Sydney landscape and the Mark Brandenburg: 'Sydney is surrounded by sandrocks and sandhills that remind me often of in sandy Mark Brandenburg.'

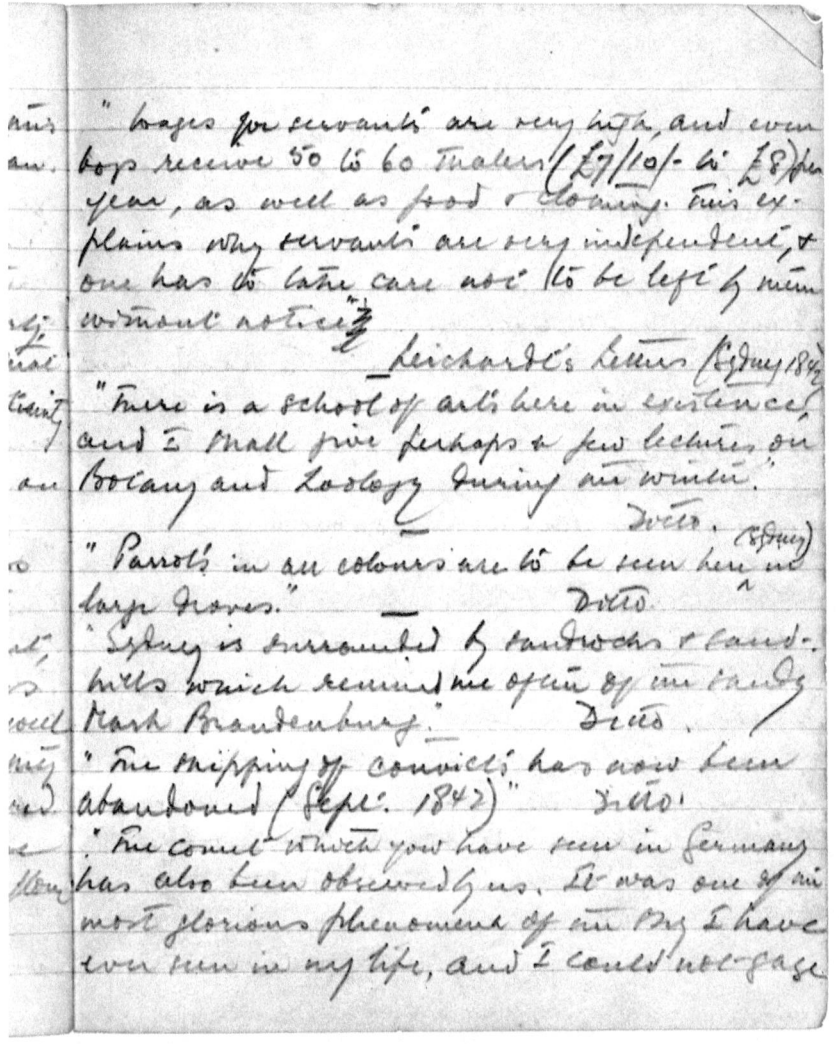

Figure 2.4 National Library of Australia, MS 9982 Papers of Patrick White, 1930–2002 [manuscript]. Series 2: Literary notebooks, 1930s–1970s; item 5: notebook containing research for *Voss* (1957), c.1955–57, part 49. Also avalilable online via the NLA catalogue.

This same comparison appears, in turn, in the opening section of *Voss* when the novel's main protagonist first meets Laura Trevelyan:

> 'After the journey in the heat,' she said with that same ease, 'you will want to rest. And your horse. I must send the man round.'
> 'I came on foot,' replied the German, who was now caught.
> 'From Sydney!' she said.
> 'It is four kilometres, at most, and perhaps one quarter.'
> 'But monotonous.'
> 'I am at home,' he said. 'It is like the poor parts of Germany. Sandy. It could be the Mark Brandenburg.'[80]

Seen in isolation, this passage emerging from the *Voss* notebook amounts to nothing more than proof that White consulted Leichhardt's *Letters* and transcribed sections of them directly into *Voss*. The argument being proposed here goes further than this, suggesting that the *Letters* do not amount to background source material only; rather, their self-conscious literary framing and their undeniably romantic sensibility are of direct thematic significance for White's portrayal of Voss.

As we have seen, a central theme of White's novel is the relationship between the subjectivity of Voss and the Australian landscape. Voss is variously described as being 'obsessed' by the landscape, of taking ownership over it 'by right of vision', of 'possessing the whole country with his eyes' and as finally becoming the 'centre' of the landscape which he surveys.[81] As many scholars have pointed out, these descriptions of Voss are heavily ironic in that the conclusion of the novel shows that the landscape ends up possessing him, and that the questing subjectivity of German romanticism is brought undone by Australian conditions. Having studied in Berlin and later in Göttingen during the twilight years of German idealism, Leichhardt was of course aware of the romantic notion that there exists a dialectical relationship between the perceiving subject on the one hand and nature on the other hand. Take, for example, this heady passage written by Leichhardt to his sister in 1843, which also appears in Politzer's edition of the letters:

> What should I say to you concerning my activities? You delight in the beautiful flower and its perfume, you delight in the verdant tree and its shadow, you gaze over the forest and meadow from the earth to the starry sky, and you feel yourself to be moved by higher feelings, since so many voices speak to you of an infinite being unknown to you. If nature moves you in such a friendly way, how much more must she do this to me, in that I have made it my task to penetrate into her deepest secrets and to discover her eternal laws, according to which she functions so magnificently, so splendidly.[82]

This passage, I submit, provides us with evidence that Leichhardt's correspondence was not simply a private affair but was consciously framed within the discourse of German romanticism. The image of a questing Leichhardt who endeavours to penetrate into the secrets of nature is, moreover, echoed in Voss's own quest to know and master the Australian landscape.

Perhaps, the clearest thematic parallel between Leichhardt's *Letters* and White's novel exists in the notion of a character compelled by a kind of indwelling necessity to explore and conquer Australia, even at the risk of death. It seems quite likely that White may have derived this idea, and the high romantic language in which it is expressed, not necessarily from Goethe or Nietzsche but from reading Leichhardt's own letters in Politzer's edition. In the following letter dated 20 October 1847, Leichhardt writes to his brother-in-law Schmalfuss concerning the failure of the second expedition of 1846–47, controversially attributing this failure to the weakness of his Australian companions. Leichhardt thanks Schlmalfuss for his suggestion that he should perhaps direct his energies into less risky enterprises than attempting the first east-west crossing of Australia, an attempt that would eventually lead to his death in the third expedition of 1848. Yet Leichhardt is unable to follow the advice of Schmalfuss, and responds with the following lines:

> You give me admirable advice in your kind letter; but I cannot follow it; it lies outside of my nature. An infinite, unconquerable urge drives me to study this nature and to solve the puzzles of this land.[83]

It is this formulation – *ein unendlicher unbezwingbarer Drang*, 'an infinite, unconquerable urge' – that resonates in Patrick White's *Voss*. In White's novel, Voss refers to his Australian quest as a kind of compulsion or daemonic possession that pursues him relentlessly. 'I am compelled into this country,' he remarks at one point early in the novel, before later commenting

> I will cross the continent from one end to the other. I have every intention to know it with my heart. Why I am pursued by this necessity, it is no more possible for me to tell than it is for you, who have made my acquaintance only before yesterday.[84]

The Significance of the *Voss* Notebook

What conclusions, then, can we draw from White's *Voss* notebook? The notebook reveals that Leichhardt's letters to his relatives were used directly by White, even to the extent that he transcribed directly from them when writing *Voss* (the extent to which such transcriptions appear throughout the entirety of *Voss* has not been systematically investigated here, and is a topic worthy of further research).

Moreover, when we look beyond the parochial Australian debates concerning the legacy of Leichhardt as an explorer, while also taking into account the context of Leichhardt's education in Berlin and Göttingen during the 1830s, we are able to situate his German correspondence within the context of late German romanticism. Leichhardt's German correspondence reveals that he had literary ambitions and that his understanding of the relationship between the self and the nature was expressed in a self-consciously romantic and literary language that echoes particular formulations used by White in *Voss*. This in turn raises the possibility that the chief German romantic source for *Voss* was not Goethe or Nietzsche, as many critics have assumed, but rather Leichhardt's own writings, and demands a reconsideration not only of Leichhardt as a literary figure but also of his direct literary influence upon White.

Notes

1 My thanks to Clemency Fisher, Tom Darragh and Rod Fensham for their assistance with my queries about the diaries of John Gilbert and Ludwig Leichhardt. Some of the material presented here is analysed in different contexts in the following papers: Angus Nicholls, '"The Core of this Dark Continent": Ludwig Leichhardt's Australian Explorations', in *Transnational Networks: German Migrants in the British Empire, 1670–1914*, ed. John R. Davis, Stefan Manz and Margit Schulte Beerbühl (Leiden: Brill, 2012), 141–62; Angus Nicholls, 'The Young Leichhardt's Diaries in the Context of his Australian Cultural Legacy', in *The Leichhardt Diaries. Early Travels in Australia During 1842–1844, Memoirs of the Queensland Museum* 7, no. 2, ed. Tom Darragh and Rod Fensham (Brisbane: Queensland Museum, 2013), 541–59.

2 See Marcel Aurousseau, 'The Identity of Voss', *Meanjin* 17, no. 1 (1958): 85–86. See also: Aurousseau, ed. and trans., *The Letters of F. W. Ludwig Leichhardt*, 3 vols (Cambridge: Cambridge University Press, 1967–68); Harold Orel, 'Is Patrick White's Voss the Real Leichhardt of Australia?' *Costerus: Essays in English and American Language and Literature* 6 (1972): 109–19.

3 These materials are listed in the National Library of Australia catalogue as follows: MS 9982 Papers of Patrick White, 1930–2002 [manuscript]. Series 2: Literary notebooks, 1930s–1970s. Item 5: Notebook containing research for *Voss* (1957), c. 1955–57 (hereafter *NLA Voss Notebook* followed by part number). A second notebook – listed as Item 4: Notebook, including material for *Voss* (1957), *Riders in the Chariot* (1961) and *A Fringe of Leaves* (1976), c. 1947–76 – contains only very limited material of direct relevance to *Voss*.

4 Hume's case is mentioned later in the *NLA Voss Notebook*, see parts 25–26.

5 See, for example, *NLA Voss Notebook*, part 30. Elizabeth Gould's correspondence was at that time unpublished but available in the Mitchell Library. She was the sister of Stephen Coxen (also listed on Figure 2.1).

6 The passages transcribed by White also appear in a volume that has only recently been published: *This Errant Lady: Jane Franklin's Overland Journey to Port Phillip and Sydney, 1839*, ed. Penny Russell (Canberra: National Library of Australia, 2002); White seems to have taken them from *The Life, Diaries and Correspondence of Lady Jane Franklin*,

ed. Willingham Franklin Rawnsley (London: Erskine MacDonald, 1923), since Rawnsley's name appears on his list (see Figure 2.2, top right). For references to Franklin's text, see *NLA Voss Notebook*, part 31.
7 Edward John Eyre, *Journals of Expeditions of Discovery into Central Australia*, 2 vols (London: T. & W. Boone, 1845); see *NLA Voss Notebook*, parts 51–57.
8 John Dunmore Lang, *Cooksland in North-Eastern Australia: The Future Cotton-Field of Great Britain* (London: Longman, Brown, Green & Longmans, 1847); see *NLA Voss Notebook*, part 37.
9 Augustus Charles Gregory, *Expedition in Search of Dr. Leichhardt, Report of Proceedings* (Sydney: Government Printer, 1858); see *NLA Voss Notebook*, parts 27–30.
10 Charles Sturt, *Narrative of an Expedition into Central Australia*, 2 vols (London: T. & W. Boone, 1849); see *NLA Voss Notebook*, parts 45–47.
11 John McDougall Stewart, *Explorations in Australia: The Journals of John McDougall Stewart During the Years 1858, 1859, 1860, 1861 and 1862* (London: Saunders, Otley & Co., 1865); see *NLA Voss Notebook*, part 48.
12 Georgiana McCrae, *Georgiana's Journal: Melbourne a Hundred Years Ago*, ed. Hugh McCrae (Sydney: Angus & Robertson, 1934); see *NLA Voss Notebook*, parts 64–67.
13 Ludwig Leichhardt, *Dr. Ludwig Leichhardt's Letters from Australia*, trans. L. L. Politzer, introd. Alec H. Chisholm (Melbourne: Pan, 1944); see *NLA Voss Notebook*, parts 21–23, 25.
14 Daniel Bunce, *Travels with Dr. Leichhardt in Australia* (Melbourne: W. Fairfax, 1859); see *NLA Voss Notebook*, parts 3–20.
15 Ludwig Leichhardt, *Journal of an Overland Expedition in Australia from Moreton Bay to Port Essington* (London: T. & W. Boone, 1847).
16 For example, a phrase appearing in the *Voss* Notebook (part 24), according to which the rushing of water resembles the sound of 'a sea-beach heard at a short distance', matches exactly an entry in Gilbert's Diary dated 5 April 1845. See John Gilbert, *Diary of the Port Essington Expedition, 18 Sept. 1844–28 June 1845*, MS. A2586, Mitchell Library, State Library of NSW, accessed 11 November 2012 online: http://acms.sl.nsw.gov.au/_transcript/2012/D15039/a4331.pdf. White is also likely to have come across material relating to Gilbert through reading Alec H. Chisholm's *Strange New World: The Adventures of John Gilbert and Ludwig Leichhardt* (Sydney: Angus & Robertson, 1941).
17 For the most recent research on what may have happened on this final expedition, see Darrell Lewis, 'The Fate of Leichhardt', *Historical Records of Australian Science* 17, no. 1 (2006): 1–30.
18 See Horst Priessnitz, 'The "Vossification" of Ludwig Leichhardt', in *From Berlin to the Burdekin: The German Contribution to the Development of Australian Science, Exploration and the Arts*, ed. David Walker and Jürgen Tampke (Kensington: New South Wales University Press, 1991), 196–217.
19 Glenn Nicholls, 'Exploration and Immigration: How Intercultural Interpretations are Changing the History of Ludwig Leichhardt', *Journal of Intercultural Studies* 21, no. 1 (2000): 25–37 (25).
20 Horst Priessnitz has referred to this process as the 'Vossification' of Leichardt. See Priessnitz, 'Vossification'.
21 Already in the nineteenth century Leichhardt became the subject of an array of studies. Two early accounts published in the late 1840s – Christopher Pemberton Hodgson's *Reminiscences of Australia* (London: W. N. Wright, 1846) and John Dunmore Lang's *Cooksland in North-Eastern Australia* (London: Longman, Brown, Green &

Longmans, 1847, cited above) – are highly positive about Leichhardt's successful first expedition. Reaction began to set in with two publications written by members of Leichhardt's second expedition: Daniel Bunce's *Travels with Dr. Leichhardt* (Melbourne: W. Fairfax, 1859) and John Frederick Mann's *Eight Months with Dr. Leichhardt in the Years 1846–47* (Sydney: Turner & Henderson, 1888), both of which are considered below. Leichhardt was also discussed in general histories of Australian exploration such as John Forrest's *Explorations in Australia* (London: Sampson Low, 1875) and Henry Stuart Russell's *The Genesis of Queensland* (Sydney: Turner & Henderson, 1888); while Forrest's account is largely neutral, Russell describes Leichhardt as a competent scientist but a totally incompetent bushman. In the twentieth century, serious biographical study of Leichhardt commenced with Catherine Drummond Cotton's largely positive account of Leichhardt's explorations in *Ludwig Leichhardt and the Great South Land* (Sydney: Angus & Robertson, 1938). Cotton's study was, however, followed by an extended personal attack upon Leichhardt in the form of Alec H. Chisholm's *Strange New World: The Adventures of John Gilbert and Ludwig Leichhardt* (Sydney: Angus & Robertson, 1941). Chisholm's tendentious account is discussed below. A more sober and objective tone resumed with L. L. Politzer's, *Bibliography of Literature on Dr. Ludwig Leichhardt* (Melbourne: Privately Printed, 1953) and two works by Renée Erdos: *Ludwig Leichhardt* (Oxford: Oxford University Press, 1963) and 'Leichhardt, Friedrich Wilhelm Ludwig (1813–1848)', in *Australian Dictionary of National Biography*, vol. 2 (Melbourne: Melbourne University Press, 1967), 102–04. Erdos offers a factual account of Leichhardt's activities but does not weigh into the debates raised by Bunce, Mann, Chisholm and others concerning the merits or otherwise of Leichhardt's character. In his 1967 introduction to the first comprehensive edition of Leichhardt's correspondence (cited above), which includes English translations of Leichhardt's German letters, Marcel Aurousseau takes issue with earlier accounts like that offered by Chisholm, lamenting in general the lack of objectivity in Australian scholarship on Leichhardt. This effort to rehabilitate Leichhardt continued with E. M. Webster's *Whirlwinds in the Plain: Ludwig Leichhardt, Friends, Foes and History* (Melbourne: Melbourne University Press, 1980) which is as much an account of those who wrote about Leichhardt as it is of Leichhardt's life itself. Webster was followed by what is the most rigorous of all Leichhardt biographies in English, Colin Roderick's *Leichhardt, the Dauntless Explorer* (Sydney: Angus & Robertson, 1988), which offers (for the first time by an Australian scholar) a detailed account of Leichhardt's German educational background, based on close analysis of his personal diaries, logs and field book.

22 The German reception of Leichhardt has, perhaps unsurprisingly, been far more positive in its assessments of his achievements and character. The first German publication on Leichhardt appeared in 1856, in the form of Ernst Amadus Zuchold's *Dr. Ludwig Leichhardt: Eine biographische Skizze* (Leipzig: Wilhelm Naundorf, 1856). Zuchold's study is in part based upon Daniel Bunce's serialised account of the second journey that appeared in the Melbourne newspaper *The Argus* during 1850. Since Leichhardt came from a part of Prussia that later fell within the borders of East Germany, a series of works on him emerged from the German Democratic Republic, presenting Leichhardt as a hero of German exploration and science. These included Hans Damm's *Ins innere Australiens. Die erste Durchquerung von Brisbane zur Nordküste* (Leipzig: Brockhaus, 1951) and Heinz Haufe's *Entdeckungsreise in Australien. Ludwig Leichhardt, ein deutscher Forschungsschicksal* (Berlin: Verlag der Nation, 1973). A recent biography by Diethmar Felden, *Durch den fünften Kontinent: Leben und Leistung Ludwig Leichhardts* (Gotha: Julius Perthes, 1996), has largely continued in this vein. Like

Roderick, Hans Wilhelm Finger has written detailed accounts of Leichhardt's life that are based upon close readings of the diaries but include little analysis of the secondary literature. These include *Leichhardt: Die ganze Geschichte von F. W. Ludwig Leichhardt* (Göttingen: Niedersächsische Staats- und Universitätsbibliothek, 1999), which discusses Leichhardt's family background and education in some depth, and *Das Unmögliche Wagen: Ein australisches Epos* (Munich: Fritz Finger Verlag, 2000), which is confined to Leichhardt's time in Australia.

23 Marcel Aurousseau, ed. and trans. *The Letters of F. W. Ludwig Leichhardt*, 3 vols (Cambridge: Cambridge University Press, 1967–68).

24 Some of the problems with Marcel Aurousseau's translation of Leichhardt's correspondence are discussed by Roderick in *Leichhardt, the Dauntless Explorer*, 8.

25 Roderick, *Leichhardt, the Dauntless Explorer*, 30. See also Roderick, 'The Education of an Explorer: Ludwig Leichhardt', in *From Berlin to the Burdekin*, 22–39.

26 Felden, *Durch den fünften Kontinent*, 12.

27 See Martin Vöhler, 'Christian Gottlob Heyne und das Studium des Altertums in Deutschland', in *Disciplining Classics: Altertumswissenschaft als Beruf* (Göttingen: Vandenhoeck & Ruprecht, 2002), 39–54.

28 See George S. Williamson, *The Longing for Myth in Germany* (Chicago, IL: University of Chicago Press, 2004), 30–32.

29 Roderick, *Leichhardt, the Dauntless Explorer*, 45.

30 Roderick, *Leichhardt, the Dauntless Explorer*, 84. On the networks that led to Leichhardt's decision to travel to Australia, see Nicholls, '"The Core of this Dark Continent": Ludwig Leichhardt's Australian Explorations', 145–49.

31 Roderick, *Leichhardt, the Dauntless Explorer*, 165–67.

32 Roderick, *Leichhardt, the Dauntless Explorer*, 228, 236.

33 Chisholm, *Strange New World*, vii, xi–xiv.

34 Alec. H. Chisholm, 'Introduction', in *Dr. Ludwig Leichhardt's Letters from Australia*, 5–6.

35 Daniel Bunce, *Travels with Dr Leichhardt* (1859; repr. Oxford: Oxford University Press, 1979), 153–59. See also Webster, *Whirlwinds in the Plain*, 144–46.

36 Ludwig Leichhardt to C. Schmalfuss, 20 October 1847, *The Letters of F. W. Ludwig Leichhardt*, vol 3, 945–56 (948).

37 In the Preface to this volume, Mann refers to a letter in which 'the Doctor [i.e., Leichhardt], in a letter to his brother-in-law, attributes the whole of his misfortunes to the bad conduct of his companions '[…] For the sake of my children, myself, and the memory of my former companions, I now publish a true version of this journey in as brief a form as possible'. John Frederick Mann, *Eight Months with Dr. Leichhardt in the Years 1846–47* (Sydney: Turner & Henderson, 1888), 3.

38 Daniel Bunce, *Travels with Dr Leichhardt* (1859; repr. Oxford: Oxford University Press, 1979), viii.

39 See Aurousseau, *The Letters of F. W. Ludwig Leichhardt*, vol 1, x–xvi; Webster, *Whirlwinds in the Plain*, 367–80; Roderick, *Leichhardt, the Dauntless Explorer*, 1–3, 442–62.

40 Irmtraud Petersson, *German Images in Australian Literature* (Frankfurt am Main: Peter Lang, 1990), 183–215; Susan Martin, 'Leichhardt in Australian Literature' in *Leichhardt: the Man, the Mystery, the Science, the History*, Symposium held at the National Museum of Australia, Canberra, 16 June 2007, accessed 23 October 2012 online: http://www.nma.gov.au/audio/transcripts/leichhardt/NMA_martin_20070615.html. For a discussion of representations of Leichhardt in Australian literature since the publication of *Voss*, see Glenn Nicholls, 'Exploration and Immigration', 31–35.

41 Henry Kendall, 'Leichhardt', in *The Poetical Works of Henry Kendall*, ed. T. T. Reed (Adelaide: Libraries Board of South Australia, 1966), 228–30 (229).
42 A. B. Paterson, 'The Lost Leichhardt', *Bulletin*, 14 October 1899.
43 Francis Webb, 'Leichhardt in Theatre', in *Collected Poems* (Sydney: Angus & Robertson, 1969), 35–45; here: 36–37.
44 Francis Webb, 'Leichhardt Pantomime', *Bulletin*, 17 December 1947: 21.
45 Patrick White to Ben Huebsch, 11 September 1956, in *Patrick White: Letters*, ed. David Marr (London: Jonathan Cape, 1994), 107–09 (107).
46 Patrick White to Marcel Aurousseau, 18 July 1970, cited in David Marr, *Patrick White: A Life* (London: Jonathan Cape, 1991), 314.
47 Marr, *Life*, 316.
48 See Nicholls, 'The Young Leichhardt's Diaries.'
49 In a recent article on Leichhardt materials held in Australian libraries, Matthew Stephens refers to the following collections of Leichhardt's papers in the Mitchell Library: MSS C154, Notebook comprising notes, manuscripts and letters, 1842–47; MSS 683/1–2, Diaries, Correspondence and Papers, 1842–47. Matthew Stephens, 'From Lost Property to Explorer's Relics: The Rediscovery of the Personal Library of Ludwig Leichhardt', *Historical Records of Australian Science* 18, no. 2 (2007): 191–27 (208). Colin Roderick notes that the log of Leichhardt's second expedition is held in the Dixson Library (*Leichhardt, the Dauntless Explorer*, 2). On Leichhardt's diaries see also Robert Sellick, 'Leichhardt's Diaries', in *From Berlin to the Burdekin*, 218–27.
50 National Library of Australia catalogue listing: MS 9982 Papers of Patrick White, 1930–2002 [manuscript]. Series 2: Literary notebooks, 1930s–1970s. Item 4: Notebook, including material for *Voss* (1957), *Riders in the Chariot* (1961) and *A Fringe of Leaves* (1976), c. 1947–76, parts 15 and 19. White mentions his interest in Jewish mysticism in a letter to Kerry Walker dated 24 June 1982, cited in Marr, *Life*, 452.
51 See Marr, *Life*, 114–37, 144–45; Patrick White, *Flaws in the Glass* (1981; repr. Harmonsdworth: Penguin, 1983), 38–39.
52 White, *Flaws in the Glass*, 104.
53 See, for example, Aurousseau, 'The Identity of Voss', and Orel, 'Is Patrick White's Voss the Real Leichhardt of Australia?'
54 See Aurousseau, 'The Identity of Voss'.
55 Patrick White, *Voss* (London: Eyre & Spottiswoode, 1957), 9, 30, 111, 67, 423.
56 White, *Flaws in the Glass*, 103.
57 White, *Voss*, 32, 23, 36, 38.
58 White, *Voss*, 38–39.
59 White, *Voss*, 203, 181.
60 White, *Voss*, 356, 382, 414, 478.
61 Irmtraud Petersson, *German Images in Australian Literature*, 203–15. For Petersson's discussion of depictions of Leichhardt in Australian literature, see also 183–202.
62 See, for example, Geoffrey Dutton, *Patrick White* (Melbourne: Landsdowne, 1962), 35; Patricia Morley, *The Mystery of Unity: Theme and Technique in the Novels of Patrick White* (St Lucia: University of Queensland Press, 1972), 129, 151; Dorothy Green, '*Voss*: Stubborn Music', in *The Australian Experience: Critical Essays on Australian Novels*, ed. W. S. Ramson (Canberra: ANU Press, 1974), 284–310 (287); Veronica Brady, 'In My End is My Beginning: Laura as Heroine of *Voss*', *Southerly* 35 (1975): 16–32; Thomas Stein, *Patrick White: Voss* (Munich: Fink, 1983), 36. All of the above quoted in Petersson, *German Images in Australian Literature*, 203–15.

63 Vincent Buckley, 'The Novels of Patrick White', in *The Literature of Australia*, ed. Geoffrey Dutton (1964; repr. Ringwood, Vic.: Penguin, 1982), 413–26 (422). Similar views are held by Barry Argyle, *Patrick White* (Edinburgh: Oliver & Boyd, 1967), 46; Brian Kiernan, *Patrick White* (London: Macmillan, 1980), 51; Ann M. McCulloch, 'Patrick White's Novels and Nietzsche', *Australian Literary Studies* 9, no. 3 (1980): 309–20. All of the above quoted in Petersson, *German Images in Australian Literature*, 203–15.
64 See *NLA Voss Notebook*, part 37.
65 Carolyn Bliss, *Patrick White's Fiction* (Houndmills, Basingstoke: Macmillan, 1986), 64.
66 See Marr, *Life*, 133; White, *Flaws in the Glass*, 39.
67 Glenn Nicholls, 'Patrick White the Parodist: The German Romantic Tradition in *Voss*', *Antipodes* 10, no. 1 (1996): 15–19.
68 Patrick White to Manfred Mackenzie, 5 January 1963, in *Letters*, 216–17.
69 Patrick White to the Moores, Dogwoods, 8 February 1958, in *Letters*, 129–31; here 129.
70 See *Dr. Ludwig Leichhardt's Briefe an seine Angehörigen: Herausgegeben im Auftrage der Geographischen Gesellschaft in Hamburg von Dr. G. Neumayer und Otto Leichhardt* (Hamburg: L. Friederichsen, 1881). For a more detailed account of how this volume came to be published, see Nicholls, '"The Core of this Dark Continent": Ludwig Leichhardt's Australian Explorations', 154–56.
71 Georg Balthasar von Neumayer, 'Dr. Ludwig Leichhardt as Naturalist and Explorer', in *Dr. Ludwig Leichhardt's Letters from Australia*, 71–96.
72 Priessnitz, 'The "Vossification" of Leichhardt', 202.
73 Here it should be noted that Leichhardt addressed and sent nearly all of his German correspondence with his family to his brother-in-law, Carl Schmalfuss; however, the individual letters themselves were also often intended for other members of the family, including his mother and sister. This explains why the letters quoted here are all cited as being from Leichhardt to Schmalfuss.
74 For context on German travel writing of the period, see Alison E. Martin, *Moving Scenes: The Aesthetics of German Travel Writing on England, 1783–1830* (London: Legenda, 2008).
75 See Alexander von Humboldt, *Relation historique du voyage aux régions équinoxiales du nouveau continent (*1814–25, trans. into English as *Personal Narrative of Travels to the Equinoctial Regions of the New Continent)*. Leichhardt had met Humboldt in Paris a year before his departure to Australia. Writing to his brother-in-law in 1847, Leichhardt says of Humboldt: 'his example was and is constantly in my view' [*sein Beispiel war und ist mir beständig vor Augen*]. Leichhardt to Schmalfuss, 21 October 1847, in *Dr. Ludwig Leichhardt's Briefe an seine Angehörigen*, 166; see also Politzer, *Dr. Ludwig Leichhardt's Letters*, 64; and Roderick, *Leichhardt, the Dauntless Explorer*, 146–47.
76 See, for example, Leichhardt's lengthy digression on the poetry of Schiller in his letter to Schmalfuss dated 21 October 1847, *Dr. Ludwig Leichhardt's Briefe an seine Angehörigen*, 167–68; see also Politzer, *Dr. Ludwig Leichhardt's Letters*, 65. Leichhardt also begins his *Journal of an Overland Expedition* with an epigraph from Goethe's drama *Iphigenie auf Tauris*: 'Die Götter brauchen manchen guten Mann/Zu ihrem Dienst auf dieser weiten Erde' [The gods need some good man/To serve them on this wide earth].
77 [*Ich habe die ganze Zeit über unablässig gearbeitet und gesammelt; allmählig, wie sich meine Materialien mehr ordnen, werde ich Euch Sachen zum Druck nach Hause senden; und wenn Schmalfuß bei einem angesehenen Buchhändler, z.B. bei Reimer in Berlin anfragte, könnte ich vielleicht für Euch*

von hier aus nützlich werden, indem ich Euch den Vorteil des Honorars überliesse. Es scheint mir am besten, eine solche Veröffentlichung in Brief form zu fassen, wie zum Beispiel Raumers Briefe über England oder Italien]. Ludwig Leichhardt to Carl Schmalfuss, Sydney, 6 September 1842, in *Dr. Ludwig Leichhardts Briefe an seine Angehörigen*, 119 (this letter was sent to Leichhardt's brother-in-law, Schmalfuss, but was written for Leichhardt's mother); see also Politzer, *Dr. Ludwig Leichhardt's Letters*, 18–19.

78 Friedrich von Raumer, *Briefe aus Paris zur Erläuterung der Geschichte des sechzehnten und siebzehnten Jahrhunderts*, Teil 2: *Italien und Großbritannien* (Leipzig: Brockhaus, 1831).

79 [*Ich fühle mich nicht unglücklich! Denn seit so langer Zeit habe ich mich gewöhnt mit der Natur zu leben und in ihrer Betrachtung und Erforschung Freude zu finden [...] Sidney ist von Sandsteinfelsen und Sandhügeln umgeben, welche mich oft an die sandige Mark Brandenburg erinnern*]. Leichhardt to Schmalfuss, Sydney, 6 September 1842, in *Dr. Ludwig Leichhardts Briefe an seine Angehörigen*, 116–17, my trans.; see also Politzer, *Dr Ludwig Leichhardt's Letters*, 16–17.

80 White, *Voss*, 13.

81 White, *Voss*, 31, 32, 165, 181.

82 [*Was soll ich Dir über meine Beschäftigungen sagen? Du erfreust Dich der schönen Blumen und ihres Duftes, Du erfreust Dich des grünenden Baumes und seines Schattens, Du blickst über Wald und Flur von der Erde zum gestirnten Himmel, und Du fühlst Dich von höheren Gefühlen bewegt, indem so viele Stimmen von einem unendlichen Wesen, Dir unbewusst, sprechen. Wenn Dich die Natur so freundlich bewegt, wie vielmehr muss sie es mir thun, der ich es mir zur Aufgabe mache, in ihre tiefsten Geheimnisse ein zu dringen und die ewigen Gesetze zu entdecken, nach welchen sie so herrlich, so grossartig wirkt*]. Leichhardt to Schmalfuss, Newcastle, NSW, 15 May 1843, in *Dr. Ludwig Leichhardts Briefe an seine Angehörigen*, 129, my trans.; see also Politzer, *Dr. Ludwig Leichhardt's Letters*, 28.

83 [*Du giebst mir herrlichen Rath in Deinem lieben Briefe; doch ich kann ihn nicht befolgen; es liegt ausser meiner Natur. Ein unendlicher unbezwingbarer Drang treibt mich, diese Natur zu studiren und die Rätzel dieses Landes zu lösen*]. Leichhardt to Schmalfuss, Sydney, 20 October 1847, in *Dr. Ludwig Leichhardt's Briefe an seine Angehörigen*, 129, my trans. Politzer's translation of 'ein unendlicher, unbezwingbarer Drang' is rather more prosaic and inaccurate, being rendered as 'an irresistible urge', *Dr. Ludwig Leichhardt's Letters*, 61.

84 White, *Voss*, 23, 36.

Part II
MANY IN ONE

Chapter 3

WHITE'S LONDON

David Marr

Patrick White chose a remarkable occasion to make his loyalties plain. The day after the news broke that he had won the Nobel Prize and Australians were claiming White as their own, he told the press assembled in his Sydney garden: 'I feel what I am, I don't feel particularly Australian. I live here and work here. A Londoner is what I think I am at heart but my blood is Australian and that's what gets me going.'[1]

He put it less politely in private. After not hearing from his old lover Pepe Mamblas for 25 years or more, the now Duke of Baena wrote to congratulate him on the prize. White replied: 'Two years ago we were in Europe, but like it less and less. London, parts of the French provinces, and the mountains of Greece are all I want to see again. I am at heart a Londoner, only by fate an Australian; I imagine it's like being born with a hump or a clubfoot: one has to put up with it.'[2]

White never doubted that returning to Australia after World War II was of fundamental importance to him as a man and an artist. The alternative, he wrote in his endlessly quoted essay *Prodigal Son*, was 'remaining in what I then felt to be an actual and spiritual graveyard, with the prospect of ceasing to be an artist and turning instead into that most sterile of beings, a London intellectual'.[3]

That he made such a fanfare of his escape and grizzled so much every time he visited the city as a lionised writer blinds us to the part London played in his life and writing. He was born there, discovered sex in the city and celebrated his first literary triumphs in London. His affection for the city was not sentimental. He complained about it all his life, with the love and despair of a native.

Even in his most reclusive years in Sarsaparilla, he never lost contact with London. He used a London bookshop and each week the airmail edition of the *Observer* arrived at his house on Showground Road. Heaps of rustling rice paper, the *Observer* was a mark of civilization in the better-off houses of Australia for decades. White's was one. His letters were alive with references to the *Observer*. He particularly loved the photographs.

'Thank you for letters and the Asprey catalogue,' he wrote to Geoff and Ninette Dutton in the 1970s. 'It is really surprising that such expensive toys are made in present-day England; one wonders who would buy them: perhaps some of those faces one sees in the business section of the *Observer*. However, I must say some of the jewels appeal to me. I shall always be a sucker for jewels and furs; if I were a woman I expect I should have become the most rapacious kind of cocotte, and probably would have got stoned for wearing bird-of-paradise plumes on top of everything else.'[4]

It irked White enormously that the *Observer*'s reviews of his work were the most hostile he had in England. It seemed a poor way to repay a loyal reader on the far side of the world. He saw plots, even the malignant hand of Clive James behind these unhappy notices. Angus Wilson's review of *The Twyborn Affair* in 1979 was an exception. It was, he told his New York publisher Alan Williams, 'the first time in decades that I haven't been done dirt in the *Observer*'.[5]

* * * * *

White believed that to be born a Gemini gave him an affinity with Pushkin, Henry Lawson and Marilyn Monroe. He was convinced the time and place of birth matters for everyone. That he was born in London was a fact on which he placed great importance, and the four months before he embarked with parents and nanny for Australia in September 1912 were 'a formative period'.[6]

The rest of his childhood was spent among Australians of a certain class who believed themselves as at home in London as they were in Sydney or Melbourne. For most it was a delusion – a delusion White would explore in his novels – but for many it was absolutely true. Their lives were spent in big houses in Australia and big houses in Britain. Marriages were made. Australian money put lead on British roofs. White's mother Ruth would set up home in London after the war and pour a little of her fortune into Glyndebourne. Being Australian and being children of the Empire was not thought the least contradictory in those years. At least in the white dominions, the ethos of the British Empire was an empire of equals.

The boy was back in London at the age of 13 on his way to school. The 1920s was the last decade in which the Australian rich in large numbers gambled with the lives of their children in English boarding schools. Young Patrick was one of those damaged by the experience and emerged with a wary suspicion of the human race and a connoisseur of bullying in all its nuances.

'My four years at boarding school in England were such hell, I shouldn't wish it for any child I know,' he told his niece Alexandra Bishop. 'The only thing I can say in favour of them is that, when anything particularly awful was happening during the War, like the Blitz in London, or when one was being shot up or bombed in the Western Desert, or escaping into Tobruk in the dark, I used to tell myself: at least none of this is quite so bad as the years at Cheltenham, because the enemy is only trying to destroy one's body, not the part that matters.'[7]

Australian boarding schools in the 1920s were as capable as Cheltenham College of breaking a boy. White never saw that the Philistine values he so despised in his schooldays were one and the same with the Philistine values he would excoriate back home. Along with the language, the crown, the Westminster system and the common law, those Philistine instincts are Britain's enduring legacy to Australia. It is a common bond we strangely fail to celebrate.

What London could give the boy was theatre, and it was through the West End that White fell in love with the city while he was still a schoolboy. With Ronald Waters, a stage-struck friend in the same boarding house, White spent hours concocting shows, designing stage sets and writing away for the autographs of actresses. One of their contemporaries in the house Ragnar Christophersen told me of the boys gathering after the Christmas holidays one year to boast how many shows they had all seen. 'We asked Paddy once and I remember he had been to thirty, which meant he must have been to the theatre or cinema on some days at least twice.'

White's first and enduring literary ambition was to have a great success in the West End. Though he bitched all his life about his family's malign attitude to his career, he finally admitted to me, as he read through the manuscript of my biography – in front of me slowly over nine agonizing days – that being a playwright had also been his mother Ruth's ambition for him: to be another Somerset Maugham, the next Galsworthy. After Cheltenham and a couple of years jackerooing in Australia – to see if indeed he might be suited for the land – and then three years in Cambridge, White came down to London in 1935, found a room in Ebury Street and began to write plays.

We know so much more – perhaps too much – of his early efforts now that his notebooks from that time have reached the National Library of Australia. 'Miracle' was perhaps his first:

> A child in the East End claims to have seen the virgin and can show stigmata. After some time the child, tormented by her conscience, confesses to fraud. The effect on the various personages. The cabinet minister who has given up his career for a life of contemplation as a result. His mistress who has also converted. How are they to react?[8]

There was a handsome Jesuit involved somehow in the plot and a rather blowsy upper crust woman wearing mauves and purple who would wander in and out of White's work for the next fifty years.

Nothing came of the unknown number of plays he wrote in his Ebury Street years: 'Marriages are Made in Hell', 'It is a Pity She is Blind', 'How Many Virgins' and so on.[9] But his love of theatre survived all setbacks and disappointments. He saw everything. After Ralph Richardson came to lunch at his house in Sydney in the 1970s, White wrote to his publisher Tom Maschler: 'all these old actors grow quite pop-eyed when they hear all the plays I have seen them in, because of course I was in London all through the Thirties, and not somewhere like Goondiwindi as is commonly thought.'[10]

A couple of his poems appeared in magazines, but his first success of any note was a revue sketch called 'Peter Plover's Party', a monologue for a flibbertigibbet performed by Cyril Richard for over a year in *Nine Sharp*.

> I read your last. It was such fun. Though personally, I don't think the woman would have eaten the potato. She would have kept it as a souvenir. Just a psychological point. And of course, your style's becoming a joy. So delightfully raw.[11]

Early success in revue marked for life his writing for the stage. He had seen Strindberg and Wedekind, admired the German expressionists and absorbed Racine, but from *The Ham Funeral* (1948) all the way to *Shepherd on the Rocks* (1987), his plays were flavoured by the spirit and conventions of revue: knockabout figures, song and dance, and direct address in the unmistakable voice of the writer himself.

White's London was a few blocks round Ebury Street, not a celebrated address, but somewhere convenient and quite respectable, within walking distance of more distinguished quarters of the town where its population of writers, actors, harlots, painters, aristocrats, antique dealers and refugees aspired to live on the way up or once lived on the way down. A handful of the characters around Ebury Street – most, as it happens, refugees – would inhabit the Jardin Exotique of *The Aunt's Story* (1948) and the grey world of that grey second novel *The Living and the Dead* (1941).

Where should the blue plaque go? Not in Ebury Street itself but round the corner on 13 Eccleston Street – now a bar – where he had taken a flat above the studio of the Australian modernist and fabulist Roy de Maistre. Though something like twice White's age, the painter was both his lover and mentor. He had a way of seducing then persuading young men of artistic bent to take themselves seriously. Francis Bacon was another of his protégés. De Maistre encouraged Bacon to abandon furniture design for painting. White meanwhile turned the top two floors of the house into a small modernist triumph with furniture all by Bacon.

Here is an important point for biographers: that two famous gay men knew each other in their early lives is not proof they have ever leapt into bed together. As far as I have been able to discover, neither White nor Bacon ever claimed to have had that pleasure with each other. They were friends for a long time until White became overawed by Bacon's fame. He wrote unforgettably of Bacon having in these early London years

> a beautiful pansy-shaped face and rather too much lipstick. He lived in a house at the Chelsea end of Ebury Street, not far from the Mozart house, with an old Nanny who used to shoplift when they were hard up.[12]

The transformation that de Maistre worked on White was to persuade him to put aside his ambition to be the next Galsworthy and work on a novel sketched in his jackerooing years back home. This was *Happy Valley* (1939), the novel that made White's name. 'I began to write from the inside out when Roy de Maistre introduced me to abstract painting,' White told Geoffrey Dutton.

> Before that I had only approached writing as an exercise in naturalism [...] Then came the terrors of abstract painting. As far as I was concerned, it was like jumping into space, and finding nothing there at first (the same thing when one first plunges into Zen.) Then gradually one saw that it was possible to weave about freely on different levels at one and the same time.[13]

On a rather self-consciously literary jaunt to the Atlantic coast of France to work on the final draft of *Happy Valley*, White began an affair with Pepe Mamblas, an apparently charming Fascist, later an envoy for Franco, who would introduce him to another London altogether: the London of rich and immensely snobbish homosexuals.

The role of young men from the colonies in this little world has not, I believe, had the anthropological attention it deserves. I know a little of it and recognise it in White's writing because I had an uncle who went over – after the war as it happens, not before – and was soon living in Belgrave Place. My father was not fooled, but it puzzled my mother when she visited in 1954 that her brother was living there with a number of servants, a Rolls and no particular source of income. Adrian later told me: 'the trip wires were always out at Victoria for fresh men just off the boat from Australia and South Africa.'

White's rich gay existence revolved round the house of Malcolm Bullock, Member of Parliament, who, after the death of his wife, the daughter of the Earl of Derby, devoted his life to theatre, gossip and the company of young men.

White told me of eating opulent meals *à deux* with Bullock while the Russian empire chairs bit into his kidneys.

To Mamblas, who was leading a shadowy existence in France down near the Spanish border, White sent sharp sketches of the figures he encountered in this society. Little masterpieces like his report to Mamblas of meeting Sybil Thorndike and Lewis Casson suggest this London world is where he found a taste for social comedy that was with him for life. Indeed this might have been its heyday. He wrote:

> I have never met an actress who acted so hard off the stage, and yet with it all, a lot of sincerity – that was what I could not understand – the queer mixture of sincerity and technique. The conversation was mostly political. They are very ardently Left. Sybil works herself into a frenzy which one suspects may develop into an epileptic fit. She sits on the edge of her chair, trying to bring out words which refuse to come, and clutching at the air as a substitute. The uncomfortable part was that I found myself also straining to sit on the edge of my chair and could almost feel my face growing into the shape of hers. Lewis Casson sat there like a block of granite against which, occasionally, she cannoned, to quiver off again. By the end of the evening I was in a state of complete awe and exhaustion.[14]

White was not in love. There was a good deal of sex associated with this existence but no love. He was never in love in London, not even with Mamblas. The city never represented that for him. He fell deeply in love in America in the summer of 1939 – not once but twice – when he went over to find a publisher for *Happy Valley*. Rather to his surprise, he landed Ben Huebsch of the Viking Press. Most of White's finest novels were written for this man, a New York Jew of great intellectual and moral clarity. The one thing London took a very long time to provide White was a publisher of stature. That was the role of New York for 30 years.

He fell so hard for his first American lover – a poet in Taos called Spud Johnson – that White decided he would abandon London and live in America. In this mood of farewell he began to sketch a novel set in London which he thought would share the scale and ambition of Joyce's portrait of Dublin in *Ulysses* (1922). He would make a quick dash back to pack his belongings and attend rehearsals for what promised to be his first play staged – *Return to Abyssinia* starring the great French actress Françoise Rosay – but return forever to America. Then war broke out. The play was cancelled but he took the berth he had on the *Vandyck* and reached England in late autumn. 'Wartime London also has its advantages,' he told Mamblas. '[M]ost of the rich, upholstered bores have fled into the fields, and altogether the secondary, mechanical relationships have disappeared out of one's life.'[15]

The novel was proving long, shapeless and murky. Years later he realised he had dived into it far too soon, thinking to himself: 'Ah, I am a writer now! Quick, I must write another.' He blamed the war only partly for what he rated his worst novel. The real fault, he told the novelist Thea Astley many years later, was haste. 'The idea had been in my mind for some time. I wanted to write a book about London and the characters were more or less assembled. But if I had hatched the thing for several more years, it might have become the book of London, instead of just another novel, and several of the characters who remained shadowy, flickery creatures might have become living human beings.'[16]

Almost word for word he put into the novel a little speech Mamblas had delivered as they left Malcolm Bullock's house one foggy night after a tedious dinner, a speech complaining about gay high society in London that ended with the Spanish attaché offering White, 'the choice of the two ways, of the living and the dead.' He told Mamblas that would be the novel's title.

Asthmatic and Australian, not yet wanted for the war and still free to travel, White returned to New York to be reunited with his second great American passion, a Manhattan doctor from the Deep South. He finished the deliberately abbreviated version of the novel and gave it to Huebsch in June 1940. White still imagined himself living the rest of his life in America but he had to face the war. It was another of the defining decisions of his life. Auden, whom he never met and always disliked, stayed on in New York. White returned to fight, not to Australia but London.

'The Blitz in Patrick White' would be a great PhD, subtitled something like: 'A Redeeming Fire'. The bombing of London was one of the great imaginative events of his life in which he formed a new and deeper attachment to the city. He was no longer a dilettante observer – or not only that – but a survivor among the craters immensely stimulated by the fire raining from the sky.

White was at the Café Royal with a young director John Wyse the night the bombing began. 'The eastern sky was ablaze, fire engines clanging,' White wrote in *Flaws in the Glass*. 'It was not yet dark. The west was a cold ice-green as opposed to the Wagnerian glow eastwards, the play of light paradoxical as our world was turned upside down.'[17] He and Wyse were thrown to the ground on Ebury Street as a bomb hit Victoria. A soldier offered them his helmet as shelter. The two fops made it to Eccleston Street and fucked under the bed. Wyse told me he had never seen White so carefree.

They had survived the blaze that destroyed the Jardin Exotique and spared Himmelfarb 'the amazed Jew' who 'walked unharmed beneath the chariot wheels'.[18] This was the same fire that consumed the ex-bawd Eddie Twyborn – back in trousers but with too much makeup like the early Francis Bacon – crossing London to join his mother at the Connaught.

And the blitz gave birth to *Voss* (1957). At some point in those apocalyptic weeks, sitting in his room swigging Calvados as the bombs fell, White read the journal of the explorer Edward John Eyre, a young man who walked across the Nullarbor in the early 1840s. Eyre was a name known from White's childhood, but he was now 'electrified' by this account of a romantic's journey through a landscape set on destroying him. The journal gave White an itch to see Australia again and the vague ambition to write a novel about an explorer.

'We now live almost exclusively in the cellars and basements at night,' he wrote to Spud Johnson. But most nights he also walked the streets. 'The alternative seemed to be extinction by staying in, and the deserted streets have been very beautiful, in a white moonlight and a yellow flashing of guns.'[19] He and the city lost their inhibitions together, for any night might be for any of them the end of the world. More than ever this was the territory of White's late masterpiece *The Twyborn Affair* (1979). He wrote: 'I learned a lot about the whore's mentality, and the variations on her one client, in fact the whole tragi-comedy of sex.'[20]

The war that took White to Africa and Palestine washed him up in London again in January 1946, a civilian once again with a new suit and a new suitcase. The city was in ruins, he was hungry and his friends were stuck in ruts. De Maistre had turned into a high society Catholic with delusions of royal connection. But here was yet fresh evidence for the 'redeeming fire' thesis: de Maistre lost a cousin when a buzz bomb hit the Chelsea Barracks. His painting *The Aunt* (1945) was based on a photograph he found of her in the rubble.[21] The painting helped clarify the purpose of his next novel, one he had been planning in one form or another for 10 years. He bought the painting and began *The Aunt's Story*.

The novel was his companion and shelter as he began another of his epic explorations: a visit to Australia to see whether that was where he and Lascaris might live. 'I landed here after fourteen years absence, and immediately realised how Australian I have been all the time underneath,' he told Mamblas.

> Even the uglier aspects of the place have their significance and rightness, to me, though I expect if you came here, a real European, you would be rightly appalled. But I am enjoying relaxing with my instinct after a long session with my reason.[22]

But something compelled him to return to London. This expensive, complicated journey was made ostensibly to sell his furniture and collect his dogs. But I believe he wanted to see the city one more time to be absolutely sure of his decision. He felt no happy palpitations when he arrived after a long journey in the hold of a troop ship.

> It costs a fortune just to exist – doing nothing and eating filth in what used to be the cheap restaurants – though from the one meal I ate at the Ritz, I should

say filth prevails. Most of the people one sees look ill, tired, hopeless, or just dull and apathetic. There seems to be a restriction on everything one attempts to do. And it is not as if one felt there was an end to it, and that one would get somewhere someday. I can see no future at all for England, and advise anyone I know to leave it.[23]

The one oasis in London was the West End and it rekindled his old ambition to be a playwright. Waiting to get out of England once again, he wrote *The Ham Funeral*. It was his farewell to London, and to the callow young man he had been before the war: a poet growing up and fighting his way out of the smothering embrace of his landlady Alma Lusty and her great, damp crumbling house. 'Send us a pitcher post-card now and agen,' she calls as he makes a break for freedom. 'Let's know you're alive and kickin! But write plain.'[24]

White's ambitions were huge. What he found on his return to the other side of the world was crucial to everything that followed. But so was everything he brought in his luggage: London standards and taste, and the ambition to be writer who would speak not to Australia alone but to the world. He brought all he had learned of the human heart in war and peace on Ebury Street, in Belgravia and the West End. He saw himself as a man of understanding in a country that did not understand. Though he felt both immediately at home and a stranger in Sarsaparilla, he was – like so many figures in the novels that would come – the stranger in the know.

He had also absorbed into his own imagination the history of the Lascaris family, a history of ruin after ruin, exile after exile. Counting the Byzantium of Manoly's supposed ancestors, the family had been expelled centuries ago from Constantinople and Nicea, a generation earlier from their rich existence in Smyrna and in the late 1940s from the disappearing Greek city of Alexandria. Both men were exiles from cosmopolitan cities they loved, an exile from which, frankly, they took a certain masochistic pleasure. And distance would allow White to imagine Smyrna, Nicea, Alexandria and London more freely than had they lived there still.

He stuck it out. Survived miserable years of doubt. Renewed his name in the literary world with *The Tree of Man* (1955) and became famous with *Voss*. In 1958 he set off with Lascaris on a long journey which had London as its final destination. He had not seen the city for a decade. 'I wonder how I succeeded in living in it for so long, overlooking so much,' he wrote to the Moores. 'It is so terribly dirty, ugly, the people so drab – also ugly and dirty – the women like uncooked dough, the men so often suggestive of raw veal.'[25] That visit was followed by visits every three or four years for the next twenty years. Each time he arrived he felt at home and made no secret of his growing delight in London while filling his letters with the same old complaints: plain faces, poor food, shocking prices, ugly streets and nosy journalists.

White feared fame but allowed himself in London to live the life of a literary celebrity: being feted by publishers, 'fending' off the press, throwing himself into the 'whirl' of the city from which he sent home reports of meetings with the famous and curious. This to the Duttons in 1971:

> We lunched with the Charles Johnstons [...] and in addition to the Princess Bagration had Princess Aly Khan and Diana Duff Cooper! The latter still has a very blue stare, but by now is rather crippled and wafty: she told us a long and tangled story about a pair of gorillas having sex in a private zoo for the entertainment of a number of Bright Old Things.[26]

London delighted both White and Lascaris as a city of amazing stories and strange encounters. A passion for gossip and human peculiarity was one of the strong bonds in their marriage. But Lascaris found other aspects of their visits less entertaining. It irritated him that his partner, so mean in Sydney, would spend so lavishly in London. He thought it a little vulgar, with the taint of the colonial made good. And White's determination to go to London every time they travelled also irritated him. White could say the next trip would be devoted to exploring Greece or spending time with the Lascaris family and friends in America, but London was always the real objective.

London meant theatre. Every visit rekindled passions Lascaris would like to see wither and die. He feared theatre as a distraction from White's real mission as a novelist. But with the appetite of a schoolboy, White dragged him to everything. He never returned to the city without a play or a film to sell.

In 1958 he brought from his desk drawer *The Ham Funeral*. No luck. He revised it a little before their next London visit in 1963. No luck again. With him on that visit he had also brought the scripts of *Night on Bald Mountain* (1964) and *The Season at Sarsaparilla* (1962) hoping to snare a London management. Still no luck. White was surprised and hurt when at the last minute the Mermaid Theatre rejected *Sarsaparilla* as indecent. Australians would gasp at the decadence of London theatre, he told his old friends the Moores. 'They have just no idea what goes on – if it isn't adultery, it's incest, abortion, up-your-jacksie Queen Elizabeth – and the language – by this time the bloodys have given way to the fucks.'[27]

White never bothered with London cinema on the grounds that good films always reached Australia, but not those that might fall foul of Australia's long night of censorship. So in London one year he took himself off to see Joe Dallesandro in *Andy Warhol's Flesh* (1968). 'For the first time I saw a nude erection on the screen,' he wrote to an old queen in the bush. 'And a very handsome one it was.'[28]

One of White's great fears when he went out to Australia was that he would, without knowing it, lose the absolute standards he had absorbed in London. Books reached Sarsaparilla of course, but not London conversation and only rarely the writers in whose company White placed himself. London visits reassured him that his standards weren't slipping. He held off beginning new novels – *Riders in the Chariot* was boiling up in 1958 – or beginning second drafts of novels – *The Eye of the Storm* in 1971 – until he had tested himself once again in London.

The Eye of the Storm (1973) was another of his works born in London. The sombre purpose of the 1963 visit had been to see his ailing mother for what he knew would be the last time. Ruth was dying, in state, in a luxurious flat in Rutland House, nearly blind but still ruling the staff from her bed. The hostility between them died away. They had wonderful long conversations. It came to White as he was crossing Kensington High Street one day that this would make a novel he must write. *The Eye of the Storm* would be set in Sydney – in his own house above Centennial Park – but later he also turned this last reconciliation of mother and son into the 'many delightful conversations, others more disquieting' of Eadie and Eadith Twyborn in the wartime Connaught Hotel.[29]

White had it in for the Connaught. One year, with great care, his publisher had booked a table for lunch. It was at a time when the hotel was hugely fashionable and the booking had been made months in advance. But Manoly Lascaris was wearing a skivvy under his jacket. The headwaiter offered 'sir' a tie. White declared: 'you are not going treat my friend like a dog on a lead' and led the party out.

London, dirty in 1958, filthy in 1963, squalid in 1968 – the formula White used in dozens of letters was 'filth almost equal to Istanbul' – seemed miraculously spruce in 1971. The new prosperity of Britain was not the only explanation. White was feeling particularly wonderful about the city because he had at last found a great London publisher.

Back before the war his first had rejected *The Living and the Dead*. The second refused to take *The Tree of Man*, which was rejected by about twenty publishing houses before Ben Huebsch fixed him up with Eyre & Spottiswoode. Try as they might, the E & S team never excited White. Rumours in the late 1960s that he was looking for a new publisher provoked an orgy of flattering attention. White toyed briefly with the idea of finding an Australian publisher, but he was just making mischief. With the Commonwealth publishing cartel still firmly in place, London houses ruled the Australian market. White had no patriotic objections.

Harold Macmillan called at Centennial Park to recruit him for the family firm. The two men spent an hour talking about Mount Athos. But Macmillan was pipped at the post by Jonathan Cape. 'I can't think of a living author I would rather publish than Patrick White,' Cape's Tom Maschler told White's agent. 'If you gave me the choice between publishing Graham Greene and publishing Patrick White, I would choose Patrick White any day – and then the statement is almost an insult to White.'[30]

Maschler and then his colleague Graham Greene (the *other* Graham Greene) became the demanding audience for whom he wrote his last – and some of his finest – novels beginning with *The Vivisector* in 1970. Maschler and Greene opened the highest reaches of literary London to him. The old claim of his class proved true for Patrick White in the Jonathan Cape years: he had never felt so at home in London. In that mood he made the rather shocking admission when the good news came through from Stockholm in 1973 that he was at heart a Londoner.

He was reasserting his ambiguous vision of himself: prophet and gossip, novelist and playwright, man and woman, Australian and Londoner. He was expressing his lifelong distaste for chauvinism. 'I'm not for nationalism at all,' he said in this same round of interviews. 'Not for flag-wagging and drum thumping.'[31] Ever since the early days of his return when Australian critics had declared his novels un-Australian, he had been particularly contemptuous of literary chauvinism. Now at this moment of triumph, he was asserting his absolute freedom as an artist. No fashion, no literary school and no country could claim him as its own.

White was not done with London. There was one more book and one more visit in the spring and summer of 1976. 'London is still my favourite place for living,' he wrote to Manning Clark.[32] And to Geoffrey Dutton: 'London is in my bones and I can't tear myself away from it.'[33] Early one morning White left his hotel in Wilbraham Place to explore his old stamping ground: the region between Ebury Street and the Thames where, in an imagined Beckwith Street, the light glimmering off the water, he would place the red-brick façade of Eadith Trist's whorehouse.

The Twyborn Affair is the London novel White had been hatching for 40 years, familiar territory revisited with absolute candour and absolute mastery. Here the all-knowing Eudoxia/Eddie/Eadith is pitted against the conventional and timid of two worlds, of here and there, of England and Australia. This was not the London he visited as a literary celebrity but the city in which he had discovered himself so long before, where he might have died, as Eddie Twyborn does, on the blazing first night of the Blitz.

> Down one of the dark tributary streets came a young soldier in battle dress and tin hat. He reached the corner in time to fall head on, making almost a straight line on the pavement, with this character from a carnival or looney bin. The young man seemed to be trying to share the brim of his protective hat with one who could hardly remain a stranger. 'Something happening at last, eh?'[34]

The nurse rang me at 5.45 am on 30 September 1990 to say Patrick had died earlier that morning. Manoly came on the line: he wanted me to ring people. Among them was my friend Anne Chisholm who was working in London on the biography I had finished only a few months before. What I didn't know at that early hour was that Patrick had made an absurd request that the press not be told of his death until his ashes were scattered. By the time I rang back to beg Anne to keep the news to herself, her husband, the great journalist Michael Davie, had rung Fleet Street. It was on the wires. Though absurd it was somehow absolutely right that the news of Patrick White's death should reach Australia from the city that shaped him, the city he most loved, his other home, London.

Notes

1 Patrick White Interview, TR 107/10/73, PNS 237, Australian Broadcasting Commission.
2 Patrick White to Pepe Mamblas, 20 May 1973, MS 7712, National Library of Australia.
3 Patrick White, *Patrick White Speaks* (London: Jonathan Cape, 1990), 14.
4 Patrick White to Geoff and Ninette Dutton, 12 November 1972, MS 7285, Bib ID 1357699, National Library of Australia.
5 Patrick White to Alan Williams, 21 September 1979, Viking Press collection.
6 *Australian Financial Review*, 11 July 1972, 2.
7 Patrick White to Alexandra Bishop, 16 February 1969, Frances Richardson collection.
8 Patrick White, 'Miracle', Papers of Patrick White, MS 9982, series 2, National Library of Australia.
9 See Papers of Patrick White, MS 9982, item 2, National Library of Australia.
10 Patrick White to Tom Maschler, 20 September 1973, Reading University Library.
11 Hebert Farjeon *et al.*, *Sketches from 'Nine Sharp'* (London: Samuel French Ltd, 1938), 43–45.
12 Patrick White, *Flaws in the Glass* (London: Jonathan Cape, 1981), 62.
13 Patrick White to Geoffrey Dutton, 19 September 1960, in David Marr, ed., *Patrick White: Letters* (Sydney: Random House, 1994), 170.
14 Patrick White to Pepe Mamblas, 19 November 1937, cited in David Marr, *Patrick White: A Life* (Sydney: Random House, 1991), 166.
15 Patrick White to Pepe Mamblas, 15 February 1940, in Marr, *Letters*, 27.
16 Patrick White to Thea Astley, 20 March 1961.
17 White, *Flaws*, 82.
18 Patrick White, *Riders in the Chariot* (Sydney: Random House, 2011), 190.
19 Patrick White to Spud Johnson, 12 September 1940, Harry Ransom Humanities Research Centre, University of Texas at Austin.
20 White, *Flaws*, 85.
21 Roy de Maistre, *Figure in a Garden (The Aunt)*, 48.1974, Art Gallery of New South Wales.
22 Patrick White to Pepe Mamblas, 26 January 1947.
23 Patrick White, 9 February 1948.

24 Patrick White, *Four Plays* (London: Eyre & Spottiswoode, 1965), 73.
25 Patrick White to David Moore, 12 August 1958, in Marr, *Letters*, 145.
26 Patrick White to Geoff and Ninette Dutton, 4 July 1971, in Marr, *Letters*, 381.
27 Patrick White to Gwen and David Moore, 14 August 1963.
28 Patrick White to Freddie Glover, 6 June 1971, Glover family collection.
29 Patrick White, *The Twyborn Affair* (London: Vintage, 1995), 424.
30 Tom Maschler to Juliet O'Hea, 5 January 1968, Bib ID 1356300, National Library of Australia.
31 Patrick White interview, PNR 1129/10/73, Australian Broadcasting Commission.
32 Patrick White to Manning Clark, 18 May 1976, Bib ID 383394, National Library of Australia.
33 Patrick White to Geoffrey Dutton, 5 May 1976, in Marr, *Letters*, 475.
34 White, *Twyborn*, 429.

Chapter 4

ELECTIVE AFFINITIES: MANNING CLARK, PATRICK WHITE AND SIDNEY NOLAN

Mark McKenna

Sydney 1959

Manning Clark and James McAuley were walking together along George Street in Sydney. They had walked half the distance when McAuley noticed a familiar face coming in the opposite direction – one which Clark would later claim haunted him for days afterwards – the face of 'a man who wanted something which no human being could give him'. As their paths crossed, the three men halted to speak with one another. McAuley introduced Clark to Patrick White. It was the beginning of an intensely felt three-decade long friendship, one that flowered through Clark and White's mutual admiration for one another's work and journeyed unevenly from infatuation and love to disillusionment and acrimony. By 1959, White had already published three of his greatest works: *The Aunt's Story* (1948), *The Tree of Man* (1955) and *Voss* (1957). While White was at the height of his creative powers, Clark had barely managed to begin his life's major work. Aged 44 he was still three years out from publishing the first volume of *A History of Australia*. Unknown to both men, their creative paths were already connected through the inspiration they had drawn from artists such as Arthur Boyd and Sidney Nolan. Behind the story of White and Clark's deeply felt, tempestuous relationship then lies a much larger one: the struggle of a relatively small vanguard of intellectual and cultural 'elites' to create a new vision of Australia in the late twentieth century.[1]

Canberra 1949

As Manning Clark moved to Canberra with dreams of writing what he called 'the spirit of place' into his history of Australia, Patrick White, preparing to write *Voss*, was reading the journals of the explorer Ludwig Leichhardt. In the same year, Sidney Nolan was flying over central Australia working on a series of paintings of the 'MacDonnell Ranges', 'Ayers Rock' and 'unnamed' ridges, sand hills and plains, flooded in what he called 'a transparent floating light'. Nolan was also reading the diaries of Burke and Wills in preparation for the first of a stunning sequence of paintings based on their ill-fated attempt to cross the continent from south to north in 1860–61.

At Melbourne University in 1946, Clark had seen an exhibition of Australian 'contemporary art' which featured Nolan's early Ned Kelly paintings, Albert Tucker's *Images of Modern Evil* and two of Arthur Boyd's most important works from the 1940s, *The Mockers* and *The Mourners*, paintings which echoed Bruegel and Bosch in their use of biblical narratives, setting the Australian landscape against the background of the Holocaust and Hiroshima. Sitting with Clark in Melbourne's Mitre Tavern, Boyd talked to him about the Australian continent's 'fragile beauty'. Shortly afterwards Boyd too set off into the bush, travelling through the Wimmera district of Victoria. Over the next three decades, Clark would make his own excursions, travelling incessantly to historical sites, walking every mile of his history of Australia.[2]

In Sydney in early 1949 and 1950, while still unknown to one another, White and Clark both saw the paintings that had resulted from Nolan's journey to central Australia. Remembering their impact, White would later ask Nolan to provide an illustration for the cover of *Voss*. In his notebooks, Nolan claimed that he had painted mountains of bare rock as Australia's 'cathedrals', dwarfing the trees and shrubs below them which appeared as little more than a 'dotted veil above the landscape'. From Cairns in 1947, Nolan told John Reed of his difficulty in 'understanding the country' he encountered. It seemed impossible, he said, to 'be articulate about it from our own particular level and tradition [...] we have only experienced the fringe of what we know to be indigenous.' Reed had already seen Nolan's first Ned Kelly paintings that year and was thrilled by his 'inspired realisation of the Australian bush'. Nolan, Reed argued, had penetrated beneath the harshness of the landscape that had so alienated Europeans in Australia, and 'revealed the deep soft beauty of the bush' 'with all its subtleties'. In fact, asserted Reed, Nolan had glimpsed something of an 'authentic national vision'. Here potentially was the expression of everything that cultural nationalists, such as Vance Palmer, Inky (P. R.) Stephensen, Clem Christesen and Max Harris (albeit from extremely different standpoints), had pined for – the creation of a national mythology.[3]

Like Nolan's Kelly paintings, with their unforgettable evocation of the lone individual in the Australian bush, Boyd's religious allegories of the 1940s attempted to portray the psychological state of Europeans in the Australian environment – not only the strange beauty of the land but also the loneliness, the isolation and the silence that the bush seemed to impose on all those who inhabited it. At the beginning of the post-war period, Boyd, Nolan, White and Clark shared the sudden realization that the work of Australian artists and writers mattered in a way it had never done before. 'It was a core of something,' said Boyd, 'of which you thought there was nothing else like it, either in Australia or elsewhere.'[4] With these singular artists, Manning Clark shared more in common than he did with any historian in the corridors of Melbourne or Canberra universities.

Oxford 1956

Sitting at his desk in Raleigh Park, Oxford, Clark struggled to begin writing *A History of Australia*. In his diary he claimed that he was striving for a history that was fully alive to the sensuality of existence and human emotion, something that might come close to what Nolan described to him as a 'sacramental feeling', a history that captured 'the magic' of the continent that had so frightened the novelist, D. H. Lawrence, with whom they both had a deep affinity. In so many ways Clark was attempting to do for Australian history what Nolan in his history paintings was doing for Australian art and Patrick White had already done for the Australian novel. In 1958, after the publication of both *The Tree of Man* and *Voss*, White explained that he had wanted to the latter 'the textures of music [and] the sensuousness of paint, to convey through the theme and characters of Voss what Delacroix and Blake might have seen, what Mahler and Liszt might have heard'. Beginning his history, Clark thought of Beethoven and Mozart who met in Vienna for the first and last time in the same month the First Fleet sailed for Australia. He wanted to give his work, he said, 'the Mozart vision of life'. As Clark railed against the lifeless prose of his academic colleagues, White attacked Australian novels that resembled 'the dreary, dun-coloured offspring of journalistic realism'. All three men were convinced of the superiority of their vision in a country blind to the originality and power of their art. While Clark steeled himself against the 'jeerers, mockers and sneerers', White condemned the dingoes that howled unmercifully at his door. Nolan, meanwhile, spoke of Australia as a 'ghost civilisation' based on a 'kind of cannibalism – 'Eat the land. Eat the trees. Eat the artists'.[5]

By the time Clark had returned to Oxford from travelling in Italy, he was ready to begin writing. On 1 October 1956, in the upstairs bedroom of a rented terrace in Botley, looking out across an autumnal Raleigh Park to Tom Tower and the spires of Oxford in the distance, Clark wrote his first sentence. Describing Governor Arthur Phillip at Sydney Cove taking possession of the continent in the name of the Crown, he began with echoes of Genesis: 'It was all there in the beginning, that seventh day of February 1788 [...] It was all there – the European past, the seeds from which it all developed – the protestant view of the world, the catholic view, the enlightenment, and that other one – man and his environment [...] European man under the gum tree, not the oak.' Thirty years later with the publication of the sixth volume, the gum tree and the oak would become 'the old dead tree and the young tree green'. Oxford, the site of his rejection at the hands of the English at Balliol in 1938, was also the place where his history began. His first drafts were written in his customary ink scrawl, a script that resembled micro-barbed wire. Remarkably, there were few crossings out. When reading the drafts today, the words from his pen appear to flow effortlessly, yet those first pages were a struggle. He had no idea of the period he would cover and he was still six years out from publication. But finally, he had found the will and the sheer bloody-minded persistence to write.[6]

Clark had begun his history in the shadow of *The Tree of Man*. In White's character, the farmer Stan Parker, Clark saw much of the spiritual searching he was struggling to articulate in Australia's past. Parker senses the divine in the Australian landscape, a moment of revelation for Clark as he prepared to explain the fate of Catholicism, Protestantism and the Enlightenment in the unforgiving environment of Australia. Hence reading *The Tree of Man* inspired him to deal with the *universal* themes of human existence and to write the history he had always wanted to write: history as art. 'If a novelist could do it,' Clark told himself, then 'I want to show that an historian can do it.' He had to find a way to show the unspoken and undocumented lives of his characters and imagine his way into their hearts and minds. The figures of the past would move in his hands like characters in a novel or film, their actions lit intensely for brief moments, coming and going on the page as people seemed to move in and out of his own life.[7]

London 1964

Spring: Clark and his wife, Dymphna, were in close contact with Boyd, Nolan and comedian Barry Humphries. Boyd had set up a studio in Highgate. In summer, Nolan's *Kelly* and *Gallipoli* paintings were exhibited in Piccadilly. Clark attended both exhibitions, mystified at first as to exactly what Nolan was trying to say, but gradually over the next five years he became more and more inspired by his work.

When they arrived in London in February that year Clark and Dymphna found an old gamekeeper's cottage at Twickenham on a narrow lane that ran down to a pub on the river. Around the cottage, Dymphna remembered an acre of garden and, 'in the days when Manning was still quite social', long dinner parties with the Boyds, Nolan and Humphries which ran well into the late evening. While Clark had known Boyd for nearly fifteen years, he came to know both Humphries and Nolan more intimately in London, and through them was drawn into closer contact with White. Meeting Humphries on Charing Cross Road in March 1964, he immediately felt a 'deep bond with him'. In Humphries – his black hair swept long down one side of his face, his voice darting in and out of character – Clark saw someone like himself, 'damned, doomed, vulnerable and anxious to uncover themselves', 'another Don Juan in hell', an artist who had been 'savaged by the reviewers' and his fellow Australians. So well did he get on with Humphries that Clark felt Dymphna was 'wildly jealous' of their 'intimacy'. No doubt, Dymphna also resented Clark's 'childish excitement' when he came into contact with 'great spirits' in whom he saw his own reflection, an excitement from which she immediately felt herself excluded or cast suddenly into an accessory role.[8]

In August that year when Clark met Nolan at the Kelly exhibition in the Qantas building in Piccadilly, he pursued the same theme that had drawn him to Humphries. They talked of 'the mockers' in Australia who failed to understand their work, unlike the critics in London. Patrick White, they agreed, was in much the same position. Over coffee Clark told Nolan about the particular moment in which they found themselves. This, they thought, was Australia's chance to 'discover' itself. For Nolan, it was also a moment of opportunity. Reflecting on his work a few years later, Nolan saw that Australian artists had 'something to paint or to write about, which [hadn't] been worked over [...] hadn't had odes written to it'. As they parted, Clark felt he was in the company of a kindred spirit – one of the spiritually elect, like White and Boyd, someone who understood what he was trying to do.[9]

Since 1961, Clark had clipped and filed every press report he read on White and Nolan and would continue to do so until his death. He craved their acceptance and friendship as an implicit recognition of his own artistic endeavour; none more so than from Patrick White with whom he 'fell in love' at first sight.

When Clark wrote to White in 1961 after reading *Riders in the Chariot* (1961), so anxious was he to impress that he drafted his letter three times. The result was a mixture of fawning sincerity and genuine excitement: 'your vision has been communicated with such grace and distinction.' *Voss* and *The Tree of Man* had already made an enormous impact on him. Now White's vision of life in suburban Sarsaparilla had overwhelmed him too. To show his 'tremendous gratitude', he sent White as gifts his favourite recordings of Bach and Beethoven, including Wilhelm Kempf's recording of his favourite Beethoven late piano sonata (opus 111). Clark explained that in the slow movement, Beethoven, like White, had communicated the vision of a man who had 'climbed a mountaintop'. The image was reminiscent of the German romantic paintings which so often graced the covers of recordings of Beethoven and Schubert for

Deutsche Grammophon. Clark told White that he had given Australia a novel that reminded him of the story of Christ visiting the house of Simon the leper, and the work of Dostoevsky.

White responded warmly by inviting Clark to dinner. Shortly after his conversation with Nolan in London, Clark received White's response to the first volume; it was a 'truly wonderful and live work', White enthused. He felt 'humbled'. A few months later came Nolan's response. He was 'thrilled'. 'I feel so much in sympathy with what you have discovered,' he told Clark. After reading *A History of Australia*, Nolan felt 'that tingling of recognition and sense of exact place and time similar to the effect of the wind on the emotions'. With the publication of the first volume, Clark had succeeded in stimulating the interest of Australia's entire literary community. After going to dinner at White's house on Martin Road, the poet David Campbell, one of Clark's closest friends, told him how warmly White had spoken of his work, describing him as 'one of the few writers of understanding and imagination' in Australia. Before long Clark became a regular visitor to the 'white-walled stone house overlooking Centennial Park'. His diary entries recorded his star-struck admiration for the one Australian novelist whose work inspired him to write history in the image of fiction. Even before the second volume was published in 1968, Clark had entered the court to which he had always sought entrance, the court of the artists, and in the 1960s in Australia there was no higher court than that of Patrick White, the only writer who had achieved significant international recognition.[10]

As Clark settled down to write the third and fourth volumes of *A History of Australia* in the late 1960s and early 1970s, Nolan and White's influence on his work deepened. While writing the history of the spread of settlement and the great journeys of exploration, his travelling increased. As often as possible, he set out like Voss to cross the continent from one end to another. His plan was to finish the third volume with the story of his 'beloved Burke and Wills'. As it turned out, his work on Burke and Wills would not appear until the fourth was published in 1978, but in the interim he made two journeys into the heart of the continent in search of the two explorers. Nolan's Kelly paintings had already shown him how the bush 'alienated' many Europeans, reducing them to 'unfeeling, unaware' people preoccupied with the question of their own survival.

In 1966 when Clark saw Nolan's *Riverbend*, he realized something far more profound. Before he left Canberra in August 1967 for Menindee on the Darling, reading André Gide as he searched for Burke and Wills, he wrote to Nolan to tell him how *Riverbend* had moved him. In September as Nolan prepared for a major retrospective of his work at the Art Gallery of NSW, Clark wrote again, reminding him that together with the poetry of A. D. Hope and White's novels since *Voss*, *Riverbend* was one of the few works of Australian art with a vision to match 'the one of those who first dreamt of planting civilization in the South Seas'. Two weeks later in Melbourne, addressing the Victorian Historical Society, he told his audience that Australians were living in 'a most exciting moment in the history of the arts'. Nolan, White, Hope, William Dobell and McAuley had produced groundbreaking works of art, Clark argued, 'not through insular nationalism, but by painting and writing about the universal problems of mankind'.[11]

In Sydney, on October 12, Clark saw the Nolan retrospective where he found the *Kelly* and *Gallipoli* paintings he had seen in London as well as Nolan's luminous paintings of Burke and Wills at the Gulf. Immediately he felt 'uplifted'. Then came the moment of realisation. Nolan's mythical figures were also Clark's figures. Pulling out his notebook, he scribbled down his response as he walked through the gallery: 'Myth – my myth too, of Kelly, Burke, Leda, Frazer, Eureka, Gallipoli.' Nolan had helped Clark to see what he was trying to achieve in writing *A History of Australia*. Five days later, he wrote to Nolan in London: 'I cannot find the words to do justice to what you have seen. For me it was like listening to one of the preludes of Bach.' Even before the publication of the second volume, Clark saw the tragic vision he wanted to convey in Nolan's haunting images of Kelly and Burke and Wills, stories of failure set in a 'primeval landscape that stretched on forever'. Now he had to do the same for his characters, especially Burke and Wills.[12]

In Burke's epic journey and tragic death, Clark created a synthesis of all that he had learned about the Australian bush since he read Lawrence and Eleanor Dark in his late teens and early twenties. Clark's Burke was Nolan's Burke and White's Voss, a man driven to penetrate a country in which 'men's souls were more woundable than flesh', where Europeans stumbled in the dark, lost and exhausted, while Aboriginal people moved with grace and confidence. Instead, explorers encountered a kind of hell, a land beyond time and history, a land outside of God's creation, possessed of an infinity all of its own. Slowly, they were brutalised by the environment, brought to their knees by starvation and thirst. Even the face of their treasured Christ was reduced to a mirage shimmering on the edge of the horizon. All the trappings of their cultural superiority were rendered ineffectual until, like Voss, they could 'advance no farther'.[13]

Sydney 1972

In the early 1970s, White and Clark were still in their honeymoon period, emboldened by the support for the arts shown by the newly elected Whitlam government and sharing dinner occasionally at Martin Road. Both men felt a duty to assert a more sophisticated and cosmopolitan image of their country.

They were among the signatories to an unprecedented open letter published in November 1972, calling for Whitlam's election. Less than two years later, together with a motley cast of intellectuals, artists and sporting heroes – among them actor and director John Bell, playwright David Williamson, novelist David Malouf and South Sydney Rugby League five-eight Dennis Pittard – they spoke at a Sydney Opera House rally to support Whitlam's re-election. Clark revelled in his newfound public role. 'A great day, in touch with the people,' he wrote in his diary, 'like being at the Carlton football ground.'[14]

The Australian Labor Party won the election in May 1974 with a slightly reduced majority but still lacked control of the Senate. Since coming to power, Edward Gough Whitlam had succeeded in branding Labor as the party of ideas and culture, the only political outfit that would cultivate and protect Australia's emerging sense of national independence. For the coterie of writers and artists gathered at the Sydney Opera House, there was also a palpable sense of release: Whitlam's election had represented an all too belated expression of cultural awakening. Finally, it seemed that Australia had a government that recognised the importance of intellectuals and artists, a government that had the courage to break itself free from Australia's colonial mentality and 'go it alone'. Whitlam's urbanity was also the antithesis of the more vulgar images of Australia that so offended Clark and White. Accepting his Australian of the Year Award in January 1974, White praised the likes of Clark and Barry Humphries for their telling critiques of Australia. Clark, White suggested, had shown Australians that their essential characteristics were the same as their nineteenth-century forebears, 'the same politicians abusing one another in larrikin style, the same class-consciousness in a classless society – money consciousness might be nearer the mark – the same violence and drunkenness in the streets'. In private, White made the point more bluntly, telling Clark that his work had shown that Australians remained 'the same pack of snarling mongrel dogs'.[15]

As ever White was extremely perceptive in his summation of both Clark and Dymphna. When they attended a production of *The Magic Flute* with him at Sydney Opera House in early 1974, White admitted to Geoffrey Dutton that he found Dymphna 'difficult to come to terms with'. 'I'm told she only blossoms when he isn't there,' he said. 'That must go for both of them.' For Dymphna, the feeling was mutual. Although White attempted to cultivate a friendship – he was keenly aware of her mother's Scandinavian background and her talent as a linguist, sending her the Swedish translations of his novels – she always felt 'awkward' in his company. Over time, she also came to resent what she described as his 'caustic and treacherous behaviour' towards her husband. While she thought Clark tolerant of White's 'emotional aberrations', she saw how uneven their friendship was. Clark was in awe of White's literary powers and his standing in Australian letters.

In 1972, Clark admitted to White that he envied his 'power to evoke the frame of life' that surrounded everyone in Australia. White, meanwhile, read the second volume of *A History of Australia* as he wrote *The Vivisector*, while Clark read *Riders in the Chariot* and *The Solid Mandala* (1966) during the writing of the first and second volumes. Sending Clark a copy of *The Eye of the Storm* in 1973, White flattered him after reading the beginning of the third volume: 'I see you have lost none of your power.' Eight months later, accepting his Australian of the Year Award, White used the same volume as 'a pivot' to help him through the ordeal, chuffed that his speech had given offence to the establishment despite it being delivered without his false teeth, which broke up while he was eating an hors d'oeuvre.[16]

Although Clark's enthusiasm for White was always more gushing than White's admiration for Clark, both men continued to share the sense that they were ploughing parallel fields, following in the tracks of Australia's explorers and painters, writing over the country's silence. Since their first meeting in the 1950s, they had continued to share a love–hate relationship with Australia. While they were both deeply devoted to understanding the country's environment and its effect on all who lived there, they recoiled from the Australians who Clark saw sitting mindlessly 'with their two car families and their boat culture', or in the words of Barry Humphries, with 'their belly telly, their tinnies, their tubes, their snow bunnies and no complications'. This was White's 'great Australian emptiness' and Clark's 'greed and titillation culture' – suburban, materialist and anti-intellectual – everything the two writers despised. Their model was European high culture – Mozart, Bach, Rembrandt and Dostoevsky – the cultural heartland from which they feared severance, and with which they hoped their own work would one day help to connect their fellow Australians. White and Clark's nationalism was not so much anti-British as cosmopolitan. Yet there were also crucial differences. Unlike White, who reflected the day after he won the Nobel Prize in 1973 that he didn't really feel Australian, Clark's public persona in the 1970s and 1980s would be built on his emotional protestations of love for Australia.[17]

Canberra 1975

The dismissal of Whitlam's government in November proved to be the turning point in Clark and White's friendship. Both men saw Whitlam's removal as a bleak reflection on Australia. They protested together, speaking on republic platforms and advocating a more democratic and independent constitution. 'This rotten, hypocritical country really deserves a revolution,' proclaimed White. Clark took the same sentiments one step further, delivering lectures and speeches across the country in which he appeared to relish the prospect of

Australia being cast into a 'cleansing fire', a revolutionary inferno that would purge the country of its conservative and materialistic instincts.[18]

In the months after the 1977 federal election, which saw the return of Liberal Prime Minister Malcolm Fraser, and well into the 1980s, Clark continued to cast Whitlam as a victim of forces beyond his control. In January 1976, he penned a feature article for the *Australian* – 'History will be kinder to Labor than the People' – which provoked a storm of controversy. Whitlam's years, said Clark, were the 'days of glory'. His government was like 'beautiful birds […] trapped under the nets of the fowlers of this world […] the men in black, those last-ditch defenders of a corrupt, decaying and obsolete society'. Australia had lost a prime minister who had believed in 'the cultivation of an Australian national sentiment', in contrast to the 'pro-British, archaic, anachronistic philistinism of their predecessors, men with the values, hearts and mental horizons of the bookkeepers, the accountants, the gravediggers of society'. It was Clark in full flight; thunderous polemic from the prophet who felt Australia had been cheated of its one chance of a truly visionary leader. Equally bitter, White nonetheless told Clark that he was being too gloomy, 'Bad as things are, I can't feel quite as pessimistic as you.' Whitlam's dismissal, with its symbolic overtones of colonial dependence epitomised in the top hat and tails worn by Sir John Kerr, sharpened the old divisions in Clark's thinking. Yet under the surface of his republican nationalism lay a contradiction that was harder to see – his longing for recognition from the very Tory establishment he derided – a feature of his personality that would now prove to be the crucial point of division in his friendship with White.[19]

In 1976, when Fraser reintroduced knighthoods, making knights and dames the most senior levels of the Order of Australia, several recipients of the Companion of the Order in 1975 decided to hand theirs back. Nugget Coombs and White led the way. However, Clark, the prominent republican, not only decided to keep his award but also attended the formal investiture by Queen Elizabeth II at Yarralumla in March 1977. Former Labor MP Barry Jones remembered White telling him that 'he was pissed off with Manning' for refusing to return his award. 'Coombs was also disappointed with Manning,' said Jones. After standing on so many public platforms and condemning the colonial mentality of Australia's conservative establishment, many of Clark's friends were surprised to find him eager to be honoured by the Queen. After the dismissal and the emergence of the republican movement in which Clark had played such a leading role, White found his hypocrisy galling: 'I must say I am terribly disappointed in you. Where do we stand if everybody caves in, accepts gongs and honorary doctorates […] and courtship from the Governor-General […] I'd be a rum puff indeed if I accepted, and you're a stuffed turkey to submit.' After Clark attended lunch at Government House three years later, when invited by Governor-General Zelman Cowen, White again made his feelings plain:

> I was horribly shocked and depressed when I read the guest list at that dinner party at Yarralumla. You are unable to see what a very foxy number that Zelman Cowen is. If, as you say, he is a friend from Uni days, you could surely have gone and had a private cup of tea instead of confusing many people who are your admirers.[20]

Clark, who only twelve months earlier asked himself 'What lingers in the face of Patrick White?' and answered 'our being at ease together', increasingly saw him as the 'man of principle', the stern arbiter of his every public utterance, and he cowered before White's wrath.[21]

In the wake of the dismissal of Whitlam's government, Clark's mind was also concentrated on securing White to launch the fourth volume of *A History of Australia*. Clark was elated when White agreed to launch the book, after assuring him that he would not be forced to endure 'the agony' of A. D. Hope's attendance. (White had never forgiven Hope, whom he referred to as 'the weasel-eyed Professor of English', for reviewing *The Tree of Man* as 'pretentious and illiterate verbal sludge'.) This was White's first book launch. 'I've never launched a book in my life,' he wrote to Peter Ryan at Melbourne University Press, 'I'm more concerned with other people's landings […] [but] I accept to launch Manning's Fourth Volume because of my admiration & affection for him.' When the day came, White belied his status as novice orator. With Whitlam, Clark, Xavier Herbert and Tom Keneally looking on, he described Australia as 'an increasingly abhorrent place for all men of good will'. 'I like to think that the evil forces, both formless and only too loathsomely palpable, will be routed by the flood of light [Manning Clark] lets in'. Where White saw light, Australia's conservatives would soon see darkness. In the early 1980s, the shared public role the two men had played in the aftermath of the Dismissal had brought them closer together as much as it exposed the points of tension between them.[22]

The deepest communication between Clark and White often took place during their walks in Sydney's Centennial Park. Walking allowed them to avert their gaze from one another, the rhythm of their steps through the open space unlocking their emotions. White confided in Clark. He told him of the risks he took with 'carnal pick ups' in wartime London and admitted that he saw his life as 'a series of blunders and recoveries'; 'And so it will be, I expect,' he acknowledged, 'till the end.' He also told Clark that he kept much to himself. 'Not even Manoly [his life partner] knew one side of him'. As for the question of faith, although he saw in death the promise of some kind of 'fulfilment' and professed an almost mystical belief in God, he could never call himself a Christian because he could not bring himself to say the words 'as we forgive those who trespass against one another'. White's confession resonated with Clark, a man who lay in bed after major heart surgery in 1983 calling out 'Corpus Christi where are you?' On 19 September, when White visited him in hospital, he gave Clark a copy of Thomas Merton's autobiography *The Seven Storey Mountain* (1948) which Clark rightly saw as a 'conversion story', explaining as it did Merton's spiritual transformation and his decision to become a Trappist monk. In biro, on the half-title page, White inscribed his gift: 'For Manning/after the ordeal/love/Patrick.'[23]

Walking through the stands of flame trees and paperbarks in Centennial Park with Clark, talking about 'grace and freedom', White bitched less about others and for brief moments, allowed his frailties to become visible. The two men continued their conversations about Nolan's work, with Clark noting White's memorable remarks in his diary, drawing strength from his communion with a 'mighty spirit'. Much of the love he professed for White was born of the sense of empowerment he extracted from being in his presence. The conversations with White allowed him to see more clearly the path his own work must take: 'I realized Volume Six must be my Australia.' Occasionally, when Clark was overseas, White revealed the depth of his affection for his friend: 'Shall be relieved when you're back, Australia feels empty without you.'[24]

Australia 1988

Throughout the 1980s, Clark openly courted what he called 'the bitch goddess of fame', behaviour which would increasingly attract White's ire, despite the fact that White had himself become more politically active, joining campaigns to save the Franklin River in Tasmania and becoming a leading spokesperson for the anti-nuclear movement. In 1988, in the midst of the bicentenary celebrations, Clark's solemn face gazed out from television screens and newspapers. On 26 January 1988, he appeared on 'Australia Live', the television program that broadcast the events at Sydney Cove around the nation. Seen against the blue-green backdrop of Sydney Harbour, Clark, with his bush hat and world-weary visage, appeared like a reincarnation of nineteenth-century man, the prophet who had returned to earth to save his people and warn them that the Day of Judgement was at hand. Throughout the year, he shifted in and out of roles easily. One moment he was the activist, launching Wilderness Society calendars and speaking of the earth as 'our common mother', the next he was the sports commentator, writing on the Australian Football League's grand final as if the result would decide the country's future. He seemed to be everywhere. When White rang Clark's home in Tasmania Circle, Canberra, and found he was out on yet another speaking engagement, he quipped to Dymphna: 'I suppose he's opening a country dunny in woop woop.' In fact, White was almost as well known as Clark. In 1987, a Sunday tabloid poll saw him voted 24th in the list of 'most admired' Australians, one below Flo Bjelke Petersen, two below Clark and three below John Howard. He was hardly a recluse from public life. Yet while White took his own responsibilities as a public intellectual seriously, speaking on a variety of republican, green and anti-nuclear platforms, what he could not bear was Clark's courting of celebrity, particularly his public declarations of love for Australian Rules Football and cricket. How could any serious writer love sport? And 'how [could] Manning be so old and so vain', he asked the historian Humphrey McQueen.[25]

In the two years that followed the bicentenary, Clark and White would stake out the shifting lines of their relationship using McQueen as an intermediary. While Clark romanticized his relations with women, his deepest friendships had always been with men. In 1983, shortly after McQueen returned from New York and Paris, he found himself invited to Clark's place for dinner, 'Manning sought me out – after nearly ten years without contact – he began to court me and I was open to suggestion. We would walk and "Tuppence" [Clark's dog] would come along.' By 1989 when McQueen left for Japan, Clark had found in McQueen a man with whom he could show every side of himself.[26]

After leaving university life and ploughing out a career as a freelance writer, McQueen was free of the taint of academia in Clark's eyes. Having acknowledged his homosexuality, he had also made the crossing that so intrigued Clark. Sensitive and sympathetic to Clark's loneliness in his old age, McQueen was also the Renaissance man with whom Clark could parade his feverish appetite for literature, music and art. With McQueen he could indulge in intellectual jousting, summing up Proust, Byron and Pushkin in throwaway lines, describing the disintegrating figures in Picasso's late drawings, or exchanging his thoughts on the music of Wagner.

> I have been playing the overture to Tristan & Isolde quite a lot lately. Dymphna dismisses Wagner as one never-ending act of self-indulgence. That is too simplistic. There are many Wagners – I like the Wagner of l'orgasme perpetuelle, and the tender, serene après l'orgasme.

As his reading ranged wider, Clark read biographies compulsively, writing to McQueen about the lives of writers and artists – Tolstoy, Modigliani, Strindberg, Plath, Jung, Dickens, Greene, Picasso and Goethe – which he consumed at the rate of almost one a week. Reading Gerhard Wehr's biography of Carl Jung, he noted Jung's remarks in a lecture he gave at Yale University in 1937.

> We can only follow Christ's example and live our lives as fully as possible, even if it is based on a mistake. No one has ever found the whole truth; but if we will only live with the same integrity and devotion as Christ, he hoped we would all, like Christ, win through to a resurrected body.

Combing the lives of others, Clark appeared to be searching for answers; perhaps, the story of someone else's life might hold the secret to the riddle of his existence. Tending his archive he compiled the raw materials of his own biography in the shadow of the lives of his artist heroes, hoping that one day he would join them in the pantheon of literary gods.[27]

As Clark's letters to McQueen gathered pace and intensity, McQueen found himself becoming 'the go-between Manning and Patrick White'. In 1989–90, Clark was constantly hanging on the 'minor miracle' of White's phone calls: 'Will Patrick ring?' 'Does he still love me?'

As early as 1980, White had offered to help Clark break free from his addiction to publicity but claimed that Clark was uninterested, 'I wish we could talk Manning. But you never will. You say repeatedly you are coming to see me. You never do, or if you do, you bring one of your children to act, I feel, as a shield.' A few days later, the two men met again in Centennial Park. White told Clark to his face: 'I don't give a fuck what they think of me. You still want them to think well of you.' From here on White played on Clark's desperate need for his approval, teasing him with occasional displays of affection ('Patrick is again writing tender, loving letters') before taunting him with savage denunciations, all of which were meticulously documented by Clark: 'Alas, my being received back by Patrick White did not last for long. I have again offended him. This hurts me, because I am still in love with him. I hope he will live long enough to receive me back.' In contrast to Clark, White could make light of their falling out. When White rang Clark to tell him how moved he had been by Clark's first volume of autobiography, *The Puzzles of Childhood* (1989), Clark reminded him that he was still 'very fond' of him. 'That's very sad,' White replied.[28]

Barry Jones recalled how White 'talked a lot about Manning' in the 1980s, usually in a mixture of 'admiration and scorn'. While White and Clark clearly talked much about one another, only Clark recorded their every meeting and conversation. Typically, he left everything behind. Another mutual friend David Malouf thought that White was preoccupied with his status as a writer and believed that 'Manning had let the team down with his frequent public appearances'. 'Patrick became ironical about Manning,' said Malouf, 'he called him the Archbishop, mocking his pontificating, and when Manning rang and said he was in Sydney, Patrick would say: "Come, but bring Axel'" (literary scholar and Clark's third son). 'He also hated Manning's sentimentality, partly because it reminded him of his own sentimentality, which he always tried to disguise'. While White accused Clark of vanity in his excessive zeal to speak in public, White had his own conceit, as Malouf pointed out: 'Patrick's form of vanity was not to speak.'[29]

Throughout 1989 and 1990, Clark's moods swung dramatically according to the reception he received during his 'audiences' with the irascible monarch of Martin Road. There was no other Australian writer for whom he held more respect, no other writer with whom he wished to be mentioned in the same breath. It was not White's friendship that he pined for; emotionally, he was much closer to McQueen. Rather, it was the companionship of great minds. Clark had sought similar if less intense friendships with writers such as Iris Murdoch and William Golding, both of whom had visited Tasmania Circle and, at least in Murdoch's case, through him had met Patrick White. Seeking intimacy with White, Clark was hankering for what Goethe called 'elective affinities', a spiritual communion between Australia's most acclaimed novelist and the country's most renowned historian, and it was this 'affinity' that White took pleasure in denying him. Yet never once did Clark foresee the fate of his friendship foreshadowed in White's frequent jibes at former friends 'Nettie Nolan' and 'Jeffer Dutton'.[30]

Occasionally, the spectre of White's rejection even entered Clark's dreams. In 1984, Clark dreamt that he was in a room with White who was dressed in drag. The only other person present was [his daughter] Katerina. The White figure asked him. 'Have you been with your lover?' Clark stumbled over the reply, not knowing whether to admit that he had a lover 'albeit a very close friend'. He turned to see Katerina weeping, 'frozen in terror'. In Clark's unconscious, White appeared as 'the stern Jehovah', the punisher who maintained moral standards he could never possibly attain. Writing to McQueen, Clark vented his frustration. 'Patrick's personal vindictiveness is rather like the envy of Australian academics – bottomless and unfathomable […] he is a brilliant denouncer […] consumed with hatred and bitterness and crankiness.'[31]

As Clark's love affair with his public audience deepened, he began to recoil from what he saw as the White 'tradition': 'compassion for the weak and hatred for the many'. White's 'elitist' contempt for ordinary Australians bridled Clark. As he told Humphrey McQueen in May 1989: '[Patrick] sees us all as inhabitants of a dreadful country which has sunk so low it can never be redeemed.' In public, Clark held his tongue, refusing Peter Craven's request to review White's memoir *Flaws in the Glass* because he did not want to damage his friendship with the novelist. In private, he lamented White's reluctance to reveal 'the other man who lives side by side with the man of many savageries' and noted his physical decline in prose that few others could muster, as in this diary entry from November 1988:

> Visited Patrick White [in hospital] at 10.40am. He has been ill – emphasemia [sic], ostio-pyrrohsis [sic], blood clot. [His] body has wasted away, shrunk in height, stooped, [he] shuffles along with a stick, cheeks sunken, lips bloodless and very thin, the mouth a wavy line. Later, when he took off his glasses, I saw the sad eyes, the melancholy pose of the face.[32]

Although White had told him months earlier on the phone that he did not want to see him or even 'hear the sound of [his] famous voice', when White was hospitalized Clark had put aside his differences to visit him in St. Vincent's, crying at the sight of his shrunken body. For a short while after Clark's open display of affection, White's affection for him was rekindled, but as always he quickly reverted to condemnation. Two weeks later, Clark, depressed, confided in his diary:

> Very depressed, very weak, another Patrick White attack on me. [He] said I was the vainest man he had ever known. Very shaken by this, as vanity has been my poison drink. Why do all relationships end with both parties aware of the flaws in the other and more aware of the flaws in themselves? Love should strengthen faith in oneself ... Why this temptation to punish the one who has inflicted such pain? That can only make life more wretched. That is part of our folly, our madness.[33]

In February 1990, White refused to allow his photograph to be used in Clark's second volume of autobiography, *Quest for Grace*. For Clark this 'left a wound that only death could cure'. Shortly afterwards, White told him yet again that his 'vanity' was the cause of the break in their relationship. He even felt sorry for Dymphna because she had to live with him. In the face of repeated rebuffs from White, Clark kept hoping that White would recant. But only weeks before White died, Clark rang to find that White had cut him completely: '23 August 1990: Today Patrick White did not want to speak to me. Why? What have I done to deserve such treatment?' In order to win White's approval, Clark had been prepared to endure humiliation. In the end not even this had saved him from being spurned.[34]

A Beach House: 1990

When White died on 30 September, Clark was at Wapengo, his coastal retreat on the south coast of New South Wales. The following morning hungry for Clark's commentary, the ABC flew journalists and cameramen in helicopters from Sydney. Clark got up early jotting down notes for his interview: 'Am to be interviewed for ABC television news & 7.30 report at Wapengo today. Points to make: There are very special people – Goethe's point – one great mystery is why the gods create such people who do their work and then are taken away. Maybe the gods sent him to condemn our greed and titillation culture [...] Patrick as the judge of all of us loyalty promiscuity [...] Patrick the lover – he wanted something no one could give him. We were all inadequate. We all let him down.' A few hours later the sound of the ABC choppers could be heard above the roar of the waves at Wapengo. Clark walked out onto the verandah looking every bit the world-weary seer the ABC had travelled so far to interview.[35]

Before the cameras, Clark eulogized White as one of Australia's greatest artists. He could never desert White publicly because to do so would be to admit that White had rejected him. Despite the fact that their relationship had soured and the inspiration they once received from one another's work had ended in disappointment, it was Clark who performed the public rites for White's passing. The two men had fallen out over their different perceptions of the writer's responsibility to his country: how to speak, when to speak, what to speak about and which audience to speak to. Ironically, they had also fallen out over the issue Clark had fought for long before White took it up in 1975 – Australian independence – and how the writer should live true to that ideal. For a short period in the 1970s and 1980s, Australia looked to White and Clark – the patrician novelist and the prophet historian – to lead a more assertive and distinctive Australian culture. As the nation's first Nobel laureate in literature, White represented the entry of Australian letters onto the 'world stage', while Clark's preacher-like demeanour and his solemn, biblical pronouncements gave Australian history the gravitas and drama it had hitherto lacked. That the 'world stage' was purely a figment of the Australian imagination did not matter. Far more important was the newfound cultural awakening and dignity that both artists helped to instil in the broader public culture: the belief that Australian literature and history were, and could continue to be, the equal of any country in the world.

In the months after White's death, Clark visited Manoly Lascaris at Martin Road, listening respectfully as Lascaris spoke of his life with White, before recording the conversation in his diary. '[Manoly told me] how [White] never gave him a cent, how hurt he was when the will was read [...] He had been left with nothing except [the] right to live in the house till he died, how he [...] would have liked to convert the house into a Patrick White Museum, but [the] will now made that impossible.' Lascaris complained that White had always expected 'others to observe a code of conduct he could not observe himself'.[36]

With White gone Clark was more isolated. The lofty view from his perch seemed even lonelier. While he occasionally saw Sidney Nolan when he visited from London, he felt that he was slowly being deserted as so many of his contemporaries were no longer alive. Clark died eight months after White on 23 May 1991, Sidney Nolan following him shortly afterwards on 28 November 1992.

To the last moment, Clark had preferred to cling to the romantic view of his friendship with White, repressing the memory of his rejection in favour of glowing tributes written for posterity. In October 1990, ministering to Manoly, he praised him for serving as both White's muse and a constant source of strength and selfless love before finishing with a eulogy that barely hinted at the ambivalence of his true feelings for White.

> In Patrick's presence we should stand in awe. He made me glad to be alive – and I always felt and feel now what a privilege it was to know a little of his love. I was and am glad that through him I met you. Coming to Castle Hill and Martin Road meant more to me than I could express in words. There were moments which were like an epiphany – moments when the fever and the fret ceased. It was like hearing music – yes, on leaving I heard music.[37]

Notes

1 On Clark meeting White, see Alan Wearne and Victoria Wearne, *The Quest for Grace by Manning Clark* (Melbourne: Penguin, 1991), 220; and David Marr, *Patrick White: A Life* (Sydney: Random House, 1991), 354, 688.
2 On Nolan's 1949–50 paintings of central Australia, see Geoffrey Smith, ed., *Sidney Nolan: Desert and Drought* (Melbourne: National Gallery of Victoria, 2003), 26–67 (Nolan's comments: 36, 38). On Boyd I have drawn on Janet McKenzie, *Arthur Boyd: Art and Life* (London: Thames & Hudson, 2000), especially chap. 3. For reproductions of *The Mockers* (1945) and *The Mourners* (1945), see McKenzie *Boyd*, 64, 67. On the 1946 exhibition at Melbourne University, see Richard Haese, *Rebels and Precursors: The Revolutionary Years of Australian Art* (Melbourne: Penguin, 1981; repr. 1988), 172–73. For Clark on Boyd, see Wearne, *Quest*, 162.
3 Marr, *Life*, 316. Nolan quotes can be found in Smith, *Nolan*, 27, 36. The Reed letter appears in Haese, *Rebels*, 254.
4 Cited in Haese, *Rebels*, 173.
5 Nolan on sacramental feeling (1956) in Nancy Underhill, ed., *Nolan on Nolan: Sidney Nolan in His Own Words* (Melbourne: Penguin, 2007), 270. White on *Voss* in Patrick White, 'The Prodigal Son', in *Macquarie Pen Anthology of Australian Literature*, ed. Nicholas Jose (Sydney: Allen & Unwin, 2009), 557–60. Clark on Beethoven and Mozart, Notebook, 19 June 1956, *Papers*, MS7550, National Library of Australia. Clark on jeerers and mockers, Diary, 1 December 1956, *Papers*. Nolan on cannibalism in Nolan to Albert Tucker, 28 May 1964 in Underhill, *Nolan*, 178–79.
6 Diary, 1 October 1956, *Papers*. The first manuscripts of the first volume, including Dymphna's editorial comments, in Clark, Box 58, Folder 1, 'Volume One Preliminary Manuscript', *Papers*. At a later date, Clark wrote on the manuscript, '(This was begun in Oxford England on 1 October 1956).'

7 On White's *The Tree of Man*, see Manning Clark, *A Historian's Apprenticeship* (Melbourne: Melbourne University Press, 1992), 19; and Marr, *Life*, 288–90.
8 I am grateful to Darleen Bungey for passing on Dymphna's recollections. On Humphries, Clark to Axel Clark, 6 April 1964, in Roslyn Russell, ed., *Ever Manning: Selected Letters of Manning Clark 1938–1991* (Sydney: Allen & Unwin, 2008), 205–6; Clark to Humphries, 5 April 1964, sent to the author courtesy of Barry Humphries; and Clark, Diary, 3 March 1964, *Papers*. On Dymphna's reaction, see Clark, Diary, 22 March 1964, *Papers*.
9 Clark on his meeting with Nolan, Diary, 8 August 1964, *Papers*; regarding Nolan at the Qantas Building, see also his entry for August 15. Clark was initially puzzled by the Kelly paintings, and his letter to Dymphna, 9 August 1964, in Russell, *Ever Manning*, 232–33. Nolan reflecting on Clark's work in 1969 in Underhill, *Nolan*, 314.
10 Clark to White, 8 November 1961 (drafted several times); White's reply, 12 April 1961, also 28 June and 6 July 1961, White's praise for the first volume in his letter to Clark, 13 August 1964: all in Clark, Box 25, Folder 209, *Papers*. Nolan to Clark, 17 December 1964 in Box 24, Folder 197, *Papers*; Campbell to Clark, 8 July 1966, in Box 6, Folder 44, *Papers*. See also Clark's description of his epiphany on meeting White in Sydney in 1959 in Wearne, *Quest*, 220.
11 'A Talk to Victorian Historical Society September 29 1967', in Manning Clark, *Speaking Out of Turn: Lectures and Speeches 1940–1991* (Melbourne: Melbourne University Press, 1997), 64–66; Clark to Nolan, 11 September 1967, Box 156, Folder 2, *Papers*. Clark on his beloved Burke and Wills, Diary, 19 October 1967, *Papers*.
12 Clark at the Nolan exhibition in Sydney, Diary, 12 October 1967, *Papers*; Clark to Nolan, 17 October 1967, Box 24, Folder 197, *Papers*; 'primeval landscape' see Nolan interview, *Listener*, 8 October 1964 in Underhill, *Nolan*, 290.
13 Patrick White, *Voss* (London: Vintage, 1994), 33, 35, 124, 267, 342, 446.
14 Clark, Diary, 13 May 1974, *Papers*; Whitlam to Clark, 17 January 1974, in Clark, Box 157, Folder 13, *Papers*; letter, *Sydney Morning Herald*, 23 November 1972; Opera House rally, Clark, Diary, 13 May 1974, *Papers*.
15 White to Clark, undated postcard (probably 1968), Clark, Box 25, Folder 29, *Papers*; White accepting his Australia Day Award, *Australian*, 26 January 1974; 'Go it alone', Clark in *Sunday Telegraph*, 12 May 1974, 17.
16 White to Cynthia and Sidney Nolan, 3 January 1971, in David Marr, ed., *Patrick White: Letters* (Sydney: Random House, 1994), 372; White to Dutton, 20 January 1974, Marr, *Letters*, 432; Clark to White, 30 October 1970 in Clark, Box 38, Folder 9, *Papers*; on their readings of one another's work, see the same and White to Clark, 7 April 1968, in Box 25, Folder 209, *Papers*; White on the third volume, White to Clark, 3 January 1974, Box 157, Folder 12, *Papers*; in the same folder, White's teeth falling out and using Clark's work as a pivot in White to Clark, 3 January 1974 (and thanking him for the gift of tickets to see *The Magic Flute*); Dymphna's thoughts on the relationship between White and Clark, private correspondence courtesy of Jan Nicholas.
17 Clark on Humphries, 'The Quest for an Australian National Identity', James Duhig Memorial Lecture, University of Queensland, 6 August 1979. On White's attitude on the announcement of his Nobel Prize, see Marr in this volume.
18 White to Dutton, 22 December 1975 in Marr, *Letters*, 466; cleansing fire see 'The Cleansing Fire Speech, 1978', in Clark, *Speaking*, 30–33; see also *Age*, 10 June 1978.
19 Clark to Peter Ryan ('man of principle') 9 March 1981, Melbourne University Press Archives; see also *Australian*, 7 January 1976, 7; White to Clark, 15 November 1975, in Marr, *Letters*, 465.

20 Clark to White, 10 August 1980, in Marr, *Letters*, 534–35; White to Clark, 16 June 1980, in Marr, *Letters*, 532; and Barry Jones to the author, Melbourne, February 2008.
21 Clark on White's face, Diary, 25 August 1980, *Papers*; 'Fman of principle', Clark to Peter Ryan, 9 March 1981, Melbourne University Press Archives.
22 White to Ryan, 16 January 1978 and Ryan, Memo, 27 March 1975, Melbourne University Press Archives; Clark quotes White's description of A. D. Hope in Diary, 21 April 1966, *Papers*.
23 Corpus Christi, Clark, Diary, 14 September 1983, *Papers*; records of Clark's conversations with White in Diary, 4 November 1981 and 16 July 1985, *Papers*. Clark's copy of Merton's novel is held at Manning Clark House, Canberra.
24 White to Clark, 18 January 1979, in Marr, *Letters*, 513–14; Clark on his walks with White, Diary, 4 November 1981, *Papers*.
25 Humphrey McQueen to the author, Canberra, June 2009; celebrity poll, *Sun*, 27 February 1987, 3; 'country dunny', Dymphna Clark to the author, Canberra, 1997; 'our common mother', see Alan Tate, 'Manning Clark Overcomes Australia', *SMH Good Weekend*, 1 August 1987.
26 Humphrey McQueen to the author, Canberra, June 2009.
27 On White and Clark, McQueen to the author, Canberra, June 2009; see also Clark's correspondence to McQueen in Humphrey McQueen, *Papers*, MS 4809, National Library of Australia, especially 6 and 22 October 1989. See also Clark's annotations in his copy of Gerhard Weber, *Jung: a Biography* (Boston: Shambhala, 1987), held at Manning Clark House.
28 Clark recording White's comments over the phone in Diary, 5 September 1989, *Papers*; see also 24 August 1980; Clark to McQueen, 5 September 1989 and 22 January 1989 in McQueen, *Papers*; White to Clark, 10 August 1980 in Marr, *Letters*, 534–35; Clark continued to see Sidney Nolan when the painter visited Australia. The last occasion the two men saw one another was in March 1988. On 8 March, Clark wrote in his diary, 'I met Sidney Nolan [...] he was charming, flirtatious, looked as though he wanted or needed someone to take charge of him.'
29 David Malouf to the author, Sydney April 2008; Barry Jones to the author, Melbourne, February 2008.
30 Clark to McQueen, 14 December 1988, in McQueen, *Papers*; regarding a meeting with Iris Murdoch and John Bayley see Clark to White, 22 February 1967, in Clark, Box 37, Folder 4, *Papers*; also see Clark to Murdoch, 31 May 1972, Box 39, Folder 16; Ken Inglis told me of dinner parties at Tasmania Circle attended by William Golding.
31 Clark to McQueen, 29 June 1989, in McQueen, *Papers*; Clark's dream in Clark, Diary, 22 June 1984, *Papers*.
32 Clark, Diary, 2 November 1988, *Papers*. His other comments on White can be found in letters to Humphrey McQueen, 8 May 1989, 21 September 1989, and undated, but late 1989, all in McQueen, *Papers*. Clark refusing to review *Flaws*, Clark to Craven, 5 October 1981, Box 7, *Scripsi* papers, Melbourne University Archives.
33 Clark, Diary, 17 November 1988; see also 2 November and 8 March 1988; *Papers*.
34 Clark, Diary, 23 August 1990, *Papers*; for 'the wound that only death could cure', Diary, 7 February 1990; for White's shrunken appearance, 21 September 1989; on feeling sorry for Dymphna, 5 July 1990; on White's physical decline, 2 November 1988.
35 Clark, Diary, 30 September 1990, *Papers*.
36 Clark, Diary, 8 October 1990, *Papers*; on Manoly, see 27 February 1991.
37 Clark, Diary, 30 September 1990, *Papers*.

Chapter 5

'DISMANTLED AND RE-CONSTRUCTED': *FLAWS IN THE GLASS* RE-VISIONED

Georgina Loveridge

In 1939, Patrick White pondered the idea of writing an autobiography. In a letter to poet, journalist and lover Spud Johnson, he wrote:

> [T]he difficult question would be: how comprehensive to make it? [...] Actually, my autobiography, if a factual one, would be pretty uninteresting and bleak. I think vanity would compel me to explore its psychological possibilities, real or imagined. Just to eke out the comings and goings of fact.[1]

Forty years later, White was 'working fitfully on a kind of self-portrait'.[2] By most accounts, the resultant book, *Flaws in the Glass* (1981) was far from 'pretty uninteresting'.[3] Mockingly re-dubbed 'Claws in the Arse', its attacks on fellow public figures, friends, family and acquaintances made front-page news in Australia and England.[4] But if not 'uninteresting', was it 'factual'? 'Real or imagined'? In fact, as I will argue in this chapter, *Flaws in the Glass* (*Flaws*) emerged as the climax, product, account and expression of White's lifetime search for the truth: as both a sample of White's aesthetic and a commentary upon it, *Flaws* provides a reading guide to his fictions. Hence, I will question the classification of *Flaws* as non-fiction and, more recently, as fiction, demonstrating instead that *Flaws* tells us not *the* truth but *about* truth.

This chapter is presented in three parts. The first questions the factuality and comprehensiveness of *Flaws* and critiques prior assumptions of its form and purpose. The second surveys critical approaches to the text to date and proposes an alternative: one which acknowledges and makes use of its meta-fictional components. The final part elucidates the complex ways in which

White interweaves modes of truth in *Flaws*, ways which in turn illuminate his writing per se.

Flaws in the Glass Dismantled

When White's biographer David Marr first read *Flaws* he 'knew it was incomplete'. Years later, Marr discovered that White's parents had invested in a publishing venture to enable his first publication, a book of poetry:[5]

> It was one of those details which completely contradicted everything that White had said about his own parents. He'd always said that they opposed his work bitterly, fought him, tried to turn him into everything except a writer, but that little detail showed me that he was in fact lying.[6]

It was neither White's first nor last public 'lie' but one in a succession of public distortions of the truth, dramatically evinced with the rediscovery of the new papers discussed by Harris, Webby and others in this volume; papers White claimed to have destroyed.

White long pursued a sustained campaign to stage-manage his memorialization and mythologization. To this end, he restricted the flow of biographical data, remaining 'biographically silent' for the first twenty years of his writing career.[7] He minimized interviews and public appearances. He self-authored, edited and censored biographical records, including the biographical notes for the dust jackets of his novels,[8] two biographical essays (for *Meanjin* and the Swedish Academy)[9] and an 'interview' with G.A. Wilkes and Thelma Herring for *Southerly*.[10] Hence in 1981, *Flaws in the Glass* emerged as the culmination of a long-term public-relations campaign. It was consistent with earlier accounts, sticking to the well-worn script he had crafted 'of affliction, exile, foreignness, hostility and misunderstanding'.[11] It was 'tightly' written, incomplete, deceptive and deceptively simple. As White wrote to Jean Lambert in 1983, 'I find it strange that you should think *Flaws in the Glass* more tightly written than anything of mine you have translated. I am always receiving letters from Australians saying the book is so easy to read they must try my novels again.'[12] The general public, literary critics and academic scholars, White's fans and his detractors, all agreed.[13] *Flaws* was, in fact, no more and no less than what White purported it to be: 'a self-portrait as truthfully and simply as I can make it'.[14]

James Bertram, for example, praised *Flaws in the Glass* as 'scrupulously honest [and] genuinely revealing about [White's] personality and predilections [...] a fiercely candid confession'.[15] And even in his scathing critique of the author, John Docker questioned neither White's certainty nor his sincerity or authenticity, writing that White was 'certain in his possession of a language of fact and truth'.[16] More recently, Annalisa Pes concluded: 'White appears to be extremely reliable and honest considering the unflattering verbal portrait he paints of himself, and of those around him.'[17]

Not surprisingly then within Patrick White scholarship, *Flaws in the Glass* has tended (and continues) not only to be read uncritically but also to be used to substantiate claims about the author's life, beliefs, artistic vision and literary works. As with White's 1958 essay 'The Prodigal Son', *Flaws* has been mined of now-familiar, oft-quoted epigrams, cited without caution, critical reflection, scrutiny or qualification.[18] However, as Brigid Rooney has warned, 'to deduce White's [...] views from a memoir like *Flaws in the Glass* [...] can be risky'.[19] It is to turn a blind eye to the history of the author, to the detail of the book and to developments in White scholarship.

Indeed to take *Flaws in the Glass* at face value is to misread it in three ways. First, this approach relies upon a literal, one-dimensional reading, insensitive to the doubling effects of White's irony, hyperbole and self-parody. Second, it relies upon a partial, selective reading, blinded to the text's inconvenient truths, to contradictions, anomalies and complicating statements that destabilize its single, objective truth, by multiplying the truths at play. In fact *Flaws* hints at its own flaws, its own unreliability. It warns of the problems of truth, the fallibility of memory, the limits of self-knowledge and self-representation and the inadequacy of language.[20] In a series of disclaimers, White warns: 'the incidents [...] become blurred', are 'difficult to disentangle from memory' or shrouded in the 'webs of mystery which cling to certain [childhood] events' (27, 77, 18). Repeatedly, he writes: 'I can't remember', 'I don't remember' and 'I seem to remember' (34, 41, 44, 77). Third, it relies upon an isolated reading, outside the context of White scholarship, without regard to emergent trends and developments. It fails to acknowledge, for example, a recurrent observation: that White's works are not what they 'seem', that on first inspection they look like 'traditional', 'classic', 'realist' works, but that, on closer examination, this is an illusion which is subverted and dismantled.[21] Throughout *Flaws* we find evidence of a similar pattern: an initial, apparent conformity to the autobiographical mode which is subsequently dismantled, inverted and undone, and with it the assumptions of truth, objectivity and cohesive subjectivity.

This is not to say that White does not invite an autobiographical model of reading *Flaws in the Glass*. He declares his commitment to the pursuit of truth both in his writing and in his personal relationships. He identifies as his aim the representation of a true self. He differentiates between fact and fiction; he asserts his mastery of both and his ability to alternate between them. But these cues and declarations are countered by statements to the contrary.

That is, on the one hand White claims truthfulness and trustfulness as personality traits: 'What I had always aspired to was, simply, truthfulness and trust', 'I [...] love and venerate [...] before all, pureness of heart and trustfulness' (100, 155). On the other hand, he describes his 'battle between personality and truth' (107). As to which wins the battle in *Flaws in the Glass*, 'personality' or 'truth', we do not learn. And if the truth is a 'razor blade' – clear-cut, and black and white – it is also a 'many-sided crystal', fragmented and kaleidoscopic. And for White all he has written about are 'refractions from that many-sided crystal truth' (151). He 'has spent a lifetime searching for [...] the truth' but what he 'believes [he] can never prove to be' the truth (70).

In order to write *The Aunt's Story* (1948), White explains 'I had first to break myself of the habit acquired while compiling factual reports in the Air Force, closer to the practice of *objective* journalism than the pursuit of truth in creative fiction' (127). Where *Flaws in the Glass* lies within this spectrum the reader is left to wonder. White also describes having 'found it hard to reconcile life and art' (84). While art is an illusion – 'the illusion referred to as art' (20) – so is life: 'the illusion of reality life boils down to' (154). The breakdown of this truth–fiction reality–illusion distinction suggests the irreconcilability of reality and illusion so that, as White puts it in *The Aunt's Story*, 'there is sometimes little to choose between the illusion of reality and the reality of illusion'.[22] Yet *Flaws in the Glass* purported to be a 'warts-and-all' account, a claim White reiterated throughout his correspondence. It was an attempt to 'try to put the warts in the places where they belong', 'to try to show the person (I think) I am, because so few of my critics seem to know', 'to try to show what I am and what I have been getting at in my work'.[23]

But the view White presents of himself is of a fractured and multiple persona unknown to himself, unknowable and un-representable. He is 'many-faceted', his 'body protean', a 'fragmented character', composed of a 'cast of contradictory characters' (153, 32, 20):

> Of course there are individuals [...] who consider they know me better than I know myself. These are the most deluded of all [...] I am this black, bubbling pool. I am also this leaf rustling [...]. In the eyes of God, the Eye, or whatever supernatural power, I am probably pretty average crap. (182–83)

By the conclusion of *Flaws in the Glass* 'the reader [has] gained [...] [s]ome understanding of Patrick White [...] but not a great deal', as critics have remarked.[24]

I believe the final product is not mere self-effacement but what Paul de Man has called 'de-facement', not self-obstruction but self-destruction.[25] As Veronica Brady first observed, 'White is using his knowledge of himself to annihilate himself [...]and weaken the impression he has made.' In so doing she suggests he 'make[s] himself an example of the truth', of its subjective, 'personal' nature.²⁶ The deconstruction of autobiographical conventions illustrates what the text states directly: the impossibility of the autobiographical project, its fraught, inevitably flawed nature.

Hence, as the title of *Flaws in the Glass* implies, White's subject is less the *figure* in the glass (himself) than the *flaws* in the glass: the obfuscations which block, cloud or distort clear representation, the problematic nature of figuration of and by the author–subject. It is the (inherently) flawed image of a flawed subject, 'refractions of that many-sided crystal truth', refuting the possibility of a single, fixed, objective truth. Hence the interest of *Flaws in the Glass* is not the flaws in White, but the floating, blotched, rippled and dimpled reflection, the inherent distortions of self-representation through language (1).

According to de Man, this is the interest of *all* autobiographies:

> The interest of autobiography [...] is not that it reveals reliable self-knowledge – it does not – but that it demonstrates in a striking way the impossibility of closure and of totalization (that is the impossibility of coming into being) of all textual systems made up of tropological substitutions [of author and subject, name and referent].²⁷

Like White's early fictions, de Man suggests an autobiography is deceptive in its appearance:

> Autobiography *seems* to depend on actual and potentially verifiable events in a less ambivalent way than does fiction. It *seems* to belong to a simpler mode of referentiality, of representation, and of diegesis. It may contain lots of phantasms and dreams, but these deviations from reality remain rooted in a single subject whose identity is defined by the uncontested readability of his proper name [...]. We *assume* that life produces the autobiography as an act produces its consequences.²⁸

Similarly *Flaws in the Glass* seems to document actual, verifiable events: the dismissal of the Whitlam Government in 1975, White's receipt of the Nobel Prize for Literature in 1973, Queen Elizabeth II's visit to Sydney in 1963 and others; it refers to known figures in Australian society, culture and politics. *Flaws* seems to deviate from White's fiction in its use of a simpler mode of representation. To all appearances it is a straightforward, ordered account, structured in three chronologically sequenced parts and subdivided by chapters and subheadings.²⁹ Finally, *Flaws* seems to be rooted in what was perceived to be a single subject, circumscribed in the name of 'Patrick White'. But ultimately these appearances are undermined: linearity doubles back and loops into circularity; chronology reverses and breaks down into discontinuity; fact and fiction blur and blend; the cohesive author–subject fragments and multiplies and the 'univocal focal point'[30] is rendered 'polyphonic'.[31] The conventions of the autobiographical mode are invoked and undone. This is White's point in *Flaws*, and one reason behind its composition: 'nobody knows anybody, whether in the beginning or the end – which is one of the reasons why I'm writing this book' (148). In his self-portrait, White states the impossibility of 'coming into being', and the limitations of textual representation.

Flaws in the Glass Re-Constructed

If the effect of *Flaws in the Glass* was defacement or self-annihilation, what is its value to scholars of White's fictions?

A survey of the current body of criticism on *Flaws in the Glass* reveals three broad approaches, each of which builds upon the other: literal, applied and self-reflexive readings. These are premised on a common set of assumptions, namely that White's art was grounded in 'personal experience and values', in what Simon During has called an 'autobiographical aesthetic',[32] that it 'imaginatively transformed and elaborated',[33] 'transmuted' and 'mythicized' everyday experiences into the material of White's novels[34] and that therefore 'the critic needs to read White's life alongside his works'.[35]

In a literal reading, *Flaws in the Glass* provides a biographical reference point, a portrait of the artist at work which provides 'insight [...] into the sources and condition',[36] the 'genesis and composition' of White's works, and their 'links to situations, people, places, which have crossed the author's life'.[37] Brady, for example, provides a detailed list of these insights: the rationale behind *The Solid Mandala*, the inspiration behind *The Eye of the Storm* and the real-life progenitor for Miss Hare of *Riders in the Chariot*. This initial reading takes details articulated directly in *Flaws* and adds these to our pre-existing knowledge of the text and its sources.

The next reading *applies* the lessons of *Flaws in the Glass* to the fictions in order to extrapolate their biographical origins, sources or inspiration. Within this applied approach, we find two strains: the first attends to details of situations, events, places and people, and traces their manifestation in the plots, settings and characters of White's novels; the second sees White's fictions as a form of self-expression and self-representation, and his characters as 'fragments of [his] own fragmented identity' (32), as 'projections of the author',[38] as 'the shreds of the author's multiple selves torn apart and pieced together'.[39] This second strand links *Flaws* as a portrait of the artist to White's fictional portraits of the artist and views these as semi-autobiographical, for example his portrait of Alf Dubbo in *Riders in the Chariot* (1968), Hurtle Duffield in *The Vivisector* (1970), E. Twyborn in *The Twyborn Affair* (1979) and Alex Xenophon Demirjian Gray in *Memoirs of Many in One* (1986).

Such attempts to 'explain the art by way of the life' have attracted fierce criticism for their elision of the religious, mystical and visionary strands in White's fictions. Art is reduced to life, the otherworldly is reduced to the secular and the symbolic is reduced to the literal. However if, as David Tacey has argued, Marr's *Life* similarly sought 'to demystify White's work, to make it secular, understandable, recognisable, ordinary, gay, political and of its time', then White was complicit in this.[40] He authorized its publication, provided information, and proof-read and signed off on the final manuscript. Ten years earlier in *Flaws in the Glass* itself, White had professed his homosexuality, outlined his socialist and pro-republic politics and linked both to his development as an artist. At the same time, however, White did not deny his use of 'a few bits' of Jung, Christian theology or Jewish mysticism as 'suited my purpose'. For White the basis of his works, their source and meaning lay between his biography and his psychology, between his real life and unconscious pasts: 'on one level certainly, there is a recognizable collage of personal experience, on another, little of the self I know' (182). On this basis, White claimed (or sought) to elude definition, generic classification and definitive interpretation of his works, whether biographical, Jungian or otherwise. Of Tacey's psychoanalytical approach, he remarked: '[H]e tries to tie his subject down in the strait jacket of his system and finds I don't fit.'[41]

The self-reflexive approach to *Flaws in the Glass* is the most recent, complex and under-developed. It moves from a literal to a figurative and self-reflexive reading and turns its attention to the text's meta-fictional aspects. While the approach applies the lessons of *Flaws* to the fictions, the self-reflexive approach applies the lessons of *Flaws* to the text itself. It reads the text for its revelations of the functions of White's fictions but more than this, for its illustration of this process. White's self-portrait provides insights into the mechanics of his fictions in two ways: through description and demonstration, that is through explanation and exemplification. Hence *Flaws* works on multiple levels to enact its own truth and to illuminate the theme, function and limitations of truth in its fictions.

In this vein, Pes uses the term 'meta-fictional tool' to describe how *Flaws in the Glass* 'gives new information on the genesis and composition of White's works and on the links of these narratives to the situations, people and places which have crossed the author's life'.[42] She acknowledges its fictional elements and fictive structure. However, for Pes it is not through its fictionality – or meta-fictionality – that *Flaws* operates, or has potential, as a meta-fictional or interpretative tool. Rather she suggests that its meta-fictional function is limited to the 'new information' it provides.

Like Pes, Jessica Geva detects fictional elements in *Flaws in the Glass* and an absence of autobiography. Pursuing this point to its full conclusion Geva classifies *Flaws* as 'fiction' and the 'least autobiographical of his works':

> White's reliability as truthful portrayer and self-portrayer is thus cast into doubt because of latent designs informing his selection and depiction of characters [as own character components] enlisted to produce and shape the image of a self he wishes to conjure up [...].

She adds, 'White indeed displays a suspect flexibility with facts that creatively relegates his ostensibly ethnographic and historical self-portrait to the realm of fiction.'[43]

As its author intimates, *Flaws in the Glass* is neither fiction nor non-fiction and neither the most nor the least autobiographical of White's works. On the contrary, it contains an indeterminate, inextricable mix of truth and fiction, reality and illusion, as did White's semi-autobiographical novels with their 'autobiographical aesthetic'. The value of *Flaws* lies in its meta-fictionality, in its dual function of description and demonstration, of explication and enactment, whereby White's creative process, the mechanics of his fictions, are outlined and modelled within the text. *Flaws* provides a blueprint for White's fictions and a meta-commentary upon them.

A Reading-Guide to White's Fictions

In his interview with Wilkes and Herring, White professed to be 'a bit of a bower-bird', in that he 'enjoy[ed] [...] the accumulation of down-to-earth detail'. In turn, he suggested, '[a]ll my novels are an accumulation of detail.'[44] In an alternative analogy, White restates this in *Flaws in the Glass*:

> I knew I hadn't a scholar's mind. Such as I had was more like the calico bag hanging from the sewing-room door-knob, stuffed with snippets of material of contrasting textures and clashing colours, which might at some future date be put to some practical, aesthetic, or even poetic use. (38)

These snippets of material, the raw materials of his art, included 'down-to-earth' detail, 'images and situations from real-life',[45] and 'bits' of other texts.[46] Rather than deny his use of real-life detail, White drew critics' attention to it:

> This awful symbol business! [...] In their pursuit of symbols many academic critics don't seem to realize that writers and painters often make use of images

and situations from real life because they have appealed to them as being beautiful or comic or bizarre.[47]

I want now to use examples from *Flaws in the Glass* to suggest White is showing us how this process worked.

Flaws in the Glass opens in Turret House, which White's parents rented for the summer of 1926. Turret House is neither White's first home nor his permanent home. Nor is it even in Australia. It is in Felpham, Sussex, England, a detail a number of critics have remarked on (3).[48] As White tells us directly, 'The house had belonged to the poet Hayley, of no importance except as the friend of genius': William Blake (3). While '[a]t that stage Blake was no more than a name' to the child-White, he haunts the adult-White's account, manifest in direct references and thinly veiled allusions to Blake's works (7). For example, as White refers to 'sweet Felpham' (7), he quotes Blake's letter, 'To my dear Friend, Mrs Anna Flaxman' (1800):

Away to sweet Felpham, for Heaven is there;
The Ladder of Angels descends thro' the air;
On the turret its spiral does softly descend,
...
And at his own door the bless'd Hermit does stand.[49]

Here the 'Hermit' is Hayley, the self-described 'Hermit of Eartham' and 'Hermit of the Turret'; the 'turret' is that of Turret House. Hence as White quotes Blake's letter, he appropriates its images. The 'Heaven' and 'Ladder of Angels [which] descends thro' the air' rematerialize in *Flaws in the Glass* in 'the ceiling of the dining-room of the house that Hayley built at "sweet Felpham"' which White explains 'had been papered over with a wrinkled sky and putti seated on cumulus cloud' (7). (While 'sweet Felpham' is enclosed in quotation marks, its source is neither cited nor explained.)

One page later, again, the child-White is 'disturbed [...] without [...] understanding', 'reached [...] in depths [...] [un]explored', and 'tossed on a sea of Welsh voices' that intone Blake's 'Jerusalem', the preface to his epic *Milton* (1804–10). During the General Strike of 1926, on the Brompton Road, White witnesses 'the voices of the Welsh miners, their high harmonies [...] [s]training towards an unattainable Jerusalem'. Blake's preface to *Milton*, with its allusion to the apocryphal story of a young Jesus Christ's ('the holy Lamb of God') journey to present-day England foreshadows a second visitation, presented in an episode subtitled 'Milton comes to Blake'. In this episode, a God-like Milton ('the Human Wonder of God/Reaching from heaven to earth') returns to earth, 'descending down into my [Blake's] garden'. In *Flaws in the Glass*, in an apparent re-working of the 'Milton comes to Blake' episode, the child-White meets his 'first poet' – A.B. 'Banjo' Paterson – who like Blake's Milton descends 'the stone steps' into the 'garden' (6). Blake writes:

> Descending down into my Garden, a Human Wonder of God
> Reaching from heaven to earth a Cloud and Human Form
> I beheld Milton with astonishment
> ...
> And Milton collecting all his fibres into impregnable strength
> Descended down a Paved work of all kinds of precious stones
> Out from the eastern sky; descending down into my Cottage
> Garden, clothed in black: severe and silent as he descended.[50]

Not unlike the 'severe and silent' Milton of Blake's *Milton*, the Paterson of *Flaws* is 'the driest kind of gentleman, his face like a wrinkled, sooty lemon' and 'whether the stranger spoke' White 'can't remember' (6). While Milton is 'clothed in black', Paterson is 'dressed in a tobacco-coloured suit'. While Milton 'descended down a Paved work of [...] stones', Paterson 'came down the stone steps' (6).

Through this doubling of Blake and Paterson, White inserts himself into a double-threaded genealogy of key literary figures: from Milton to Blake to White, and from Paterson to White. Within this re-configuration, White stands as the heir to both the English and the Australian literary traditions. The links between White and Blake, and between *Flaws in the Glass* and *Milton*, are reinforced in the links between Lulworth and Turret House, and their respective gardens.

In thus dismantling and re-constructing common elements, *Flaws in the Glass* enacts a process outlined in the text itself:

> All the houses I have lived in have been renovated and refurnished to accommodate fictions. The original structure is there for anybody who knows: 'Lulworth' for *Voss*; 'Dogwoods' for *The Tree of Man* and *The Solid Mandala*; Martin Road for *The Eye of the Storm*; the cottage, the homestead, the sheds, the dunny at 'Bolaro' for *The Twyborn Affair* [...]. In the theatre of my imagination I should say there are three or four basic sets, all of them linked to the actual past, which can be dismantled and re-constructed to accommodate the illusion of reality life boils down to. (153–54)

It is this process which is illustrated in two early passages in *Flaws in the Glass* (below). The first refers to Turret House, the second to Lulworth, despite overlaps between the two.

> The house had belonged to the poet Hayley, of no importance except as the friend of genius. He had a mad wife he used to chain to the flint columns

of a summerhouse so that she could take the air. There was a cemetery with headstones carved to commemorate the lives of pets. There was a medlar tree, umbrella-shaped, under it the stench of rotting fruit. (3)
We cried for the cats and dogs we buried under crosses made from the spines of palm leaves, in graves stuck with wilting marigolds. [...] Thunderstorms were more frightening than death, and the Mad Woman [...] in what for me was the best part of the garden [...] under the custard apples and the guavas, outside the latticed summerhouse, when our father came down the stone steps bringing some friend I had not seen before [...] Mr Banjo Paterson [...] my first poet. (5–6)

Between these two descriptions, we find a recurrent set of elements: the poet, a 'mad' woman and a garden, a summerhouse, graves of deceased pets and fruit trees. Across just two pages the two scenes are mapped onto a common template, a consistent set of real-life and intertextual coordinates, comprising physical fixtures, characters, atmospheric elements and literary conventions, in particular gothic flourishes. In a two-way dynamic, the gothic elements of Turret House (the chained-up 'mad wife', the pet cemetery, the decaying 'rotting fruit') are transposed to Lulworth where they re-surface in the 'Mad Woman' (a drunken vagrant, discovered in the lower-garden) and in its pet 'graves' and 'wilting marigolds'. Like the mad wife/woman, the poet-figure haunts both scenes in multiple guises: as 'the poet Hayley' (3) of 'forgettable verses' (7), 'the friend of genius', William Blake, and as 'Mr "Banjo" Paterson', White's 'first poet' (6). The poets of past, present and future, English and Australian, commingle, united in a transnational literary trajectory, a common destiny into which the child-White is projected.

The two excerpts demonstrate the internal dynamics between these two functions: the accumulation of down-to-earth and intertextual detail and the dismantling and re-construction of an original structure grounded in the actual past. The first Turret House forms the site of an accumulation, a layering of real-life, concrete and intertextual detail. Gothic elements add an additional intertextual layer. Within the second function of Turret House is the product of a dismantling and re-construction of an original structure, of which Lulworth is a second example.

From these dual processes, Turret House emerges not (or not only) as a site of 'disconnections',[51] but as a multivalent, unifying symbol, with private, general and literary connotations. It is the real-life house, taken by White's parents for the summer of 1926; the literary-historical house of poet William Hayley, friend and patron of William Blake; the textual house, depicted in Blake's poem, 'To my dear Friend', the neighbour of Blake's cottage, the fictional site of Milton's visitation; and the avatar of Lulworth with its common components.

Hence from their origin in the 'actual past' of real-life experience, White's sets extend into an abstract past of virtual or vicarious experience, a past read about, remembered, imagined or dreamt, filtered through memory, imagination and the unconscious mind. In *Flaws in the Glass*, these pasts interpenetrate, infuse and inflect one another. Through the twin-functions of accumulation, and of dismantling and re-construction, White's real-life raw materials are re-assembled and re-imagined: augmented, altered and adapted.

White did not want to be tied down as a man or as an author, or to have his texts tied down. In interviews he was consistently, defiantly, evasive or non-descript. He rejected attempts 'to tie [him and] his subject down in the strait jacket of [their] system[s]'.[52] Instead he acted to stall, deflect or delegitimize categorisation, to dismantle traditional conventions, to disable familiar models of reading and to throw the reader (or better, the critic) off track.

Rather than to limit, indeed, *Flaws in the Glass* acts to multiply the origins, sources and referents of White's works. It provides vague, partial acknowledgements of their biographical, literary, theological, mystical or psychological elements but tempers them with counter-statements: assertions of an unconscious, irrational element, beyond detection, inspection and interpretation (182). White alerts us to three elements: the biographical, the textual and an 'unknown' element. He directs us to the nexus between these elements as the site of meaning[s], the dialectic of memory, the imagination and the unconscious mind. Circulating between these coordinates, meaning remains elusive, unfixed; it is endlessly deferred, in a constant state of play.

White's system of dismantling and re-construction, with its in-built mechanism of self-renewal, also internalised the modernist impulse to 'make it new *again*'.[53] Removed in time and space, White confronted on the one side post–World War II Europe, 'an actual and spiritual graveyard', and on the other, 'The Great Australian Emptiness',[54] a cultural blank and intellectual void. Suspended between these two poles, White's was a dual task of clearing and re-filling cultural space, of dismantling and re-constructing the modernist and the Australian literary traditions. Thus, the value of *Flaws in the Glass* lies less in what it states than what it does. What it states – its so-called confessions – is problematic: ambiguous, contradictory and at times 'lies'. What it does, its systems of accumulation and of dismantling and re-construction, is mimetic of White's fictions and casts light on their aesthetics, modes of signification and meanings.

Notes

1 Patrick White to Spud Johnson, 17 July 1939, in David Marr, ed., *Patrick White: Letters* (Sydney: Random House, 1994), 23.
2 Patrick White to James Stern, 22 December 1979, in Marr, *Letters*, 527.

3 Patrick White, *Flaws in the Glass: A Self-Portrait* (London: J. Cape, 1981), 153. All subsequent references to this edition appear in parentheses in the text.
4 David Marr, *Patrick White: A Life* (London: Jonathan Cape, 1991), 607–8.
5 David Marr, *The Burning Piano: A Portrait of Patrick White* (Australia: Australian Broadcasting Corporation Television, 1993), cited in 'Why Bother with Patrick White?', accessed 19 November 2012, online: http://www.abc.net.au/arts/white/opinions/marr.html. In *Patrick White: A Life*, Marr describes White's 'refusal to celebrate the first achievements of his career': his first poem ('The Ploughman') and two published anthologies, *Thirteen Poems* (1930) and *The Ploughman: And Other Poems* (1935), receive no mention. See Marr, *Life*, 597.
6 Marr, *The Burning Piano*. At the end of his life, White 'finally acknowledged the truth' to Marr. In his essay, 'Patrick White: The Final Chapter,' *The Monthly* 33 (April 2008), 38, Marr writes: 'On some of the sticky issues he finally acknowledged the truth, even admitting one morning that despite all the abuse he had heaped on his mother over the years, his life was the realisation of her ambition for him: to be a writer.'
7 Marjorie Barnard, 'The Four Novels of Patrick White', *Meanjin* 15, no. 2 (1956): 156–70 (156). As Barnard records, neither the Mitchell Library catalogue nor *Who's Who in Australia* (a catalogue of biographies of prominent Australians) contained information on White's life, while E. M. Miller and F. T. Macartney's *Australian Literature* (1956) offered only scant details: that he lived in Castle Hill, after an extended period abroad. See E. Morris Miller and Frederick T. Macartney, *Australian Literature: A Bibliography to 1938, Extended to 1950* (Sydney: Angus & Robertson, 1956), 491.
8 Marr, *Life*, 595.
9 See [Patrick White], 'Comment: A Note on Patrick White', *Meanjin* 15, no. 2 (1956): 223–24; and 'Patrick White: Autobiography', Nobelprize.org, accessed 19 November 2012, online: http://www.nobelprize.org/nobel_prizes/literature/laureates/1973/white.html. The *Meanjin* essay was written in the third person (in 'disguise'). See Marr, *Life*, 595.
10 G. A. Wilkes and Thelma Herring, 'A Conversation with Patrick White', *Southerly* 33, no. 2 (1973): 132–43. White drafted the transcript himself using a list of questions and brief notes taken by Wilkes during the interview. See Marr, *Life*, 595–96.
11 Marr, *Life*, 597.
12 Patrick White to Jean Lambert, 30 January 1983, in Marr, *Letters*, 576.
13 As David McCooey notes this was 'above all, the most common response to *Flaws in the Glass*'. See David McCooey, *Artful Histories: Modern Australian Autobiography* (Cambridge: Cambridge University Press, 1996), 170.
14 Patrick White to Dorothy Green, 25 January 1981, cited in Marr, *Life*, 597.
15 James Bertram, 'Review of Patrick White's *Flaws in the Glass*', *NZ Listener*, 1981, qtd in 'Why Bother'.
16 John Docker, 'Romanticism, Modernism, Exoticism: Patrick White in Biography and Autobiography,' *Southern Review* 26, no. 3 (1993): 358–76 (362). Docker nonetheless admonished 'the narrator's dated structuralism, essentialism [...] modernist magisterialism [...] his racism, his relishing a language of ethnic and racial insult [...]'; 'his wide-eyed wonder about himself as an artist', his 'self-admiration', and his 'trumpeting of his writerly virtues', which Docker found 'increasingly repetitive, insistent, and tedious'. Docker, 'Romanticism', 368, 362.
17 Annalisa Pes, '*Flaws in the Glass*: Patrick White's Selves' in *The Protean Forms of Life Writing: Auto/Biography in English, 1680–2000*, ed. Angelo Righetti (Naples: Liguori Editore, 2008), 75–90 (77).

18 On the prodigal use of 'The Prodigal Son' see Marr, *Life*, 595.
19 Brigid Rooney warns of 'the dubious, the insincere and the inauthentic' in *Flaws*, which she argues complicate a literal reading of the public, political White and impede a deduction of his political (and, we might infer, personal and artistic) views. In contrast to Docker's literal reading, Rooney detects elements of self-parody, exhibitionism and hyperbolic narcissism. See 'Public Recluse: Patrick White's Literary–Political Returns', in *Remembering Patrick White: Contemporary Critical Essays*, Elizabeth McMahon and Brigitta Olubas, eds (Amsterdam: Rodopi, 2010), 3–18 (5–6).
20 In a series of disclaimers, White warns, 'the incidents [...] become blurred', are 'difficult to disentangle from memory', or shrouded in the 'webs of mystery which cling to certain [childhood] events' (27, 77, 18). Repeatedly, he writes: 'I can't remember', 'I don't remember' and 'I seem to remember' (34, 41, 44, 77).
21 For example in 1956, A. D. Hope wrote of *The Tree of Man*: '[A]t first sight it has all the earmarks which traditionally distinguish The Great Australian Novel [...] [but] White [has] chosen to disguise his novel in the old Bunyip skin. What he is writing about has nothing essentially to do with Australia'. A.D. Hope, 'The Bunyip Stages a Comeback', *Sydney Morning Herald*, 16 June 1956, 15. And in 1992, Alan Lawson described *The Aunt's Story* (1948) as '*appearing* to offer a couple of very familiar narrative conventions [...] appearing to conform to a couple of traditional ways of writing and producing meaning, by offering [...] *models of reading* in which we have been well-trained. It then undoes these models'. Alan Lawson, 'Bound to Dis-integrate: Narrative and Interpretation in *The Aunt's Story*', *Antipodes* 6, no. 1 (1992): 9–15 (9). Meanwhile in 1993, Michael Wilding wrote: '[A]t first glance those huge, substantial novels like *Voss* or *The Tree of Man* look like classic novels [...] But that is very much an illusion'; and 'The initial impression of White's work as bulky realist fiction evaporates when you look at, or for, the detail [...] They gesture at a realism which is then denied or inverted'. Michael Wilding, 'The Politics of Modernism' in *Prophet from the Desert: Critical Essays on Patrick White*, John McLaren and Mary-Ellen Ryan, eds (Red Hill South, Vic.: Red Hill Press, 1995), 24–33 (24, 35). See also George Turner, 'Looking at a Portrait: An Approach to *Flaws in the Glass*', *Overland* 87 (May 1982): 20–27 (27).
22 Patrick White, *The Aunt's Story* (Sydney: Vintage, 2008), 325.
23 Marr, *Letters*, 525, 527, 533.
24 Turner, 'Looking', 27.
25 Paul de Man, 'Autobiography as De-Facement,' *MLN* 94, no. 5 (1979): 919–30.
26 Veronica Brady, 'Patrick White, *Flaws in the Glass: A Self-Portrait*, Cape, London, 1981, 260 pp.', *Westerly* 27, no. 1 (1982): 102–9 (104).
27 de Man, 'Autobiography', 921.
29 'Flaws in the Glass' details White's childhood, education and early career, from his birth in London in 1912 to his repatriation in 1947. 'Journeys' retraces White's travels with partner Manoly Lascaris in Greece between 1958 and 1971. 'Episodes and Epitaphs' returns to the present, to an account of recent events and figures which have shaped him as an artist and public intellectual.
30 Pes, 'Selves', 75.
31 Brady, '*Flaws*', 105.
32 Simon During, *Patrick White* (Oxford: Oxford University Press, 1996), 79.
33 During, *White*, 80.
34 David English, 'Is the Book of the Life a Good Book?: Autobiography in Patrick White, Dorothy Hewett and Beverley Farmer', *Southerly* 57, no. 3 (1997): 200–210 (206–7).

35 During, *White*, 79.
36 Brady, '*Flaws*', 105.
37 Pes, 'Selves', 84.
38 Brady, '*Flaws*', 104.
39 Pes, 'Selves', 76.
40 David Tacey, 'Patrick White Marred' *Quadrant* 35, no. 10 (1991): 7–11 (8).
41 Patrick White to Kerry Walker, 24 June 1982, in Marr, *Letters*, 566.
42 Pes, 'Selves', 84.
43 Jessica Geva, 'Patrick White: (Auto) Biography – a Veiled Confession?' *Antipodes* 26, no. 1 (2012): 19–25 (20).
44 Wilkes and Herring, 'Conversation', 139.
45 Wilkes and Herring, 'Conversation', 140.
46 Marr, *Letters*, 566.
47 Wilkes and Herring, 'Conversation', 140.
48 McCooey, *Artful*, 143–44; Pes, 'Selves,' 77–78; Peter Shrubb, 'Flaws', *Quadrant* 25, no. 12 (1981): 28–32 (28–29).
49 William Blake, 'To My Dear Friend Mrs Anna Flaxman', accessed 19 November 2012, online: http://www.english.uga.edu/nhilton/Blake/blaketxt1/Letters/12.htm.
50 William Blake, *Selected Poems*, ed. W.H. Stevenson (Ringwood, Vic.: Penguin Books Australia Ltd., 1988), 187–88.
51 Shrubb, 'Flaws', 28. See also McCooey, *Artful*, 143–44 and Pes, 'Selves', 77–78. White himself describes Turret House as having 'no connection with any other part of my life […]' (1).
52 Marr, *Letters*, 566.
53 Tim Armstrong, *Modernism: A Cultural History* (Cambridge: Polity Press, 2005), 35.
54 White, 'The Prodigal Son' in *Patrick White Speaks*, eds Paul Brennan and Christine Flynn (Sydney, NSW: Primavera Press, 1989), 13–17 (14–15).

Chapter 6

PATRICK WHITE'S LATE STYLE

Andrew McCann

O God have mercy on all turds, whether dropped by elephants, goats or humans – Ameen.
– Patrick White[1]

If there is a dominant strain in recent Australian literary criticism, it probably involves the attempt to fuse postcolonialism and religion. Its key term is 'the sacred', and for many critics Patrick White looms large among those writers whose work most obviously embodies it. In his 1996 book on White, Simon During used the phrase 'late colonial transcendentalism' to describe White's gravitation to 'the timeless and the spiritual'.[2] Almost two decades later, a much more politically engaged conception of the spiritual has largely displaced the adversarial quality of During's approach. This is hardly surprising, given the specific pressures on the field of Australian literature. During's book mobilizes the resources of literary and critical theory partly to interrogate the social organization of White's canonicity and to reveal some of the ideological effects of his work. In the years since its publication, the field of Australian literature has had to rearticulate its relationship to a broader public sphere partly by stressing the importance of a national canon as a space within which to think through a range of issues bearing on the formation of a postcolonial culture and identity. And with considerable government and institutional support underpinning these efforts, symptomatic readings of figures that constitute the cornerstones of that canon have a questionable utility. At the same time, broader trends in the humanities have led to a gentle disquiet with the forms of hermeneutics that have dominated literary studies for a long time now. The shift that Hans Ulrich Gumbrecht describes in *Production of Presence* – away from the production of meaning premised on the division of subject and object, and towards the experience of 'material presence' – is generally congruent with much of the thinking that now drives recent Australian engagements with the sacred.[3]

Today, White's readability, both inside and outside the specialized space of Australian literary studies, owes a great deal to the intersection of these frameworks. David Tacey's popular *Edge of the Sacred*, for instance, sees in White an important resource in the fashioning of a revivified sense of Australian spirituality, linked to the radical alterity of landscape and the rejection of largely secular, instrumentalized ways of knowing.[4] More recently, Lyn McCredden has articulated a vision of the sacred that steers the concept away from a timelessness shut off from tangible, material realities. Instead, she articulates a vision of the 'sacred and material in constant exchange' such that the sacred has to be understood in 'dramatic tension with earthed, bodily and sexual realities'.[5] For McCredden, the concept does not dissolve or transcend the material; it is in fact the paradigm that discloses it.

The broader political and cultural usefulness of this approach is clear in a recent publication called *Intimate Horizons: The Sacred in Australian Literature*, co-authored by McCredden, Bill Ashcroft and Frances Devlin-Glass. The book consolidates a great deal of recent thinking about the sacred and clearly articulates the political payback that is at stake in it. The utility of the sacred simply put is that it anchors a rubric through which we can understand how an inclusive and affectively resonant sense of belonging (though not necessarily national belonging) can be imagined in a largely secular, instrumentalized society. Hence the insistence on the material, embodied dimension of the paradigm is also about the possibility of a renewed relationship to the 'earth'. This is not, it should be stressed, the earth in the abstract sense of a global space, but the earth as it is delimited by our lived relationship with and presence on it. It goes without saying that, in an Australian context, the articulation of this sort of 'presence culture', with its 'intimate relationship to place', involves displacing the instrumental thinking of Western modernity and developing instead ways of being and imagining that 'strike a deep resonance with Aboriginal culture'.[6] In this way, the authors of *Intimate Horizons* can also locate, at least implicitly, the transition from the colonial to the postcolonial in changed attitudes to the sacred. In defiance of During's hermeneutic of suspicion, White's transcendentalism expresses a kind of postcolonial unconscious evident in the way his characters refuse abstract experience and embrace instead their material situatedness. From this perspective, the sacred is the paradigm in which we become properly postcolonial, not a relic of an older, anachronistic imperialism.

The question of literature's utility is implicit in this work. For all its scepticism with regard to instrumentality, the great attractiveness of the approach set out by *Intimate Horizons* is that it makes literature useful: that is, it secures literature's function, which is to say its material integration into a social and political context that literary texts seem to renew and disclose simultaneously.

It is not coincidental that, as Ken Gelder and Jane Jacobs tell us, Paul Keating apparently recommended Tacey's book to his cabinet as 'required reading'.[7] The institutional imperative driving what is really a minor form of political theology (albeit one with the good intention of displacing conventional Western conceptions of sovereignty) cannot be ignored. The sacred, better than virtually any other way of framing contemporary Australian writing, enables us to maintain an Anglo-Australian canon as a matter of urgent political exigency. At the very moment that the global erosion of national cultures and the reorientation of the humanities towards popular cultural forms threaten to sink the whole field (or at least question its relevance), the canon emerges at the centre of a project of postcolonial, national renewal.[8]

Much of Patrick White's work no doubt lends itself to the framework I have suggested here. A number of major novels – *The Tree of Man* (1955), *Voss* (1957), *Riders in the Chariot* (1961) and *A Fringe of Leaves* (1976), for instance – articulate ways of being that are at odds with the means–end rationality of a secular modernity. Brigid Rooney nicely captures the character of these novels when she talks about White's 'mythic, biblically charged national fictions'.[9] It is hard to deny that this religious ambition is central to White's oeuvre. And yet this emphasis also seems to ignore something that I think is equally obvious in White's work: its ability to empty out, to travesty and to rephrase as ruin the very signifiers of its own theological orientation. What I want to call, after Theodor Adorno, the moment of Patrick White's 'late style' involves the very inoperativity of the tropes, forms and structures that underpin White's usefulness as a political–theological resource. In this inoperativity, we might also find the possibility of re-describing aspects of White's project in a way that emphasizes a hitherto neglected set of aesthetic and critical resources.

I am not the first person to draw the connection between White's work and Adorno's concept of late style. In a terrific discussion, Elizabeth McMahon has used the idea of late style to re-describe White's career from the perspective of the intersection of 'lateness and queerness' that defines *The Twyborn Affair* (1979), in order to 'align an iconic national graphesis with a homographesis'.[10] Her discussion makes brilliant use of Adorno to show how *The Twyborn Affair* recasts 'familiar topoi, structures, and settings' from White's earlier novels and in the process presents itself as an 'allegory of reading White's fiction'.[11] For McMahon, the 'unproductive productiveness' of this gesture – what I am calling its inoperativity – organizes a 'perverse genealogy or generation' that becomes the prism for a powerful account of White's queerness.[12]

My approach in this essay shares much with McMahon's. But the importance of the notion of late style for me emerges through its relationship to a strand of aesthetic theory in which the materiality of the artwork problematizes its ability to stabilize a relationship to its theological or cultic origins. What is at stake here is precisely the viability of the sacred. In grasping this, we can read the moment of late style as the moment at which the material underpinnings of the aesthetic take on a radical, demystificatory role that interrupts the narratives of use that now cleave quite closely to White's work. As will become clear later, this is not simply to refuse the notion of the sacred outright, but to grasp the modern artwork as a sort of threshold in which we become cognizant of the sacred at the very moment of its impossibility.

The novel I am going to focus on here is *Memoirs of Many in One* (1986). Together with *The Twyborn Affair*, it forms an arc that largely defines the end of White's career. In that arc, White displaces the ostensibly national orientation of his spatial imaginary and embraces instead an elaborately constructed world that could be loosely described as Levantine (though Mediterranean or Byzantine might be just as accurate). This is the world inhabited by Eudoxia Vatatzes and her Greek lover; its spirit persists in Eadith Trist. This world also appears as an object of longing and fantasy in *Memoirs of Many in One*. In that text, White casts himself as the editor of the memoirs of Alex Xenophon Demirjian Gray, a Greek from Asia Minor who, via Smyrna and Alexandria, ends up in Centennial Park battling the inanities of Anglo-Australia and recalling, or hallucinating, a series of extravagant adventures in abjection.

The novel's Levantine geographical imaginary offers a powerful alternative to the limits of Australia. While it clearly evokes White's wartime experience of Alexandria, it is also a way of conjuring a heterotopian space of aesthetic and sexual possibility. The novel is intensely interested in the materiality of performance, and pits that performative, transformative ethos against various visions of an Australia that is somehow resistant to it. At the same time, it is the very intransigence of an Australian vernacular and its clichés (associated with masculinity, the banality of the quotidian, suburbia, the outback, 'the yartz' etc.) that measures those figures of fantasy. The result is a playful incongruity that, in other cultural contexts, could easily be construed as in bad taste. The menacing and the tragic constantly become farcical, as the paraphernalia of art always seems to fail against the 'glare and mediocrity' (126) of Australia. The result is not the peculiar sort of anti-national nationalism that we find in some of White's more epic novels, but a distinct sense that the textual apparatus that discloses the confluence of the sacred and the sexual is now too burdened by its materiality to function in any other mode but that of parody. In other words, inoperativity defines the course of the novel, and as a result it is constantly interrupting its own theological orientation with the increasingly absurd excesses of its signifiers.

But the novel's overwhelming interest in the performativity of the sacred, I want to argue, does not merely function in the interests of parody. It also begins to reveal what is really at stake in the sort of political theology that now finds in White one of its greatest resources. The meaningful opposition here, I want to suggest, is not between the sacred and the secular, as we might think, but between the forms of signification – symbolic and allegorical – that underwrite that opposition. The terms, often confused with each other, involve a distinction that is crucial to post-romantic aesthetic theory. Simply put, the symbol incarnates an idea and as such belongs in the very cosmology it evokes. It thus partakes of the timeless and the metaphysical. An allegory, by contrast, is a representation of an idea, and as such is subject to the mutability and arbitrariness of signification. A symbol is a sign taken as a wonder. An allegory is merely a sign, though one that alludes to a lost horizon of symbolic significance. In the slippage from the one to other, we have a succinct encapsulation of the problem of the sacred.[13]

Memoirs of Many in One is all about this slippage. In it, the religious orientation of White's fiction is overwhelmed by the signifiers that are supposed to evoke it. What we are left with is a disjointed series of comedic scenarios that foreground the material character, the stuff or the 'clobber' of the sacred, rather than the thing itself. We are now in a world where a 'glob of spittle', whatever else it might represent, is also simply a 'glob of spittle'. In the very inoperativity of otherwise familiar tropes and gestures, we can glimpse an entirely different vision of Patrick White from the one that currently dominates the critical landscape. *Memoirs of Many in One* effectively un-writes the possibility of identification contained in the notion of the sacred. It is the moment at which we encounter the artwork moving against its own assumptions of transcendence and unity, producing instead a series of fragments that powerfully emblematize the ruin of art itself.

A quick sense of how the novel works in relationship to White's work more generally might be in order. At the conclusion of White's story, 'The Night the Prowler', we have one of his most emblematic scenarios, in which the life of a suburbanite is rewritten as the life of a saint. Felicity Bannister has appalled her parents by turning her back on marriage to a career diplomat who is about to be posted to Rome. She refuses suburban respectability, ceases being a 'clean and healthy' girl and goes through a transitory period in which she experiences a fading sense of sexual excitement by breaking into and vandalizing suburban houses. Near the end of the story, having done her best to embody a refusal of those facile aesthetic norms linked not so much to beauty but to a demeaning suburban pleasantness, Felicity encounters a naked old man with no bladder control, 'stretched out on a soiled mattress': 'She looked around desperately. If only she could lay hands on – alcohol, say, she might find bed sores to rub.' In the end, she has to resign herself merely to comforting 'the fetid skin, with its crust and semi-cancerous moles'.[14]

It is a moment at which saintliness emerges in proximity to the abject. White's prose builds its virtuosity on the resonance of this relationship. It culminates in religious epiphany: 'the masses of hitherto colourless, or at most dust-coloured wall, were illuminated: the tributaries of decay had begun to flow with rose; the barren continents were heaped with gold'.[15] The text concludes after the old man dies, with Felicity caught up in the vague but propitious state that White calls 'the dizzy course of perpetual becoming'.[16] Like many other moments in which White's interest in abjection is evident, it is a narrative that unironically echoes a fairly conventional form of Christian hagiography, in which one turns one's back on worldly concerns and instead embraces physical decay and waste as a way of approaching God and of soliciting his love.[17]

Alex Gray is also interested in these possibilities. In a reprise of the moment in *The Tree of Man* at which Stan Parker finds God in a glob of spittle, she remembers 'the French mystic demonstrating her piety and self-abnegation by picking up from the street a gobbet of beggar's spittle and forcing herself to swallow it' (94). This interest in the religious dimension of abjection leads her to adopt a man wandering about in Centennial Park whom she thinks might be a mystic. His name is Joe, and once inside the house Alex shares with her daughter he does not hesitate to cough up some phlegm onto the Afghan rug. Later, he is on hand for a moment of unexpected communion that depends on Alex's faulty memory:

> I am on my way upstairs. I hear a noise. It can only be a male. When a husband or lover has the upper hand over wife or mistress whose sensibility he no longer respects, he farts in her presence. I believe I recognize that sound.
>
> On the half-landing I am seized by the wrist, by a steely, yet clammy, male hand. The force of obsession brings us close together, breast to breast, mouth to mouth. I am pervaded by the stench of cabbage, halitosis, and metho.
>
> A voice whines, 'What'uv yer brought me 'ere for? Whaddayer expect a bloke to do?' (102)

After this, Alex attempts to hide old Joe from her daughter by shoving him into her built-in cupboard, which she refers to as a 'priest hole', with an unopened can of bully: 'mystics, desert fathers, prophets, have never expected comfort have they?' (104). After she contemplates becoming 'Centennial Park's Very Own Saint', she drifts off into another remembered/hallucinated scenario in which she appears as 'Sister Benedict' and is accompanying a group of nuns on a pre-epiphany picnic consisting of ginger beer and raw kippers. A hairy, black mole under the Reverend Mother's left nostril looms large but the main focus is on the geriatric Sister Bernadette, her frail limbs, munching gums and the prospect of her chewing on a bit of raw fish. This scenario has its own absurd drama that hinges on the undecidable relationship between utter banality, abjection and the ecstatic. In the meantime, Alex has forgotten about the mystic until the bolt of the wardrobe door rattles:

> I hear the bolt give. I've got to accept it. I fling open the wardrobe door. The Mystic plunges head first through the racks of – let's face it – musty dresses. He is bleeding at the mouth. He is clutching the half-opened tin of Fray Bentos bully. 'The key they give yer with the tin don't work,' he bellows 'Bring a bloke a bloody can-opener.' (112)

The outburst provokes an equally peeved response from Alex Gray, one that farcically rehearses the indistinction of symbol and allegory and invites us to see the whole incident as a specifically eucharistic comedy: '"Listen", I tell my deranged Mystic. "You should know the difference between meat and flesh. You should know when your faith is being tried by your reactions to our Lord bleeding on the Cross – and what the Holy Spirit expects of us believers".' (112)

Like virtually everything in this novel, the scenario seems to replay moments with which White's readers will already feel familiar, but it strips those moments of their aura and of their ability to function in the symbolic idiom that enables us to think of the White text as primarily theological in orientation. As a result, the possibility of symbolic identification (in characters or readers) is gone. Instead we have farce: the absurdity of Alex's expectations and the frailty of the forms they inhabit. The literally abject character of this material – phlegm, blood and tainted fish – seems to reflect on the abjection of the signifier itself as it shifts from the symbolic to the allegorical; from being the living embodiment of the unity of which it is a part to a material sign that can allude only to what it will inevitably fail to make incarnate.

When Alex, as Dolly Formosa, tours the outback putting on a programme called *Dolly Formosa and the Happy Few*, we get a sense of how this devaluation of the sacred inspires a new set of artistic practices that orient to an ironic sense of aesthetic anachronism. Against a background of corrugated iron sheds and ceremonial Pavlovas (including passion fruit seeds stuck in hollow teeth), Alex appears in towns with names like Aberpissup, Peewee Plains and Baggery Baggery, performing a series of episodes from Shakespeare, and her own, under-appreciated, dance sequences and reveries. White's familiar hostility to the quotidian dimension of Australian experience is clearly evident here, but we would be missing the point to see this scenario as one that is meant to foreground the rift between high cultural paradigms and their reception. Instead, it is the very assumption of that rift that is being ironized.

Dolly Formosa has set herself the task of 'challenging "bardolotary" with truth', which she unwittingly does, not by performing the hollowness of its pretensions but by allowing a culture of transcendence to break down into its clobber, or its stuff: 'I lie amongst my sumptuous costumes', Alex tells us, 'their velvets and brocades, the trappings of Athens, Egypt, and Illyria, attempting to protect them from the glare and mediocrity of the Australian bush' (126). When Alex plays Cleopatra, coated in make-up as thick as Nile silt, marvelling at her dirty navel and bloody talons, she unmistakably evokes the sense of grotesque grandeur that radiates from Elizabeth Hunter or Eadith Trist. Yet the moment is also shambolical. The failure of the performance invites us to read a phrase like the 'glare and mediocrity of the Australian bush' as merely the concentration of an anxiety about the broader failure of aesthetic illusionism, and the embarrassment that it seems to evoke.

All three figures – Alex Gray, Eadith Trist and Elizabeth Hunter – act out the decadent melding of decaying flesh and baroque ornamentation. They are the opulence of the aesthetic in the form of the human ruin, make-up plastered across hairy upper lips. By the time we get to the Sand Pit Theatre, a sort of parody of Beckett that intends to have Alex springing out of the sand to proclaim that she is the 'spirit of the land: past, present and future' (though tellingly she forgets her lines), it is as if White has had enough of his own reception. The sacred, and the attempt to fabricate some sort of autochthonous sensibility in relationship to it, requires laughter to stave off the yawns. I do not mean to suggest that the novel is a lament, although the image of Alex protecting her costumes against the 'glare and mediocrity of the Australian bush' does communicate a certain creative pathos that may well have been White's own. What the novel explores is an aesthetic idiom based on the triumph of the everyday over the aesthetic, the triumph of mere stuff over its auratic potential. But contrary to Australian cultural studies, which sees the democratic potential of contemporary Australia embodied in this shift, White's performance is about a sort of ironic formlessness. It is the modernism of Eliot and Joyce, in reverse; chaos triumphing over the ordering possibilities of religious or mythic frameworks. Or rather, it is the unambiguous distillation of what those frameworks have perhaps assumed all along: after the shattering of religious cosmologies – the fall of the symbol into the allegory – the only thing left for a theologically oriented art form that is true to its own materiality is to dwell in the rift between the divine and the historical. In *Memoirs of Many in One*, that rift is full of the clobber – the topoi and stage props of White's own novels – that appear now as fragments imbued with the pathos of their absent meaning.

But if there is pathos, there is also the comedy that often overwhelms it. *Memoirs of Many in One* is like a peal of laughter that redraws the rift between the sacred and the profane, the symbol and the allegory, as the very ground for a new set of aesthetic possibilities that emerge at the moment of exhaustion; the moment, that is, at which a longing for transcendence collapses into the materiality of the signifier. We can see this not only in the novel's dominant thematic orientation but also in its structure, which, as Alex puts it, presents a series of 'splinters and masturbatory devices' (164). The broken, which is also to say the episodic, nature of the text is crucial here. If the phrase 'masturbatory devices' evokes something compromisingly contrived, the word 'splinters' carries with it the sense of fragmentation, disunity and destruction that is so often used by Walter Benjamin to describe allegory: 'In the field of allegorical intuition the image is a fragment, a rune. Its beauty as a symbol evaporates when the light of divine learning falls upon it.'[18]

In the cultural landscape of contemporary Australia, at least as we might envision it through White's novel, these 'splinters and masturbatory devices' in their episodic, scenic dimension and their stress on forms of artifice that verge on bad taste have a discernible relationship to the comedic genre of the 'routine': short sketches that have the brevity and the ephemerality of stand-up comedy. If Alex Gray (or White for that matter) aspires to being an Antipodean Tiresias, she ends up being a sort of Levantine Dame Edna. The result is surprising for those of us used to wrestling with Patrick White as an avatar of high modernism and its apparently anachronistic modes of cultural value. By returning us to the materiality of his own textuality, to the trope detached from its ability to secure meaning, the novel also short-circuits the opposition between high and low cultural forms. We have always known that White and Barry Humphries shared a great deal. Here we can see that affinity in a new and startling light. Dame Edna replaying the dreams of suburbia as baroque excess could almost be the model for Alex Gray. Both dwell in the pathos and the comedy of their own materiality; both are figures that can trace their provenance not only to the Australian quotidian but also to the foundational dramas of modern aesthetics.

Of course, the novel itself cannot help but offer some framework for understanding why White seems to turn against the grain of his own work in the way I am describing here. With White as the editor standing comfortably but conspicuously to one side, and with the body of the text being ostensibly a notebook, we get the sense of a subjectivity that is allowed to flaunt itself with more abandon than might otherwise be the case. The 'dramatis personae of this Levantine script', White writes, 'could be the offspring of my own psyche' (16). The very informality of the text suggests this sense of experiment and play, of material liberated from the rigours of monumental fiction. Later, White, in his capacity as editor, describes himself as the 'great creative ego' who has exploited the life of Alex Grey to 'develop my own obsessions, both real and imaginary' (192). That Alex Grey is also approaching her death plays an important role here as well. What would spur this sense of abandon and indulgence more emphatically than an acute sense of the artist's mortality (White, of course, died four years after the book's publication). It is as if we can hear the laughter of mutability rupturing the constraints of form and coherence.

Still, the notion of unfettered expressivity is a fairly conventional way of explaining the eccentricities of late style, as Theodor Adorno points out in his 1937 essay on 'Beethoven's Late Style'. In a mere four pages, Adorno attempts to explain the damaged quality that seems to attach to the late career productions of major artists confronted with their mortality. These works are frequently 'furrowed or even torn', Adorno writes. They lack harmony. They indulge in a sort of dissonance customarily attributed to an anguished subjectivity, or personality, attempting to 'break through the smooth surface of form in order to express itself'.[19] Hence the sense of a 'liberated spirit' scorning the 'sensuous charm' that, elsewhere in Adorno's work, is associated with the solace of aesthetic autonomy. At least on the face of it, this really seems to capture the dynamic in *Memoirs of Many in One*.

But this emphasis on subjectivity, or personality, Adorno goes on to write, is wrong in at least one important point. Put simply, death is a property of living creatures, not the things they create. Hence, it only appears in art indirectly, 'as allegory'.[20] The challenge of Adorno's essay is to identify the aesthetic dynamic that accomplishes this. By stressing the conventional aspects of late works rather than their expressivity, he is in a position to recast the question of subjectivity in a way that returns us to one of the dominant motifs of his thinking: the failed or ruined artwork as a hallmark of the modern. Hence,

> The power of subjectivity in late works of art is the sudden flaring up with which it abandons the work of art. It bursts them asunder, not in order to express itself but so as to cast off the appearance of art. What is left of the works is ruins, and subjectivity communicates itself, as if by means of ciphers, only through the hollowed-out forms from which it escapes. Touched by death, the hand of the master liberates the mass of material that it previously shaped; the cracks and crannies it contains are testimony to the ultimate impotence of the self in the face of existence; they are the master's last achievement.[21]

The remaindered quality of late style nicely evokes the sensibility of *Memoirs of Many in One*: 'splinters, fragmented and abandoned' as Adorno writes, clichés purified 'of the illusion of control by subjective spirit'.[22] Late works are the moments of illumination in which art extinguishes its magic, renounces alchemy and reveals instead the drama of its materiality. The symbolic is reduced to the allegories of which it always consisted; we are no longer pilgrims looking for God, but wanderers in a fossil world of formal anachronisms. For Adorno, as for Benjamin, this is the essence of modernist epiphany; both privilege not the artwork that secures a sense of the sacred or the symbolic, but the artwork that fails to, the artwork that is constitutively unable, to transcend its materiality. Hence 'in the history of art, late works are the catastrophes', Adorno writes.[23] It is a comment that clearly echoes Benjamin: 'allegories are, in the realm of thoughts, what ruins are in the realm of things.'[24]

Allegories, ruins, catastrophes: these are the points at which we leave the space of theology and re-enter the space of history, if only to grasp more clearly the messianic horizon that has withdrawn from the ruins it leaves in its wake. And this, I think, is White's final achievement: to turn against his own theological tendencies and to grasp the artwork not as a miracle of transcendence but as a ruin. I do not mean by this that we are encountering the end of art or the death of literature, but that the switch from the symbolic to the allegorical produces a new sense of what art might accomplish, yet one that cuts against the grain of art itself, confuses hierarchies of cultural value and opens up the possibility of Patrick White as crass and as profane as he is rigorous and uncompromising. It is paradoxically by grasping this form of inoperativity – the very moment, that is, at which White's work fails in its usefulness – that we perhaps come closest to the presence of White not as a resource but as a stubborn refusal to become one, and as an interruption in a certain narrative of identity and canonical recuperation. Today, White has become a figure much like the statue at the end of *Voss*: an icon in the service of a fairly uninspiring cultural nationalism. That he had the good sense to glimpse his own project in ruins at the end of his career might well prove to be a more powerful and enduring legacy.

Notes

1 Patrick White, *Memoirs of Many in One* (London: Jonathan Cape, 1986), 116. All subsequent references to this edition appear in parentheses in the text.
2 Simon During, *Patrick White* (Oxford: Oxford University Press, 1996), 18.
3 See Hans Ulrich Gumbrecht, *Production of Presence: What Meaning Cannot Convey* (Stanford, CA: Stanford University Press, 2003). Gumbrecht's work plays an important role in some of the Australian criticism touched upon below.
4 See David Tacey, *Edge of the Sacred: Transformation in Australia* (Blackburn, Vic.: HarperCollins 1995), which includes an extended discussion of *Voss* (89–107) and touches on other figures – Judith Wright and David Malouf, for instance – who are now routinely associated with the sacred.

5 Lyn McCredden, '*Voss*: Earthed and Transformative Sacredness' in *Remembering Patrick White: Contemporary Critical Essays*, Elizabeth McMahon and Brigitta Olubas eds, (Amsterdam: Rodopi, 2010), 109–23 (110–11). See also Bill Ashcroft, 'The Presence of the Sacred in Patrick White' in McMahon and Olubas, eds, *Remembering*, 95–108.
6 Bill Ashcroft, Frances Devlin-Glass and Lyn McCredden, *Intimate Horizons: The Post-Colonial Sacred in Australian Literature* (Hindmarsh: ATF Press, 2009), 2, 21.
7 See Ken Gelder and Jane Jacobs, *Uncanny Australia: Sacredness and Identity in a Postcolonial Nation* (Melbourne: Melbourne University Press, 1998), 9.
8 Though it is tangential to the concerns of this essay, I also think it can be argued that this material raises a series of issues around the content of postcolonial politics. As several powerful and extremely persuasive essays by Marcia Langton have suggested, albeit implicitly and without any real interest in the field of literary studies, the issues confronting Indigenous Australia have much more to do with the pragmatic, governmental domain of the biopolitical than they do with the mainly aesthetic production of presence that appears in Anglo-Australian visions of the sacred. See Marcia Langton, 'Trapped in the Aboriginal Reality Show', *Griffith Review* 19 (2007): 143–62, and 'The End of "Big Men Politics"', *Griffith Review* 22 (2008): 11–38.
9 Brigid Rooney, *Literary Activists: Writer-Intellectuals and Australian Public Life* (St. Lucia: University of Queensland Press, 2009), 42.
10 Elizabeth McMahon, 'The Lateness and Queerness of *The Twyborn Affair*: White's Farewell to the Novel'. in McMahon and Olubas, *Remembering*, 77–91 (78, 79).
11 McMahon, 'Lateness', 81, 82.
12 McMahon, 'Lateness', 84.
13 My use of these terms is drawn from Walter Benjamin's *The Origin of German Tragic Drama*, trans. John Osborne (London: Verso, 2003), 164–65, and Beatrice Hanssen's fine explication of it. See Hanssen, *Walter Benjamin's Other History: Of Stones, Animals, Human Beings, and Angels* (Berkeley: University of California Press, 1998), 66–72.
14 Patrick White, 'The Night the Prowler', in *The Cockatoos: Shorter Novels and Stories* (London: Penguin, 1978), 120–68 (152).
15 White, 'Night', 153.
16 White, 'Night', 154.
17 I have in mind here Élisabeth Roudinesco's discussion of Joris-Karl Huysman's biography of Lydwine of Schiedam. According to Huysman's account, Lydwine of Schiedam refused her father's attempts to marry her off. Believing that 'God can only become attached to the horrors of the flesh', she embraced her own physical disintegration and performed the kind of spectacle of abjection that would fascinate fin-de-siècle decadence. See Élisabeth Roudinesco, *Our Dark Side: A History of Perversion*, trans. David Macey (Cambridge: Polity, 2009), 15.
18 Benjamin, *Origin*, 176.
19 Theodor W. Adorno, 'Beethoven's Late Style', in *Can One Live After Auschwitz? A Philosophical Reader*, ed. Rolf Tiedemann (Stanford, CA: Stanford University Press, 2003), 295–98 (295).
20 Adorno, 'Late', 297.
21 Adorno, 'Late', 297.
22 Adorno, 'Late', 297, 298.
23 Adorno, 'Late', 298.
24 Benjamin, *Origin*, 178.

Part III
THE PERFORMANCE OF READING

Chapter 7

PATRICK WHITE'S EXPRESSIONISM

Ivor Indyk

I re-read *The Eye of the Storm* (1973) recently in the light of my own experience with elderly parents, and understood for the first time just how overwhelming the *experience* of reading a Patrick White novel could be. Partly this results from the range of emotion suffered by his characters (and the reader); partly it has to do with the fineness of discrimination with which these emotions are charted. Moods of exaltation or joy alternate rapidly with those of anger or anxiety. On the other hand, his characters never allow themselves to remain in a depressed state for long: repair is undertaken, relationships mended or restored, tentatively, for the moment. The result is an extraordinary dynamism and efflorescence of response around what is, in itself, a static and attenuated situation. Nothing could be more static than the last period of life of an old bedridden parent, nothing more fluctuating and unstable than the expectations and emotions which jostle around that persistent reality in the minds of its witnesses – or fluctuate within the elderly one, unknowable to those in attendance.

The contrast between the storm and its eye, between the far-ranging play of emotion and the old woman who is its still, blind, barely articulate cause, gives the work an epic quality. Because of the way that emotion in White's novels overflows the physical boundaries of its human agents, animates objects and landscapes and creates atmospheres, its expression has the scale of a meteorological phenomenon. The reader is immersed, overwhelmed. Nothing is final, nothing resolved – death brings finality but not to those who observe it. *The Eye of the Storm* works by repetition, accumulation – scenes build, gather, swell and release their tension, but never completely. There is always a residue, an irritant, which generates the scenes to come. It is in this sense that nothing is ever done with, or settled. The horizon seems endless, the experience of being within this proliferating drama complete and exhausting.

It is difficult to be true to this experience and at the same time to respond in the manner thought suitable to a critic without being reductive. What the novel seems to require is careful navigation rather than criticism. Of course White is a modernist: the portrayal of consciousness, his willingness to break the rules of syntax to achieve his expressive purpose, his theatrical conception of the self and the moments of transcendent illumination, all testify to the fact. White's focus on emotion puts him at the expressionist end of modernism, and the plasticity and colouring of his figures recalls the *fauvistes* and the German expressionists in particular. But his method is also baroque in its attenuations and contractions of time and place, now seeing things close up, now pursuing them through elaborate expansions. In *Voss* (1957) the emotions are magnified across continental distances, yet in *The Eye of the Storm*, where the primary locus is a bedroom, and the physical distance between people no more than a few metres, in the moments and days before death, 'when two minutes can encompass aeons of slow rot', and the present opens to the vertiginous perspectives of memory, not only to Mrs Hunter but also to all the characters in orbit around her, the expansiveness is even more pronounced.[1] The German cabaret performer Lotte Lipmann, who cooks for the old woman, may be a modernist icon, but the barbaric idol she makes of her mistress when she dresses her up, 'frightening in its garishness of purple crimson, lilac floss and fluorescent white, in its robe of battered, rather than beaten rose-gold, the claws, gloved in a jewelled armour, stiffly held about the level of the navel' (120), is unmistakeably baroque. Perhaps, it is impossible not to be baroque when you are operating in territory this close to death.[2]

And there is another point to be made here, about the Australian writer's eclecticism, which White ostentatiously exhibits in novels like *Riders in the Chariot* and *The Twyborn Affair* (1979), the ability to combine different styles of presentation without too much regard for historical propriety. There has been some use recently of the phrase 'baroque modernism', particularly in discussions of architecture and film, where it is often applied to practitioners from Spain, South America or Eastern Europe – that is to say, cultures under the sway of Catholic or Orthodox religions which may be thought disinclined to keeping emotion, or their own traditional customs, completely subservient to modernist restraint. White's expressionism is coloured and no doubt intensified by his reaction to Protestant inhibition, so he would have found common ground here with those coming from Catholicism in the opposite direction. White was quite explicit about his quarrel with Protestantism and the restraint it requires. There is his wonderful description of what the Catholic-Protestant Dorothy de Lascabanes' soul would look like at the moment of death, 'no bland Catholic balloon automatically patted on its way, but a kind of shrivelled leather satchel, as she saw her original Protestant soul, stuffed with doubts, self-esteem, bloody-mindedness, which Catholic hands, however skilled, might not have succeeded in detaching from her' (589).

White is all for inflating that shrivelled satchel, and on a scale well beyond the containing confines of a Catholic balloon. His description of the storm which gives this novel its title, seen from the stillness of its eye, is all baroque without a trace of modernism, 'visibly spinning and boiling at a distance, in columns of cloud, its walls hung with vaporous balconies, continually shifting and distorted' (424). The eye itself, on the other hand, *is* modernist territory – 'this lustrous moment made visible' (425), where all emotion is spent, and the self-dissolved is ruled over by a procession of seven swans. One recalls Yeats, of course, in this celebration of the moment's grace, and also Eliot's 'Lady, three white leopards sat under a juniper tree' – though in this case the swans are black.

It isn't necessary to make a distinction between the epiphanic White and the White whose domain is the drama of the emotions, as they are cut from the same cloth – it is a question of where you make the fold. What is interesting about White's lustrous moments is that they are moments free from emotion, or in which emotion has been transcended – moments of trust or selflessness or complete accord with another. They are marked by clarity, limpidity, stillness or a sense of oneness which renders the self insignificant, such as the one Elizabeth Hunter enjoys with the husband from whom she had separated, in his last illness, 'moments when their minds were folded into each other without any trace of the cross-hatchings of wilfulness or desire to possess' (63). The eye of the storm has graceful swans, and seabirds at rest on the marbled waves, their wings folded. Emotion, on the other hand, is turbidity, disturbance, imperfection and trouble, felt as an unfolding whether in response to an impending threat or as a preparation for flight. After the moment of stillness, old Mrs Hunter feels the resumption of emotion as a storm returning, as a menacing turbulence, 'what had been a benison of sea, sky, and land, was becoming torn by animal passions, those of a deformed octopod with blue-suckered tentacles and a glare of lightning and poached eggs' (550).

There is a Protestant sense here too, that the emotions belong to the fallen world. Chief among the emotions for White is guilt, produced by a sense of failure in relationships, of not having loved or given enough. White gives to Elizabeth Hunter the phrase 'I the guilty I will never be eaten away never purged' (196), which can be read as either 'I the guilty, I will never be eaten away' or as 'I, the guilty I, will never be eaten away' as if guilt were the precondition of individuation, which is so for White because the 'I' only defines itself in its relations to others, and those relations are fraught with a sense of failure or betrayal. Guilt in this sense is always bound up with disappointment – particularly in those primary relations between parents and children where expectation is at its most powerful and therefore most easily disappointed. Though their compensatory response to disappointment may achieve towering proportions – as it does in Voss, for example, or Hurtle Duffield, or each of the four riders in the chariot – the cause usually has its roots in the intimate surrounds and fraught domesticity of childhood. Guilt, like disappointment, also has humble or ordinary social origins, though White's determination to hold the glass close to emotion lest it be allowed to disappear under inhibition or repression ensures that its expressive proportions are anything but humble. Elizabeth Hunter's 60-year-old children Basil and Dorothy both think of themselves as murderers because they intend to commit their mother to a nursing home in order to limit the drain on their inheritance. (Three nurses, a cook, a cleaner and a gardener would soon take care of that.) It's not unusual for children in their sixties to have such thoughts and in any case to commit an elderly parent to a nursing home is not exactly a crime. That it should be felt as murder by two children who don't know how to express emotion except by composed theatrical gesture (in Basil's case) or a persistent but unfocussed anxiety (in Dorothy's) is more an indication of White's determination to magnify the feeling of guilt in them than it is an objective statement of fact.

Two points about the emotions in White's work need to be stressed. First, though White's focus on guilt may suggest that his characters exist in a fallen world, the emotion itself is social rather than religious in origin. There is Lotte the cabaret artist's credo, 'And if I cannot worship, I have to love somebody' (150) – it is precisely the lack of a religious sense, of a recourse to the divinity as a source of authority, which gives human relationships their supreme importance. Thus guilt is accompanied in White's novels by a host of related emotions, all essentially social in this way – shame, resentment, embarrassment, suspicion, longing, lust (opposed in White's world to sensuality, which is the body at ease with itself, freed from the turbulence of emotion), offence, loneliness, vulnerability, anxiety, cruelty, selfishness and spite.

Second, though the emotions may assume attenuated or grotesque proportions under the pressure of White's expressive intent, they are not necessarily large emotions in themselves. Quite the contrary, just as their causes might lie in domestic or social disappointment, so they seem by nature to be slight or fleeting, at least on first appearance. It is White's close focus that gives scale and an exaggerated visibility to what in the real world might be observed as barely a tremor of feeling, or no feeling at all. Impatience, forgetfulness and shortness of temper can be as much a source of guilt (in Sister de Santis, for example) as the betrayal implied in an adulterous act (in Elizabeth Hunter). In Dorothy guilt is aroused simply by 'little acts of unpremeditated kindness on the part of others' – the thought that she might be unworthy of a compliment throws her 'into a panic of despair' (292). For the solicitor Wyburd, the most buttoned up of all the characters, it is enough for him to be told of the plan to put his old client in a nursing home to feel that the contents of her house have turned against him. 'The light was retreating from rooms in which furniture had begun to swell and brood. At intervals ill-regulated clocks were sounding the hour [...] the clash or tinkle of the sounding clocks was the worst accusation yet: of his part betrayal of a trust.' Then his body turns against him and the staircase metes out punishment. 'All the way up the stairs his feet seemed to pad dishonestly; the sickness in his stomach made it the predominant part of him; his knee was grazed by the formally tangled iron hedge which stood between himself and the hall below [...]' (276).

It is characteristic of White to appreciate how an object – in this case a staircase – might amplify the sense of shame, as if it had as much expressive power as the creeping feeling the emotion might create upon one's face, or along one's arm. 'Stairs are worse,' Dorothy considers, 'the sounds made by comparatively modest garments will swell voluptuously when thoughts are attuned to them' (524). It is also typical of White's close focus, tuned to capture the gradations or fluctuations of emotion, and then to magnify them, that it should also pick up and enlarge the fine detail of objects or parts of the body in that focus too – the faded sage of a tabouret, the relief of veins on the back of a hand, 'the drops of perspiration lying in the saucer of a temple' (37). These details become charged with a projected emotion, which then flares back at the projector from them. Sister de Santis is unsettled by 'a glare from furniture and a bedpan scarcely covered by a towel' (14) – it is her own spiteful thought about her patient coming back as embarrassment to assail her. Dorothy de Lascabanes, suffering the anxiety of foreignness, finds herself intimidated by the telephone but calmed by her toothpaste and her sponge. Sponges are important to White – 'seeping into crevices, smoothing the wrinkles out of thoughts'; here it is a sponge which produces the thought, 'Objects, including the human ones, are often more powerful than people' (104). The large piece of *filet de boeuf* which Dorothy fishes out of her mother's rubbish bin, skewered to the ferrule of her lace and ivory parasol, revolves like a 'silent klaxon', broadcasting the guilt of the maids who have thrown it out – but since it is she who has spied on them the guilt rebounds on her, turning her expression into 'that of a flogged and panting horse, nostrils pinched, veins in relief on saturated skin' (229). The theatrical Basil likes shaving, because it makes him feel 'less frayed, splenetic, awful', protected from both past and future, but if he nicks the lobe of his ear he is in real trouble, since it is 'the worst possible place, [and] leads from fury to wretchedness and depression' (236). Some objects stand out because, against all the odds, they are expressive of delight – Lotte's pair of flawless schnitzels, for example, which she brings in on a molten silver dish edged with 'a considerable display' of starched white cloth, 'the slices of lemon shaved to a transparency, the anchovy fillets lovingly curled' (147) – the details are heart-breaking in their innocence, especially when you consider the tortured background of the cook. Other objects promise the sweet pleasures of memory but then turn with menace, like the ancient boot that Basil puts on in the shed that houses his father's old Bentley, and then can't take off, even though his sister pulls on it too, in what seems like a fight 'for their self-justification and freedom from awfulness' (509). Basil has already injured his foot once on this excursion and has a limp from before, so one feels a terrible clumsiness at work here, not only in the repeated maiming but also in the intractability of the boot, as the object in a ritual governed by emotion and memory, and conducted in all innocence, leaves its initiate crippled with embarrassment.

The magnification of affect also underwrites the exquisite discriminations of emotion in White's writing, its ability to pick up the finest nuances and modulations of feeling and to make them stand out in a powerful way. White's characters are all excitable, not because they're neurotic necessarily, the usual criticism levelled against them, and against modernism, by realist critics, but because they're alive.[3]

'I've always excited myself if the opportunity arose. I can't stop now – for anyone'(11). That's the testament of the old lady, Elizabeth Hunter, one of those complex pragmatic mothers that stand out in Australian literature, irrespective of class, combative and vulnerable at the same time, because she responds to the moment as it comes with an intensity which commands equally intense opposing reactions, in herself as much as in those who surround her. Sweetness is accompanied by dread, revelation by accusation and supplication by intimidation. It isn't simply the paradoxical nature of the emotions which White is displaying here: since relationships are defined by expectation, and therefore the disappointment of expectation, so every gesture outwards to another entails the possibility of hurt or rejection or recoil, and therefore guilt, shame, fear – or conversely again, the relief from guilt and shame offered by spite or cruelty or penitence. The old woman is nothing if not resilient, her mind constantly in motion, which is why her children are driven to panic. Wyburd describes the atmosphere in the dying woman's house as 'the hectic shimmer of apprehension' (283), and it is precisely through this lens that White's characters normally react to life.

How finely the emotions are observed in this shimmering glass, and in such combinations – helplessness confused by spite, longing hidden under repugnance, discomfiture laced with a spirit of horror! Elizabeth Hunter's attitude to her husband's doctor is 'a mixture of dislike, apprehension, and petulance' (197) – he responds to her with contempt. Brother and sister cling to each other in their parent's marital bed under the shock of emotional revelations 'which were not quite grief, passion, despair, horror, but something of them all'. It is a moment which comes close to incest (a motif White also employs in *The Solid Mandala* (1966) to suggest the intensity of the sibling relationship), yet it also contains a fine discrimination of feeling, as Basil is replaced in his sister's mind by her husband: 'It seemed to her that if she had been fond of, instead of trying to love Hubert, he might have responded. Love can freeze the limbs; affection thaw the instincts' (526).

Dorothy reacts to the Norwegian on the island as potential lovers do in White's novels, with a mixture of fear, prevarication, evasion, offence, bewilderment and humiliation. The embedding of one emotion inside another is what gives White's style its complexity – since the emotions always carry their opposites in train, even if just as an echo or a shadow, no reaction is ever simple or unalloyed. In her last meeting with the old woman who had slept with her husband many years before, 'Lal Wyburd felt herself contained in what might have been an envelope of vapour, or sentimental pity, inside which, again, her mind was reared in horror, not for the decayed humanity she had at her mercy, but beyond the mask, still the legend of Elizabeth Hunter's beauty' (537).

These are distilled moments. White's novels are played out in dramatic scenes, which prolong and complicate the moments of feeling that are their focus, allowing their magnification and modulation. His expressionism is in this way essentially performative. It is as if his characters need a scene in order to express themselves: the sense of occasion, the presence of an audience, even if it is only oneself or another, the consciousness of staging emotions that would otherwise be too complicated or too shameful to express at all. The famous actor Sir Basil is the most obvious performer in *The Eye of the Storm* – he is one of those figures who express the paradoxical nature of self-consciousness which is so acutely portrayed in White's work, because it is both a constriction on emotion and one of the most powerful of emotions. But all the characters act out parts; it is how their emotions take shape. White thought of himself as composed of a cast of contradictory characters which, too shy to act out himself, he embodied in his novels.[4] The same may be said of these characters, who are also composed of parts, taken in the theatrical sense. They are anxious actors on the whole, capable of glory, but most human when they stumble or find themselves in the grip of an awkward emotion. Then you see it clearly expressed – their sense of limitation, their overwhelming need.

This is perhaps most obvious in the reactions of daughter Dorothy, Princesse de Lascabanes, who is the most revealing character in many ways, because she is also the most volatile, the most easily disturbed. There is the scene in which she appears at her mother's bedside for the first time only to be met by the accusation that she has only come for the money like her brother. Dorothy denies it, 'Oh God, Mother, don't you allow for the possibility of human affection?' and then deflects the accusation, by allowing it to apply to her brother, 'Basil is capable of anything.' – 'That was so unquestionably true it did away with her own spasm of shame by drowning it in a wave of loathing.' Shame for herself gives way to loathing for him (it is interesting how physical White's differentiation of emotion is here – shame as a spasm, loathing as a wave), but is immediately followed by a retraction – 'No, it didn't; she detested lies: most of all those half-lies she was sometimes driven to tell.' So the accusation is sent back to her mother –'You're so *unfair*!' – in a whinge which 'developed through a moan into a downright blub'. The childlike display of unhappiness has an immediate effect on the mother, who is 'chastened, as well as impressed, by the emotional outburst it was in her power to cause'. Soon both are crying together, mother and daughter confirmed in their roles, 'softly, deliciously' (64).

The great Sir Basil is no less vulnerable to the disturbance of emotion, indeed more so, because of the way his self-consciousness as an actor first checks and then compounds his reactions. The unlikely romantic dalliance between himself and Sister de Santis is an attenuated procession of anxieties and embarrassments, culminating in the appearance of the 'not-too-well pickled Labrador' in the water before their restaurant table, a corpse with a wire around its neck, hence murdered not just drowned – it reduces him to hysteria, produces a 'nameless anguish' in her. She falls down, he remembers his failure in the role of King Lear, 'on his last performance as the old king he had never felt so personally bereft, so bankrupt; technique could not protect him from it. This last gasp; and the poverty of a single bone-clean button. In this you may have conveyed the truth, if in nothing else' (356).[5] White's expressive scenes often take this course – after the openings and withdrawals, the offerings and the resentments, the parade of hesitant and anxious gestures, the whole complex of emotion is embodied in an object, a boot, the corpse of a dog, King Lear's button, a vase of roses.

White's emphasis on part and scene does not suppose their regulation by a larger whole: on the contrary the novels proceed by elaboration, proliferation, accumulation and, in the case of *The Twyborn Affair*, by mutation, precisely in the absence of such an assurance. In *The Eye of the Storm* as the scenes unfold or intertwine, through the operations of memory or the circulation of motifs previously invested and now reinvested with significance, a later scene will recall an earlier, or an earlier anticipate a later, so that similar emotions are made to resonate in different settings, overlaying and complicating their expression; or two scenes enacted contemporaneously in two different consciousnesses, suddenly intersect as the transmission of consciousness passes from the perspective of one character to that of the other. So Elizabeth Hunter wakes from a penitential reverie in which she has relived her husband's death and her feelings of guilt at betraying him to find a vase of roses at the foot of her bed, offered by Sister de Santis out of her own drama of guilt, enacted during the night while her employer slept.

In this drama Sister de Santis farewells a visitor to the old lady's house, warning him of the dangers posed by three steps near the bottom of the badly lit garden path where at least two people have broken their legs. The three steps, and the accompanying prospect of broken legs, recur in the novel, one of those object-motifs that radiate anxiety every time it is invoked. Her solicitude for the visitor makes her feel lonely, then angry; late at night her agitation spills over into desire, in a fantasy of seduction; when lust subsides, disappointment and embarrassment take its place; she prays at the foot of her mistress's bed. Mrs Hunter wakes, sees her there and folds the nurse back into her own dream of guilt. Sister de Santis descends the stairs and scrubs out the kitchen in an act of penitence. It brings her a temporary relief. By now day has come. She goes down into the dew-laden garden, to pick the roses, in a ritual of 'innocent sensuality'. A man passing on his way to work greets her in Greek – her mother was Greek – the rhythm is familiar, but she doesn't understand what he has said. Anxiety returns. She fears for her patient, takes the roses in a vase up to her bedroom. The old lady wakes, fresh from the expiation of reliving her husband's death. The power of the roses is so great that she imagines she sees them, though she is blind. At the same time Sister de Santis hears, in her mother's voice, the peasant-migrant's greeting, and understands it. 'What a sunrise we are making!'

The logic of this long sequence – in fact, a number of scenes played end to end – is that of White's expressive drama in general. There is, as the basic rhythm, the alternation between extended awkwardness and momentary grace, between the subjection to emotion's tumult, and its temporary resolution. There is the interweaving of the characters' experiences, not unlike an operatic performance in structure, with soliloquy-arias alternating with duets at moments of confrontation or understanding. As the scenes accumulate, the power and complexity of the emotions turn the characters into vehicles of expression, it augments and dissolves them as individuals. In this way the feelings of the characters flow out beyond their identities and mingle or cross, becoming in time part of a grand epic or operatic chorus.

I say epic, both in recognition of the scale of White's orchestrations and because of the social range of his characters, across class and religion and countries and time – and the way he inhabits the individual consciousness of the character only to reach beyond it – means that he is writing, as were Joyce and Faulkner, not of individuals finally, but of a people, Australians. It is a remarkable thing about this people, that they are defined not by their heroism or their endurance, as the popular media would have us believe, but by their nervousness and vulnerability. Their embarrassment and awkwardness in their dealings with each other is an expression, both of their capacity for feeling and of their honesty – and is in this respect, a measure of their moral worth.

Notes

1 *The Eye of the Storm* (London: Jonathan Cape, 1973), 84. All subsequent references to this edition appear in parentheses in the text.
2 The centrality of death to the allegorical figurations of the Baroque is dealt with at length by Walter Benjamin in the *The Origin of the German Tragic Drama* (1963; Verso: London, 1998). But while White's figures often taken on an allegorical dimension it is their nervous vitality in the proximity of death that is their most striking feature.
3 For example, Katharine Susannah Prichard, 'Modern Trends in Literature' and 'Some Thoughts on Australian Literature', in *Straight Left* (Sydney: Wild and Woolley, 1982), 197–98, 202–4.
4 Patrick White, *Flaws in the Glass: A Self-Portrait* (London, Penguin, 1983), 20.
5 The reference is to Lear's dying words, 'Pray you, undo this button. Thank you, sir', *King Lear*, V: iii, l.311.

Chapter 8

THE DOUBLING OF REALITY IN PATRICK WHITE'S *THE AUNT'S STORY* AND PAUL SCHREBER'S *MEMOIRS OF MY NERVOUS ILLNESS*

Aruna Wittmann

Introduction

This chapter reads two accounts of madness from different discursive fields alongside one another. It looks at how these accounts – one from a fictional text, *The Aunt's Story* (1948) by Patrick White, and the other from a memoir, Paul Schreber's *Memoirs of My Nervous Illness* (1903) – share common features.[1] I wish to show how a comparison of these texts can help us understand three key aspects of White's style in this novel: the erasure of narrative presence, the mixing of narrative viewpoints and the doubling of narration in which two points of view co-exist.

Many critics have noted the transitional place *The Aunt's Story* occupies in White's oeuvre, seeing it as resting on the cusp of a change from early to late styles. They note its heightened poetic language, which stems in part from a successful assimilation of modernist precursors, and a more experimental use of syntax. In this third novel, they consider White as reaching a high point in purely stylistic terms, one from which he retreats in subsequent works.[2] *The Aunt's Story* also stands at the pivot of many personal transitions: in it White pays homage to Europe while embarking for home and Australia.[3] He also turns away from a life of multiple relationships to a single, settled love. In a larger sense then love and home are what are at stake behind the stylistic innovations. That the narrative strives for, and often achieves, the texture of madness is a measure of White's skill and personal daring. I would like to suggest that further investigations into White's psychobiography, tracing his experience and fears of madness, would yield new pathways into his work. This chapter will, however, concentrate on stylistic effects. These recreate encounters with radical, altered states while debating the issue of sanity. Reading these stylistic effects against those used in Paul Schreber's memoirs points to many useful similarities; in a final analysis, however, fictional and discursively normative representations of madness show major divergence.

Paul Schreber is perhaps the twentieth century's most famous psychiatric patient. The memoirs he published on leaving hospital give a vivid account of his nine-year long illness. They provided the case history Freud used to develop his theory of psychosis.[4] Schreber was a 51-one-year old, married High Court judge when he fell mentally ill for the second time. Though he entered psychiatric care of his own accord, he was transferred against his wishes into a secure asylum where he regarded himself as a prisoner. It was after eight years in this second asylum that Schreber started to write his memoirs. His main aim was to show the courts that he was able to function in the outside world in spite of holding delusional beliefs. The following is a quote from the psychiatric report presented at court, which gives an overview of Schreber's delusional system:

> He is called to redeem the world and to bring back to mankind the lost state of Blessedness. He maintains he has been given this task by direct divine inspiration, similar to that taught by the prophets; he maintains that nerves in a state of excitation, as his have been for a long time, have the property of attracting God, but it is a question of things which are either not at all expressible in human language or only with great difficulty [...] The most essential part of his mission of redemption is that it is necessary for him first of all to be transformed into a woman. Not, however, that he wishes to be transformed into a woman, it is much more a 'must' according to the Order of the World, which he simply cannot escape, even though he would personally very much prefer to remain in his honourable manly position in life. (Addendum A, *Memoirs*, 333)

Schreber fought two appeals against involuntary confinement, in 1900 and 1902, winning the second. The Grounds of Judgement which released him state:

> The Court is in no doubt that the appellant is insane [...]. What to objective observation is hallucination and delusion is for him irrefutable certainty [...]. But it is not sufficient grounds for placing plaintiff under tutelage that his mental processes are pathologically disturbed. (Addendum E, *Memoirs*, 422)

One could view the court's judgement as a confirmation that two levels of reality or two systems – one mad and one sane – not only coexisted but could do so safely in the outside world. Schreber himself states in the preface: 'it is also in my opinion of little importance whether, in view of the relationship contrary to the Order of the World which arose between God and myself, ideas which I formed at the time were more or less faulty' (Preface, *Memoirs*, 4). Here he admits that he might have been severely deluded but suggests that it does not matter because some of his delusions are true for him and can, therefore, claim the general interest of the reader. Schreber seeks the reader's assent and makes a very definite claim on our judgements about what holds true in the common, social world. He recognizes that he is deluded but has a psychological need to share his delusions. The desire to share one's delusions is what Patrick White also tries out with his characterisation of Theodora Goodman, the main protagonist in *The Aunt's Story*.

The novel is divided into three sections, which could be read as corresponding roughly to White's analysis of cause, process and outcome of illness. In the first section, White presents increasing social alienation as he shows us the widening gap between a normative reality and Theodora's at-a-distance interpretation of it. We are drawn into her point of view and side against reality, as she becomes our main focus of sympathy. That *she* becomes aware of two orders of reality is clear in the passage below, for example:

> Once when the Syrian left, Theodora went with him some of the way. In the white-lit winter evening her legs grew longer with the strides she took. Her hair flew. She had increased. She walked outside a distinct world, on which the grass quivered with a clear moisture, and the earth rang. In this state, in which rocks might at any moment open, or words convey meaning, she stood and watched the Syrian go. His silence slipped past. The hills settled into shapelessness. She was left with the trembling of her knees. (30)

The epiphanic state in which the world becomes indistinct, merged and shapeless is presented by White as a source of beauty, mystery and value. It is a world in which meaning bursts forth, as if out of rocks. There is, however, a collateral danger associated with this state, which White immediately presents in the next paragraph:

> Afterwards, trailing through the shrunk yard, there was no external evidence that the Syrian had been. The meat-safe still creaked on its wire hook, and the kitchen window's yellow square denied the immensity of shapelessness. Even Theodora Goodman's hair hung meekly in damp tails. (30)

The ordinary world loses in beauty and value when compared with the epiphany. The hyper-real state seems to steal from the ordinary so that flesh is no longer 'trembling' or 'quivering' but simply a meat-safe, something mechanical and dead. That the epiphanic moments that happen fleetingly for Theodora have become permanent for Schreber is clear not only from what he says discursively about his perceptions (he insists that he has become imbued with rays which both torture him and give him extra clear sight)[5] but is also evident when he tries to describe the natural world around him. Of moths he says, for example:

> So-called Moonshine-Blessedness fluttered towards me in long flights (the image is hard to describe, one might perhaps compare it with so-called gossamer, not in single threads but in a kind of denser texture); this was to represent the female state of Blessedness. It was of two kinds, one flatter and one more robust; perhaps the former can be regarded as Child-Blessedness. (*Memoirs*, 13)

One way of understanding the distorted perception of reality that is happening here is suggested by Eugene Minkowski. He was a psychoanalytic phenomenologist who worked with Eugen Bleuler in the famous Burgholzi clinic in the 1920s and '30s. He hypothesized that what happens in a schizophrenic mindset is a conglomeration of time and space, such that everything seems to happen in one plane – at the same time and in the same place. He divides what he calls lived space into two, light and dark:

> Everything is light, precise, and clear in light space. In dark space everything is obscure and mysterious. One feels as if in the presence of the unknown, in its positive value, and the phenomenon of mystery seems the best and the most immediate way to express this characteristic of lived obscurity.[6]

He suggests that dark space obliterates distances, bringing everything close. It is against a uniting backdrop such as this merging that patients watch their own sensory phenomena, which stand out as something distinctive but mysterious. Minkowski says the sick individual stands helpless in front of such happenings and tries to work out what they are. He does not have access to a strictly space/time ordered, scaffolded world in which an adult and a baby moth fly towards the onlooker. For Schreber these are mysterious beings, abstract states of mind or little gods of Blessedness, which he tries to incorporate into his own system.

Most writers, White included, have access to such liminal, often luminous, states of perception and consciousness. The difference between a fictional rendering and prose written from within delusional madness seems to be one of quantity and the extent to which doubling is consciously recognized. To recognize the doubling of reality is therefore an indication of sanity.

I shall now go on to look at three of White's stylistic devices – erasure of narrative presence, mixing of perspectives and the co-existence of different viewpoints – tracing parallels in the memoirs which indicate that White and Schreber's texts inhabit essentially similar worlds.

Erasure of Narrative Presence

Mounting de-socialization and the increasing free flow of perception is what Patrick White shows us in *The Aunt's Story*. What starts off as Theodora's whimsical abstraction at the beginning of the novel, when she sees herself as little more than a pair of hands flitting above the 'china and mahogany world' (11) of the objects in her mother's bedroom, gradually turns into the more menacing disassociation of consciousness we see occurring in the *jardin exotique*: 'A slight breeze began to play with the cactus fingers. They creaked. The pads of the prickly pear moved in the air as dignified as blotting paper. Age and wisdom, intensified to a point that was unwise, rustled their eyelids, and looked' (141). The impossibility of self-possession is presented discursively in the narrative elsewhere, but what we see in this extract is White attempting to remove Theodora's narrative presence while keeping her point of view. The reader is discomfited because the familiar, reassuring presence called Theodora is now replaced with abstractions and body parts, which are then identified with cacti. The vicious, devouring aspect of the garden is seen to eat up Theodora quite literally. Or again, as in the passage below, Theodora's presence disappears into Lieselotte's paintings. Her sense of being in the room is replaced with her ability to fly in and out of the windows of both the room and the pictures it contains. White names the transformation Theodora effects: she becomes 'flaming like a bird of paradise'.

> Theodora saw that they were in a large room, somewhere high, the light purified by an immensity of surrounding space, the walls pierced by the open windows of pictures. And now she was drawn to the many windows, and the world these contained, the hanging gardens flowering with miraculous questions, the glass pagoda from which her own soul looked out, flaming like a bird of paradise. (167)

Similarly, the cumulative effect of reading Schreber's *Memoirs*, despite the insistence of the 'I' on every page, is one of extensive self-distancing. His description of watching butterflies in the asylum garden provides an example of the fraught, tortured nature of his thought when faced with simple perceptions.

> Whenever a butterfly appears my gaze is first directed to it as to a being newly created that very moment, and secondly the word 'butterfly – has been recorded' is spoken into my nerves by the voices; this shows that one thought I

could possibly no longer recognise a butterfly and one therefore examines me to find out whether I still know the meaning of the word 'butterfly'. (*Memoirs*, 221)

The diminution of ego functioning we see occurring in both Schreber and Theodora could be understood in many different ways. Minkowski relates the diminution, which White presents as erasure of narrative presence, to a takeover by dark space. He suggests light and dark space coexist in normal life; pathology results when the usual relation between them becomes disrupted. When dark space takes over, the patient becomes trapped in a bleak world that progressively wipes out distinctions:

> The morbid world penetrates the individual and robs him of everything intuitive and personal [...]. And it is this diminution of the intimacy, of the personal character of the ego, which our patients' complaints seem to express – complaints related to the deprivation of freedom.[7]

It is salient to note, of course, that the sudden opportunity for freedom presented by her mother's death is what drives Theodora's quest for individuation. But the madness White tips his character into suggests that Theodora pursues freedom to the point of delusion, paradoxically losing her free agency. Although White seems to endorse the dark knowledge held in the black rose at the end of the novel, the symbol feels empty. We are returned to a literary world and asked to find our meaning as readers therewith, in a realm of metaphor cut loose from the mind and body of the main character.

Mixing of Narrative Viewpoints

In the highly experimental second section of the novel, White uses many different stylistic devices to show Theodora becoming more isolated and deluded. The method of suddenly leaving her own narrative to enter the imagined narratives of those around her makes the *jardin exotique* section particularly difficult to read. One such transition is her assumption of the role of the sensible Ludmilla, the General's sister:

> Through so much business, of dialogue and forks, the General's note still floated. Its madness shocked the room into an appearance of reality, in which tables and chairs assisted the rite of eating, and the bamboo étagère had never stood any nonsense. Tufted with sparse palms, the upright structure of the étagère made the reasonable Ludmilla more distinct. Though even she had disappointed, taking God too often from the cupboard, and tramping the roads to Kiev. (150)

The French word *étagère*, which is the term for a shelving unit, seems to catapult Theodora from the reality of the dining room where she is still herself looking on as an observer into taking part as a participant in the General's life by becoming his sister. For the character it is the upright appearance of the bamboo unit which performs this transfer of agency. One could follow the phallic thread to see where it leads. At the level of authorship, it seems to be the introduction of the French word itself, which causes the transfer into a new mixed narrative mode. *Étagère* comes from word *étage*, meaning floor or storey, which suggests a sudden switching between different levels of consciousness. Theodora's process of dissolution is often portrayed through this device of switching between her own and the viewpoints of characters or objects she assumes. The various hotel guests seem to exist only to offer her the opportunity to do this. White shows us Theodora moving into them and their stories as if to take possession, or to give her access to a world she is losing access to in her own right.

Schreber does this too. He calls it 'a future transmigration of souls' and tells us in his *Memoirs* that he was 'cast in several roles consecutively: a Hyperborian woman, a Jesuit Novice in Ossegg, a Burgomaster of Klattau, an Alsatian girl who had to defend her honour against a victorious French officer, and finally, a Mongolian Prince' (*Memoirs*, 88). The extraordinary list of people Schreber encounters in self-transformations is a measure of his learning and historical imagination. He tries to account for the very specific nature of the roles assigned to him:

> The fate of becoming a 'Hyperborian woman' seemed a sign that the earth had lost so much heat that general glaciations had either occurred already or was imminent; That I was destined to be a Jesuit Novice in Ossegg or a Burgomaster in Klattau or even an Alsatian girl in the situation specified above, I took as prophesies that Protestantism had either already succumbed to or was about to succumb to Catholicism, and the German people to their Roman and Slavic neighbours; the prospect of my becoming a 'Mongolian Prince' appeared to me as a sign that all Aryan peoples had proved themselves unsuitable to defend the realms of God, and that a last refuge would now have to be taken with non-Aryan peoples. (*Memoirs*, 88)

Schreber's self-analysis here points to his end-of-the-world scenarios and fears. His anxieties focus on being taken over – by ice, Catholicism and non-Aryans – which he combats by going over to the enemies' side, as if in identification with the aggressors. One could ask *vis-à-vis* Theodora's similarly invasive insertion of herself into others' stories – what are the characters that she assumes and to what purpose? A quick overview suggests that she becomes Katina's nanny, Alyosha Sergei's sister, Mrs Rapallo's maidservant, Wetherby's hated mother – they are all passive and observational positions in relation to the main characters.

Co-Existence of Viewpoints

In the second section, White develops a narrative style which allows him to switch between different perspectives without warning. He does this with all his characters, but mostly we follow Theodora as she dwells inside her subjectivity, either in her perceptions about herself, for example, of 'retreating from the jaws of roses' (138–9) of the wallpaper of her hotel room or in her perception of others. We also get another type of mixed perspective – the co-existence of active and passive viewpoints – where Theodora is both the active agent and the observer of her own actions, as in the following passage:

> I am preparing for bed, she saw. But in performing this act for the first time, she knew she did not really control her bones, and that the curtain of her flesh must blow, like walls which are no longer walls. (196)

The self-watching exterior gaze foregrounds the difference between being and doing. In the novel's final section, White tries to find a style to express the disjunction of the active and passive but does not succeed, I would like to suggest. Something about the nature of the fictional medium which endorses and allows metaphoric slipping between different levels of reality blocks his ability to portray radical self-alienation. In the following passage, for example, White shows us Theodora as thinking an act into being, but when she tries to find the act to match the thought, she finds metaphoric complexity instead:

> Now that the man in the laundered shirt slept, Theodora Goodman could search her own purpose, her own contentment. I am going home, she said. It had a lovely abstraction to which she tried to fit the act. She tried the door of a house and went in. There were the stairs, and the cotton quilt on which she threw her jaded hat. (259)

What White struggles to achieve – a convincing impression of madness characterized partly by the disjunction between being and doing – Schreber achieves effortlessly. He does not have to struggle against a fictionalizing medium – we recognize the delusionary quality of some of his statements because we judge them against a normative reality. The following where he talks about being turned into a woman is an example:

> When the rays approach, my breast gives the impression of a pretty well-developed female bosom; this phenomenon can be seen by anybody who wants to observe

me with his own eyes. I am therefore in a position to offer objective evidence by observation of my body. (*Memoirs*, 248)

One reason for the often convoluted language Schreber uses is his need to negotiate between what he fears his readers would see, that is no breasts, and what he would like them to see. It is because of issues such as these that he constantly uses phrases like 'gives the impression of' or 'as far as I know'. He is mindful of the patience and tolerance of the reader, leading us by slow degrees, by using familiar structures like chronology and appeal to established authorities (for example, Emil Kraepelin's *Textbook of Psychiatry*) to convince us of the truth value of his delusions.

Louis Sass sees what he calls Schreber's double bookkeeping, that is his attempt to keep hold of two orders of knowledge, as a hyper-reflexive activity which arises from a need to control who sees and knows. He suggests that in a case of schizophrenia like Schreber's the symptoms are caused by a hypertrophy of thought, a profound inward turning of attention and a subsequent alienation from the emotions, instincts and the body. He argues that the body then becomes an object in its own right. It is no longer an instrument for the conduit of feelings and emotions.[8] Theodora's desire to know everything which White highlights throughout could also be understood in light of this desire for control.

Conclusion

As well as similarities in the symptoms of the illness they portray, White's and Schreber's texts show a striking structural parallel which I would like to look at by way of conclusion. Madness in both writers is associated with, or at least accompanied by, some kind of feminization. One of Schreber's fixed delusions, which he firmly held even after discharge, was the conviction that God wanted him to be turned into a woman. Only by this feat would Schreber be able to copulate with God and repopulate the world with new human beings. Schreber saw his feminization as a religious duty which went against all his usual moral principles. Though Schreber documents the extreme pain he experienced in the initial stages of changing gender, which he called unmanning, in later years he came to embrace being female as providing temporary relief from his sufferings. He accepted the unmanning and turned it into an active sexual participation with the rays which had been torturing him. In the passage below, one can see how Schreber manages to reconstruct a manageable, working sense of reality from what were otherwise frightening and painful experiences.

> This state of Blessedness is mainly a state of voluptuous enjoyment, which for its full development needs the fantasy of either being or wishing to be a female

being, which naturally is not to my taste. I must however submit to the necessity of the Order of the World which forces me to accept these ideas, if my bodily state is not to be made unbearable by pains, by bellowing produced by miracle, and by insane noise. (*Memoirs*, 291)

Zvi Lothane points out that Freud made the mistaken assumption, common for his time, that Schreber's gender transformation was suggestive of an underlying homosexual desire. Freud believed that Schreber's repressed love for his father became transformed into its opposite, hate, which then became transferred onto his psychiatrist Dr Flechsig. Thus Schreber's paranoia that he was being persecuted by Dr Flechsig, and later by God, was a direct result of a re-emergent infantile homosexual desire. Lothane points out, however, that 'it is the gender of the subject that rules in Schreber's understanding of voluptuousness, not the object of desire'.[9] Thus, Freud's attribution of repressed homosexual desire as the main driving force behind the illness is an inference. For Freud, feminized feelings in the body suggest desire for a man, whereas Lothane shows that Schreber continued to fantasize about women even after his newly acquired feminization. Schreber complained of losing his manliness and feared being changed into a woman but he never ceased to complain of the lack of female company, especially that of his wife. Rather than as a symptom of a repressed homosexual desire, Lothane considers Schreber's illness a response to the literal unmanning or removal of rights that hospitalization imposed on him, coupled with unresolved guilt about sexuality in general. Lothane also contests the sexual abuse theories propounded by William Niederland and Morton Schatzman who believed that Schreber had suffered actual physical, emotional and sexual abuse in his childhood home at the hands of his educationalist father.[10]

Where Freud reads a drama of repressed desire, and Schatzman reads child abuse, Lothane reads depressive mourning (Schreber and his wife had suffered their sixth miscarriage just before Schreber's illness), compounded by maltreatment during hospitalization. Louis Sass, as a phenomenologist, does not look for an etiology but suggests instead that what is at issue in Schreber's illness is neither repressed childhood sexuality nor the abuse of power by parental figures but rather an internally staged epistemological fight. He takes issue with psychoanalysis' regression hypothesis because for him the extreme state of self-consciousness shown by Schreber is incompatible with a whole-scale regression to childlike states. Schreber in Sass's analysis is caught between an active masculine knowing and a feminine being. He cannot occupy either position exclusively, but choses to do both. Sass points to how Schreber finds relief by dressing up in women's clothes and staring at himself in the mirror. In this state, he is both the observing consciousness and the feeling being who is observed. He resolves an epistemological conflict by the act of cross-dressing: 'but I have to imagine myself as man and woman in one person having intercourse with myself, or somehow have to achieve with myself a certain sexual excitement […]' (*Memoirs*, 250).

Sass suggests that a schizophrenic's world is so highly theoretical that the body and the mind become postulates. The body as an inhabited part of the ego separates from the thinking apparatus so that all sense of natural appetite for the world is lost. Sass writes, 'and it may be this separation (of body and soul), rather than the polymorphous infantile sexuality postulated by psychoanalysis, that accounts for the uncertain sexual identity in so many schizophrenics'.[11] The search for an understanding of what a schizophrenic mindset might be like brought Sass to a consideration of the forms and mechanics of modernism, which for him consisted in a hypertrophy of consciousness at the cost of the natural rhythms of the body.[12] The highly conscious, acutely self-referential aspects of modernism which tries to incorporate the primitive and the irrational within itself is an image which perhaps captures something of what Schreber was trying to do with his paradoxical act of cross-dressing in front of the mirror.

Cross-dressing or drag is also what we see Patrick White perform in *The Aunt's Story*. A male writer poses as a woman who is herself less female than the stereotype would require. White therefore shows up the performative aspect of gender identity, but in his portrayal, as well as in the tragic case of Schreber, we see madness as the end point reached. White makes it clear that Holstius at the end of *The Aunt's Story* is a hallucinated figure who offers Theodora a way of living which is totally at odds with common, everyday reality. Though Holstius comes across as a positive fatherly figure, an amalgam of all the good men in her life, Theodora's social alienation at the end of the novel is almost complete:

> They will give you warm drinks, simple, nourishing food, and encourage you to relax in a white room and tell your life. Of course you will not be taken in by any of this, do you hear? But you will submit. It is part of the deference one pays to those who prescribe the reasonable life. (283)

White's late modernist text and Schreber's early modernist one are both trying to resolve a rift in consciousness, which they themselves partly theorize as a split between the masculine and feminine. They do not offer any easy solutions, however, preferring to highlight the individual's sense of helplessness when confronted with the disjunction or lack of fit between biological sex, gender identity, object love, gender performance and society's expectations. Schizophrenia or schizophreniform types of psychoses may or may not be a modernist malaise, but as this study has shown, there are similarities in the types of mental states they convey with those in a fictional modernist text. Schreber's *Memoirs* and Patrick White's *The Aunt's Story*, therefore, offer ways of understanding, especially when studied together, the madness which artists, writers and critics have always sensed behind modernism. They also offer an approach to the more belated idea, the modernism of madness, which Minkowski, Sass, Freud and others have been engaged in trying to formulate; an understanding of the painful states of being which Schreber calls 'contrary to the Order of the World'.[13]

As a coda, and given what this chapter has shown to be White's extensive investigation of madness as an ontological state, one could perhaps counter some of Simon During's criticisms of White in his paper 'Patrick White, Saul Bellow and the Problem of Literary Value'.[14] There, During takes White to account for not being sufficiently adept at using the 'advanced, academised flows of humanist knowledge' that were available to him.[15] Although During is talking about the late 1960s and the early 1970s when White's *The Solid Mandala* (1968) and Saul Bellow's *Mr Sammler's Planet* (1970) were published, and not about the late 1940s which is when *The Aunt's Story* (1948) came out, yet nevertheless one could argue that White's life-long interest in actual states of madness has a literary political consequence which During does not adequately acknowledge. Perhaps, it is less the case that White cannot use these 'advanced, academised flows' than that his project lies elsewhere. His progressively more attuned explorations of madness within the context of contemporary Australian society are not just metaphorically motivated, that is the madness of character is not used solely as a metaphor of what is wrong in the wider social world, but are an attempt to capture what are actual liminal states, some of which defy language to an extent that they are not able to be captured in common everyday discourse, and certainly not in advanced, academic ones. Perhaps, White refrains from the Freudian commentary on Waldo's inherently ambivalent, conflicted and confused gift of a doll to Mrs Poulter because the logic of his presentation compels him to do so. The 'pastoral mode'[16] which During critiques might be an attempt on White's part to express some of the lacunae, forced pacificity and lack of self-consciousness that Waldo, in spite of being the more socially able of the two brothers, feels. So one could see the Waldo/Arthur figure in *The Solid Mandala* as a continuation of the character of Theordora Goodman in *The Aunt's Story*. Therefore, one could consider Patrick White's writing of madness in the different modes – from modernism to pastoral – as an ongoing investigation into how the actual or possible madness within us fits in.

Notes

1 Patrick White, *The Aunt's Story* (Sydney: Vintage, 1994). All subsequent references to this edition appear in parentheses in the text. Daniel Paul Schreber, *Memoirs of My Nervous Illness*, trans. and ed Ida MacAlpine and Richard A. Hunter (New York: New York Review Books Classics, 2000). All subsequent references to this edition appear in parentheses in the text.

2 See, for example, the discussion of Patrick White's style by Carolyn Bliss, *Patrick White's Fiction: The Paradox of Fortunate Failure* (London: Macmillan, 1986); William Walsh, *Patrick White's Fiction* (Sydney: George Allen & Unwin, 1977); and Rodney Stenning Edgecombe, *Vision and Style in Patrick White* (Tuscaloosa: University of Alabama Press, 1989).
3 Simon During, *Patrick White* (Oxford: Oxford University Press, 1996), 23.
4 See 'Psychoanalytic Notes on an Autobiographical Account of a Case of Paranoia (Dementia Paranoides)' (1911) in Sigmund Freud, *The Standard Edition of the Complete Psychological Works of Sigmund Freud Volume XII*, trans. James Strachey (London: Vintage, 2001), 9–84.
5 See Schreber's account of his visions 'seer of spirits' in *Memoirs*, Chapter 6.
6 Eugene Minkowski, *Lived Time: Phenomenological and Psychopathological Studies* (Evanston, IL: Northwestern University Press, 1970), 429.
7 Minkowski, *Lived Time*, 426.
8 See the discussion of the 'double book keeping' of schizophrenia in Louis Sass, *Paradoxes of Delusion: Wittgenstein, Schreber and the Schizophrenic Mind* (Ithaca, NY: Cornell University Press, 1994), 21, 43.
9 Zvi Lothane, *In Defense of Schreber: Soul Murder and Psychiatry* (New York: Routledge, 1992), 436.
10 See William Niederland, *The Schreber Case* (Hilldale, NJ: Analytic Press, 1984) and Morton Schatzman, *Soul Murder: Persecution in the Family* (London: Penguin, 1976).
11 Sass, *Paradoxes*, 48.
12 Louis Sass, *Madness and Modernism: Insanity in the Light of Modern Art, Literature and Thought* (Cambridge, MA: Harvard University Press, 1992).
13 'The art of conducting my life in the mad position I find myself – and I do not mean here the relationship with my environment but the absurd relation between God and myself which is contrary to the Order of the World – consists in finding a fitting middle course in which both parties, God and man, fare best' (*Memoirs*, 251).
14 Simon During, 'Patrick White, Saul Bellow and the Problem of Literary Value', *Australian Literary Studies* 27, no. 3 (2012), 1–17.
15 During, 'Problem', 15.
16 See During's discussion of the pastoral mode: 'And that is because the pastoral mode does not allow White to be quite certain of the degree to which his characters can be granted self-consciousness, while the narration's limited intellectual range cannot call upon a discourse that can sufficiently present Waldo's implied Freudian psychology.' During, 'Problem', 13.

Chapter 9

DESPERATE, MARVELLOUS SHUTTLING: WHITE'S AMBIVALENT MODERNISM

Gail Jones

In the conclusion to his masterwork *Minima Moralia* (1962), Theodor Adorno meditated on the 'irrationality' of post–World War II culture. Modernism he claimed was governed by 'occultism', by a regressive form of deranged thinking in which a kind of banal supernaturalism offered emotional recompense for the shattered real. If the war had destroyed reason, if history was represented in camps, ruins, death and displacement, there were forms of delusional certainty that might offer another kind of authority, in this case unimpeachable because finally inscrutable. Just as Zygmunt Bauman asserted the 'modernity' of the Holocaust so Adorno suggests the grim register of modern times. '[T]he veiled tendency of society towards disaster,' he argues, 'lulls its victims in a false revelation, with a hallucinated phenomenon.'[1] Occultism in his terms refers to forms of the relinquishment of agency for fate, surrender to commodity fetishism ('a world congealed into products'),[2] a subject position characterized by paranoia and neurasthenia, and the substitution of fantasy, spectacle and superstition for reliable historical and material knowledge. In Adorno's later work he examined, as an ideological exemplar, the astrology columns of the *Los Angeles Times*, finding therein the confirmation of his sense that historical understanding had been converted through mass culture to alienated hocus pocus.[3]

I wish to consider in this chapter how might we theorize the modernist irrational in the work of White – specifically in his immediate post-war novel, *The Aunt's Story* (1946) – but also to place it alongside an argument that respects and considers seriously the audacity of his images, the genuine claim of his work to a radical stylistics and a dissenting novelty.[4] I want too to include recognition of the painterly aspiration of the imagery – preoccupied, to a large extent, with colour, abstraction, shapes and spatial form, which situates his phantasmagorias, his imagistic exorbitance, in the context not only of postcolonial modernisms, in dialogue with the visual arts, but also in a particular metaphysic of the image, not foundational or propositional, not subject to realist verification, but idealist, formalist and wrought (perhaps *overwrought*) with what we might call auratic confidence. Moreover since it is the hocus pocus, the spiritualism, that is often controversial in White's work, I want likewise to examine it afresh here, to ask how it is founded and by what narratorial logic it proceeds.

In *The Aunt's Story* there is a scene in which Theodora, the mystical aunt of White's tale, wanders the streets of Sydney:

> In the streets in which Theodora walked at dusk, the sky was restless. Its fever fluctuated. The violet welts and crimson wounds showed. The trams gushed sparks. All along the streets the hour was fusing even the fragments of unrelated lives, almost of Theodora Goodman. The faces clotting at corners were not so very obscure in this light. The veins were throbbing with the same purple. It was about this time that Theodora noticed the big white flower, glittering and quivering with pollen, grow slowly from the pavement, sway and bend, offering its thick arum skin.
>
> Theodora felt the gust of the white woman. She felt her eyes. She saw the wet lips that many nights had pulped. [...] Out of the past Pearl fell. (124–25)

My first point is a formal one, to do with stylistic occultation. Typically, White invests in scenes of mystification, in which his protagonists encounter radically incommensurable orders of being, rendered in a mode of baroque embodiment.

Theodora is here in an 'unreal city', hyper-modernist; she encounters the revenant of her former servant, Pearl, now a prostitute, in terms that abstract her as a raw and fleshy emanation of the dusk. Pearl is both of the world, immediate in hyperbolic and dismembered ways – the welts, the gashes, the throbbing, the gushing, all expressive of a kind of sexual wound – and pure abstraction, a whiteness, a flower, a token of paranormal connection. In her state of pyschaesthenia, Theodora precariously knits artifice and being-in-the-world; White's carnality is here almost preposterous, yet he wants also to transvalue the encounter so that it is – indeed – a superintendent fusing of lives. Reminiscent of the work of Albert Tucker (I have in mind an image like *The Victory Girls* of 1943 in which prostitutes are represented in violent distortion as merely breasts and oversized mouths),[5] this encounter is arguably at the expense of Pearl, cast as a modernist type so that Theodora might have her moment of connection.

Describing modernist painting, T. J. Clark has argued that formal oscillation, 'a desperate, marvellous shuttling between a fantasy of cold artifice and an answering one of immediacy and being-in-the-world' typifies the fitful charter of modernist image making.[6] These tendencies cannot be reconciled, Clark argues, in the epistemological and social regimes of a modernist aesthetic. Irresolution is in his view the signature mark of modernist art. What struck me was how succinctly this description identifies a kind of tension in White's work, the word 'shuttling' suggesting textual agitation and indeterminacy.

Three pages later White writes:

> But Theodora would have blocked her ears with wax. She could not bear to face the islands from which Pearl sang. Now her veins ebbed, which had flowed before. Almost overhead hung an almost stationary electric bulb. Pearl saw this too. Her white face was streaky grey.
> 'Sometimes it winks,' Pearl said. 'Sometimes it just looks.' (127)

So added to the wasteland-ish 'unreal city' is *Ulysses* (the Cyclops, the Sirens); this is an allusion both consolidated and confounded throughout the text. Theodora's mother is at one stage figured as Penelope, her father as Ulysses, then Theodora is Ulysses, *becoming-man* as it were; moreover the novel is beset with a pan-classicism in terms of geographic idealizations – there is Egypt figured as Meroë, there is Greece and Turkey, referenced as a Yeatsian Byzantium; there is also a mystical Syrian (a travelling salesman), a charismatic Greek cello player and various modernist personages, assembled as Theodora's avatars in the Hôtel du Midi, in the centre of the text and in the centre of Europe.

Gertie Stepper, an earlier servant, refers to the Syrian as a 'Horiental' (29); in this comic misnaming is a kind of oblique reference to the lost significance of the spiritual in Australia, which White locates in the Eastern Orthodox church – that of golden iconography – and the intuition that 'from the deserts the prophets come',[7] that it is in empty rocky, spaces that trans-individual and trans-historical mysticism is possible. This is occultism of an antiquarian kind – not astrology columns, predictable and banal, the adherence to which Adorno called 'woeful idiocy',[8] but the mystical tradition filtered by White's modernist contemporaries – alchemical, densely figurative, adverting to timeless verities not as received authority but practised in bodily and mental extremity. The individualist quest for the past *as* the future is typical, it seems to me, of high-modernist disillusion and an unfortunate cynicism as to the feasibility of a model of redemption that is instead social and political.

White's occult practice is in part purely literary-ideological, an adherence to the high-modernist subsumption of ordinary life into glorifying myth. But the passages I've quoted suggest what Walter Benjamin calls the 'essence of melancholic immersion', in which fragments become allegories of loss, and intention, he says, 'faithlessly leaps forward to the idea of resurrection'.[9] (It is the word 'faithlessly' that interests me here: I don't have time to explore this but this is my way of thinking through the heterodox, non-Christian mode of resurrection practised through images.[10])

At the same time, however, there is a commitment to the stuff of the body, to the mess and perplexion of corporeality that functions almost as a substrata of skepticism about idealized and occulted experience. In White's novels characters fart, spit, belch, have indigestion; they suck their teeth, taste their sweat, are subject to errant desires and inconvenient *impingements* – to use Judith Butler's term for the way narrative situations submit to bodily imperatives in even the most idealized forms of address.[11] And then there is mortality: 'Greeks are happiest dying,' says the Greek cello player (108); White is fascinated by decay and degeneration, arguably a signal form of the colonial modernism of declining empire.[12]

Although thematically Theodora must die to be reborn in a spiritual apotheosis, she is figured not as a holy innocent but as a kind of murderer. The embedded story of Jack Frost, a pastry-cook from Clovelly (in Sydney) who murdered his wife and three girls in post-war madness, is also one of Theodora's displaced identifications – there is a scene in which Theodora contemplates the local church, made cardboard and flimsy by the summertime humidity (96) – and what follows is a description of the murder, committed on a Sunday morning, secular and shocking.

> The Jack Frost murders had struck a chord of mass hysteria, which was always waiting to sound, and now particularly, since the war, since people had been left high and dry by other horrors. (98)

This is the kind of mass experience Adorno is interested in, the index of cultural anxieties, repressed desires and ideological confusion. But the imagistic texture here is peculiar. Locals remember Jack Frost's tarts, cakes and cream puffs, sitting nested on paper doilies (96–97), and are shocked by the apparently anomalous violence in what White calls 'the wasteland in the suburbs' (97). When Section Two of the novel, the 'Jardin Exotique', ends in a conflagration that proleptically implicates the Second World War, White confirms that his is not a version of spiritual quest beyond the body and history, but cognizant of both trauma and historical violence. The Jewish twins in the hotel, the Desmoiselles Bloch, are governed, almost palpably, by their all-too-human future to come. There is a kind of assertive vulgar materialism, a being-in-the-world, to cite Clark again, which exists alongside bizarrely oracular dialogue, saintly aspiration and what might otherwise be regarded as a politics of disengagement or retreat.

Neither is White wholly convinced by the famous Yeatsian dictum that artists must shoulder what the priest can no longer carry.[13] Although attached to a kind of hieratic model of the artist, and the mystic as a special kind of artist, White's metaphysics of bodily presence also complicates his apparently Yeatsian hierophancy. Moreover, his affiliation is as much with jagged imagism as with the suave European prose tradition, and the non-realist 'Jardin Exotique' section may be read as an almost Vorticist explosion; its imagery is reminiscent of surrealism (a poet who resembles a walking cello), its characters sometimes types of modernist writers (there is a fanatical futurist in the Marinetti style) and its shifts of identity, a kind of system of contagion, is a version of inter-subjectivity and neurotic transference that owes much to post-Freudian psychology. Assembled in the Jardin are all the figures of European high art: Chekovian and Dostoevskian Russians, Jamesian Americans and English poets. These suffer the auto-da-fe from which, in narrative terms at least, it is only Theodora who emerges into the future.

Like many readers, I have long been fascinated by the Jardin of *The Aunt's Story*. After what looks like a fairly conventional opening to the novel – the death of the mother, a narrative of childhood, the heroine's emancipation – White submits Theodora to rash disintegration. In what resembles dream-work she becomes, prismatically, every character. Mystical flowers, pollen, gold and fire reappear; Theodora communes with and in a sense becomes a ghost; characters are decadent, unemployed and sadistically motivated, speaking always of destruction and the casual cruelties they share. Yet what is compelling is the experimentation with subjectivity and time and the ways in which it allows objects in the narrative to be read as what Walter Benjamin called *the dialectical image*. These link material culture with its history, crystallize a way of seeing that connects stasis and time, offer not transcendence but 'profane illumination'.[14] Notoriously vague Benjamin was interested in expressing the history that resides in images, the way 'progress' might be interrogated by the coexistence of catastrophe.[15] The Jardin is like the Arcade of Benjamin's meditation, a space in which objects are not symbolic of ideal unities but full of details redeemed from neglect, discredit and deathly 'enshrinement' by our tender and resurrecting attention.[16] Just as Pearl connotes a constellation of historical references and is poignant in her abjected historical role, so Theodora negotiates her selves, her identifications, through her own modest history recapitulated in literary and fascist Europe. At the centre of this section is a nautilus, a fragile shell, a traveling symbol, which is the icon of both integrity and destruction. It is, significantly, a natural fetish rather than a commodity or reification, and in this it prepares the way for the pastoral resolution to the novel.

In the third section of the novel, the short conclusion, Theodora arrives in New Mexico,[17] disembarks from a train, disposes of her tokens of identification (passport, money, tickets and name) and finds herself speaking in intimate alliance to a man who is not there. Pacific and dreamy, told in the phenomenology of madness or enlightenment, Theodora discovers that 'true permanence is a state of multiplication and division' (284). There is light, wheat and rural quiet. In a fascinating comment on the pastoral paintings of Pissarro, Clark writes, 'What matters is that the hieratic be inseparable from the commonplace, and that flatness be twisted together – weirdly, unresolvedly – with inwardness and depth.'[18] Clark is speaking of the gold-leaf effects of certain painterly techniques, of the sense of calm depth beneath a stippled surface and of the solar intelligence, as it were, that might render a scene radiant but not lose the ordinary and specific loveliness of things. White of course had more than a passing interest in visual arts,[19] and what is significant here is the sense of visual paradigm at work; not only dialectical images, those soliciting historical awareness, but a sense of the artefact achieved, the culmination of a knowing. So the irrational here is not religious, exactly, not hocus pocus; rather it is a meditation, I think, on interdependence, death and the transitivity of self. One could argue that there is no 'social' at the novel's end, only a crazed interior, but this is to neglect the long rehearsals of the Jardin that insist on the inescapability of one's own history, even if one is a mystic. There are overextended symbols of modernist convention – the black rose that trembles on Theodora's hat, for example – but there are also farm boots squeaking, the sipping of milk, the eating of bread and the kindness of strangers.

At the end of *Minima Moralia*, the miserable Adorno writes: 'The only philosophy that can be responsibly practised in the face of despair is the attempt to contemplate all things as they would present themselves from the standpoint of redemption.'[20] Like Benjamin he is not without eschatological desires; and not all supernaturalisms, clearly, are the same. The auratic confidence of White's image making may at least be read as a fastidious refusal of the supremacy of the commodity; and the often wretched physicality of his characters, which White inflicts, if you like, indicates a wish to preserve above all another kind of materialism – somewhat apoliticial, certainly, but with its own clever negotiation of modernist forms and ideologies, its own refusal of authoritarian history. Europe is rejected for the robust new world; Australia, read not through the 'belatedness' thought characteristic of Australian modernism,[21] is the necessary stage to another revelation. For Benjamin the point of profane illumination was to break the historical continuum, to remind us of the 'now-time' of fulfilled experience.[22] White's modernism, for all its typical ambivalence, is also vigorous, assertive and rudely material. Moreover, it is driven by the desire, I would suggest, for an artefact of completion, a painterly artefact, dare I say, finally *iconic*.

Notes

1 Theodor Adorno, *Minima Moralia: Reflections from Damaged Life*, trans. E. F. N. Jephcott (London: Verso, 2010), 239. Zygmunt Bauman, *Modernity and the Holocaust* (Cambridge: Polity, 1989).
2 Adorno, *Minima*, 239.
3 Thomas Adorno, 'The Starts Down to Earth', *Telos* 19 (Spring 1974): 19–30.
4 Patrick White, *The Aunt's Story* (Sydney: Vintage, 1994). All subsequent references to this edition appear in parentheses in the text.
5 Albert Tucker, *Victory Girls*, NGA 71.42, National Gallery of Australia, accessed 4 April 2014 online: http://artsearch.nga.gov.au/Detail.cfm?IRN=82187.
6 T. J. Clark, *Farewell to an Idea: Episodes from a History of Modernism* (New Haven, CT: Yale University Press, 1999), 10.
7 A. D. Hope, 'Australia' (1939), *The Australian Poetry Library*, accessed 8 April 2014 online: http://www.poetrylibrary.edu.au/poets/hope-a-d/australia-0146006.
8 Adorno, *Minima*, 241.
9 Walter Benjamin, *The Origin of German Tragic Drama* (1928) cited in Eric L. Santner, *On Creaturely Life: Rilke, Benjamin, Sebald* (Chicago: University of Chicago Press, 2006), 87.
10 At one stage David Marr describes White as 'a believer without any formal faith'; the context is a story of White heading out to buy a set of Tarot cards in London in 1963, introduced by the painter Lawrence Daws. David Marr, *Patrick White: A Life* (Sydney: Random House, 1991), 451. From an Anglican background, 'White's upbringing had done more for his prose than his faith'; Marr, *Life*, 283.
11 See, for example, Thomas Dumm and Judith Butler, 'Giving Away, Giving Over: A Conversation with Judith Butler', *Massachusetts Review* 49, no. 1–2 (Spring/Summer, 2008): 95–105 (99).
12 Rod Edmond, 'Home and Away: Degeneration in Modernist and Imperialist discourse' in *Modernism and Empire: Writing and British Coloniality, 1890–1940*, Howard J. Booth and Nigel Rigby, eds (Manchester: Manchester University Press 2000): 39–63.
13 'The arts are, I believe, about to take upon their shoulders the burdens that have fallen from the shoulders of priests, and to lead us back upon our journey by filling our thoughts with the essences of things, and not with things'. W. B. Yeats, 'The Autumn of the Body', in *Ideas of Good and Evil* (London: A. H. Bullen, 1903), 303.
14 See Walter Benjamin, 'Surrealism: The Last Snapshot of the European Intelligentsia' (1927).
15 Benjamin *The Arcades Project*, 473
16 See also Susan Buck-Morss, *The Dialectics of Seeing: Walter Benjamin and the Arcades Project* (1989; Cambridge, MA: MIT Press, 1991), 221.
17 According to Marr, *Life*, 242.
18 Clark, *Farewell*, 68.
19 See Helen Verity Hewitt, *Patrick White: Painter Manqué* (Melbourne: Miegunyah Press, 2002).
20 Adorno, *Minima*, 247.
21 See Bill Ashcroft and John Salter, 'Modernism's Empire: Australia and the Cultural Imperialism of Style', in Booth and Rigby, *Modernism*, 292–34.
22 'The employment of the theory of dialectical images [...] represents an attempt on Benjamin's part to transpose the theory of "ideas" or "monads" of the *Trauerspiel* study from an idealist to a materialist framework [...]. The major difference between the two renditions of the theory is that the later form abjures references to the tradition

of Western metaphysics and instead draws its inspiration from concrete aspects of contemporary social life. Nevertheless [...] both attempt to deduce and image of transcendence while remaining wholly *within* the boundaries of the empirical world of experience. The ultimate concern of both approaches is the *redemption* of phenomena from the profane continuum of historical existence and their transformation into images of fulfillment or *now-time*.' Richard Wolin, *Walter Benjamin: An Aesthetic of Redemption* (New York: Columbia University Press, 1982), 125–26.

Chapter 10

'TIME AND ITS FELLOW CONSPIRATOR SPACE': PATRICK WHITE'S *A FRINGE OF LEAVES*

Brigid Rooney

If, as some say, timing is everything, the temporal rhythm of Patrick White's drafting of *A Fringe of Leaves* (1976) – in two bursts more than a decade apart (1961 and 1975) – must have had a bearing on its curiously doubled temporalities, its thickening and interleaving of past, present and future.[1] Events in White's life at the time of drafting may also have contributed to the studied theatricality of its recurring settings, or chronotopes: of boat, shipwreck, island, church and forest clearing. Mikhail Bakhtin provides a painterly description of the literary-artistic chronotope:

> ... spatial and temporal indicators are fused into one carefully thought out, concrete whole. Time, as it were, thickens, takes on flesh, becomes artistically visible; likewise, space becomes charged and responsive to the movements of time, plot and history. This intersection of axes and fusion of indicators characterizes the artistic chronotope.[2]

While this applies to any novel, it resonates with White's fictional vision in particular ways. In *Riders in the Chariot* (1961), for example, there is a telling description of Alf Dubbo's painting, 'The Chariot Thing' in which artistic illusion – standing for fictional fabrication – affords an unlikely access to truth. When viewed from an angle the painting fleetingly achieves an optical illusion, 'a reversal of the relationship between permanence and motion', in which the banks of the river seem to move, while the river lies still: 'So he encouraged an illusion which was also a truth, and from which the timid might retreat simply by changing their position.'[3]

While the irreversible flow of the river allegorizes phenomenal time, the painting's optical inversion – the solid riverbank flowing against the fixity of the river – allegorizes the literary-artistic project itself. Art suspends and thickens time, and liquefies place. All that is solid melts, and all that melts solidifies. There is a cryptic quality to White's chronotopic imagery. It promises without quite revealing truths. Or more precisely, it dwells on an infinite deferral between promise and revelation. A spatio-temporal reversal is effected by the optics of the image from the standpoint of the viewer. By implicating spectator and spectacle, White's vignette of Dubbo's painting also evokes the agonistic theatre of public appearing; it reverberates with self-consciousness about its own image production. In this chapter's discussion of *A Fringe of Leaves*, I pay attention to its painterly and theatrical scenes – or chronotopes – and how they function as enclosures of revelation and encryption. Through these time-infused spaces, protagonist Ellen Gluyas Roxburgh's outward journey reverses to become an interior journey into the self. In my reading, the novel's timing – its writing and reception – conspire with its narrative composition. From this angle, I suggest we may glimpse how configurations of time and space in *A Fringe of Leaves* illuminate and encrypt both the settler-colonial condition and White's own literary project.

The Timing and Early Reception of *A Fringe of Leaves*

According to David Marr, the idea for *A Fringe of Leaves* germinated in 1958 when White first heard from Sidney Nolan about the 1836 Eliza Fraser shipwreck, with its castaway and frontier captivity ordeal.[4] Both men were staying in Fort Lauderdale in Florida in a climate, White remarked, that 'makes one feel like a beachcomber, a tropical wreck [...]'.[5] Having heard of Eliza Fraser from Barrett Reid and read about her in the John Oxley collection in Brisbane, Nolan visited Fraser Island in 1947, where he began, *in situ*, his culturally influential paintings of the subject. These remarkable works stimulated not only White's novel but also, as Anthony Hassall has shown, South African writer Andre Brink's *An Instant in the Wind* (1976). Yet White began research for the novel – after dispatching *Riders in the Chariot* to Viking Press – as early as June 1961, sailing from Sydney by coastal steamer, the *Manoora*, north along the eastern coast to Brisbane, in Eliza Fraser's wake. After visiting the painter Ian Fairweather on Bribie Island, White travelled by train to Maryborough from where, after some difficulties, he was flown by light aircraft to Fraser Island, first circling the island by air and then walking through its rainforest on foot. Marr contends that the environment – seascape, island, rainforest and coast – made a profound and lasting impression. In Maryborough White spoke with Wilf Reeves, an Aboriginal informant who contested, according to Marr, dominant settler accounts of the Eliza Fraser story. White began his first draft of *A Fringe of Leaves* in the midst of – and as antidote to – the excitement of rehearsals for the Adelaide University Guild's debut production of *The Ham Funeral*. The distractions of opening night and the play's controversial reception added to a blockage White was already suffering and he put the first draft aside. He began his second draft in May 1975 in the declining months of the Whitlam Government, at a time of national uncertainty and at a highly theatrical juncture in his career. Awarded the Nobel Prize for Literature in 1973, White was now an outspoken activist, a literary figurehead on the national stage, a crusader against urban development and in 1974 a campaigner for the re-election of Whitlam's government.[6]

Both White's Nobel Prize win and his turn to activism were touchstones for early reviewers of *A Fringe of Leaves*. Reminiscent of *Voss*, this new novel was reassuringly masterly while presenting new variations on familiar themes.[7] Not unexpectedly Leonie Kramer cast a cold eye over its style and approach. Her *Quadrant* review provoked counter-readings by Suzanne Edgar, Veronica Brady, Dennis Haskell and others.[8] In these and subsequent readings, Ellen Roxburgh emerges as a site of critical fascination through which the novel's allegorical, ethical and political dimensions may be construed; for Laurie Hergenhan *A Fringe of Leaves* – as historical fiction – works allegorically to provide 'a parable of the present'.[9] In her evocation of, and divergence from, the historical Eliza Fraser, Ellen is the key to White's themes of integrity, love and compassion, and of a savage nature that mirrors the brutality of civilization.[10] *A Fringe of Leaves* was also said to express a new turn in White's writing: though still ironic, no character is wholly caricatured and its conclusion seems to bring a new beginning, a restored faith in human possibility.[11] While some reportedly balked at its representation of Aboriginal people, Veronica Brady (among others) argued that the novel conveyed its sympathy by undermining Eurocentric dichotomies of civilization and savagery.[12] It is true that the narrative attributes the greatest savagery to the convict-driven respectable white world that Ellen must re-enter; and the narrative is more concerned with the injustice of the penal system than it is with the wrongs of frontier dispossession. These early readings have long been overtaken (especially in the post-Mabo era) by postcolonial critique which finds in captivity narratives a problematic reprise of the 'white Aboriginal' figure. In light of this critique, and even though White's mid-1970s novel was written too early to engage with these debates (and may even be considered as a contribution to the wider cultural conversation that informs present critical horizons), it is impossible to remain innocent of white-settler fiction's role in recuperating settler selves and belonging and, by extension, nation in a way that assimilates, annexes and displaces Aboriginal culture and claims.[13]

So it was a different cultural horizon within which Veronica Brady read the frontier in *A Fringe of Leaves* (as she did in 1983) as having 'Janus-like possibilities' by looking back to an Aboriginal (primitive-natural) model that deconstructs white Australia and forward to the nation's incorporation of a fuller range of human experiences.[14] Brady's observation is negatively mirrored in Simon During's (1996) critical appraisal of White's Janus-like timing in the Australian literary field; During sees him as anachronistic, as the last representative of an outmoded Anglo-Australian squattocracy.[15] Unsympathetic reading positions can, however, yield new perspectives. In her review of *A Fringe of Leaves*, for example, Leonie Kramer dislikes the way White's leisurely rhythm drags against the momentum of dramatic event: 'The pace', she says, 'is slow', giving rise to 'a curious sense of lethargy'. Contributing to this temporality is the novel's stage management – what Kramer sees as its melodramatic contrivances and its disconnection between actions and character: its gestures, she says, are 'decorative rather than illuminating'.[16] Further, she contends White's familiar syntactic device (of the conditional tense) lends a 'spurious subtlety to the narrative', creating 'an illusion of depth and complexity in character not conveyed by the action itself'. Yet despite Kramer's discomfort, these are the very qualities in *A Fringe of Leaves* that constitute what Guy Davidson identifies as the camp aesthetic of White's ornamental surfaces.[17] White's habit of conjuring illusory depths through surfaces, evident elsewhere in his writing, takes specific form in *A Fringe of Leaves* through the narrative's troping of theatricality, spectacle and mirroring and through its particular blend of novelistic realism with melodramatic excess.

Not only the timing and reception of *A Fringe of Leaves* but the narrative itself is marked by a Janus-like, forward–backward, prospective–retrospective gaze. Ellen Roxburgh is the stabilizing point that marks the workings of this gaze. Commentators have noted that in her progress through changing landscapes and social regimes, Ellen exhibits a combination of passivity and strength; her ability to straddle different worlds disrupts colonial binaries.[18] She also figures a textual and meta-textual crossroads: as White's female 'avatar' she expresses both his literary and public roles (calibrated by the epistemology of the closet) and his late colonial position in Australian culture.[19]

Everywhere in *A Fringe of Leaves*, not only in the case of its protagonist but also through its littoral landscapes and its tropes of transport and theatre, we find figures of liminality. The liminal is a zone that recurs, as Andrew McCann has shown, in White's earlier works.[20] But in *A Fringe of Leaves*, the zone of the edge is developed as a fully elaborated theme and narrative attribute. It is established in both spatial and temporal terms, extending through a series of chronotopes – where chronotopes are understood as spaces cross-hatched with the flow of time. In particular we find carriages or vehicles with their contained interiors, within which the contraflows of narrative time are condensed. Layered and folded figures of time–space are key narrative units in White's modernist myth making.[21] Hence in the calm prelude to the scene of shipwreck in *A Fringe of Leaves*, we find the passengers 'lulled by air and motion and the mystical permutations of canvas':

> Time, and its fellow conspirator space, subtler for its present watery guise, were never in more perfect accord, and when on the seventh day the ship nosed gently into fog, the impression of limitless unity was increased, if not for all the voyagers, for Mrs Roxburgh, unquestionably. (162)

Dramatically doubling each other as co-conspirators, time and space are figured here as narrative agents: that is, they are metaphorically pictured as the constitutive elements of Bakhtin's chronotopes. Time and space invest themselves in sea/air ('watery guise') and 'ship', making these spaces the vectors through which narrative event, the plotted story, is drawn. The loaded reflexivity of White's metaphoric language may be what creates Kramer's sense of 'lethargy': continual notice is given to the workings of narrative itself, its structuring metaphoricity, its chronotopic orchestration and its speculative, counterfactual status (reinforced by White's constant use of the conditional mood).[22] In this light we can consider the way White's vehicles produce densities of meta-narrative meaning. His vehicles are not only metaphoric but also play upon the idea of metaphor as vehicle. The etymology of metaphor is to carry across, to bear, to transfer and to transport.[23] As is well understood, 'vehicles' are supremely novelistic – and cinematic – motifs. Trains, boats, planes and automobiles routinely signify both the regulated machine time of modernity and subjective temporalities involved in processes of reading or viewing. Vehicles are figures that metaphorize contradictions between movement and stasis experienced by readers phenomenologically, in the tension between the scaffold of linear plot and its sequencing, between temporally unfolding narration and its divergent orientations towards time.[24] Similarly, the act of reading a novel, which cultivates the self's private interiority, can be thought of as conditional to its public display.[25] In *A Fringe of Leaves*, how do vehicles contribute to the narrative's chronotopic system? What kind of vehicle is Ellen herself? What role does she play in White's literary occupation of Australian space?

Of carriages as chronotopes

The opening *in medias res* of *A Fringe of Leaves* puts us alongside three occupants of a horse-drawn carriage travelling through colonial Sydney. Mr and Mrs Merivale and Miss Scrimshaw are being carried away from Circular Wharf where they have just been visiting the Roxburghs, whose ship the *Bristol Maid* is about to embark for England. Their dialogue dramatizes the tenuous respectability of Anglo-colonial Sydney's genteel class through whose carriage window appears an alien world of bleached grass and scorched earth (10), as a class that barely holds itself aloft from truculent emancipists with their indecent rumours of frontier murder. The scene works as a theatrical set-piece, a prologue to the main action, which concludes with a performative flourish: 'The occupants of the carriage were rolled on into the deepening afternoon, and finally, like minor actors who have spoken a prologue, took themselves off into the wings' (24).

A succession of scenes inside moving carriages serves as narrative vehicle for Ellen Roxburgh's journey from the claustrophobia of colonial society, through the rendering down of self through privation, exposure and nakedness, to humility and sensual awakening and into moral strength, empathy and love. As Hergenhan puts it, Ellen's journey involves a 'moral education'.[26] The movement of the horse-drawn carriage – in the first chapter – replicates the narrative's mobility of view and tropes the cultivation of interiority and selfhood through sentimental journey. In so doing White seems to tap into, re-function and adapt the tradition of the sentimental novel to the settler-colonial context. For Terry Eagleton, eighteenth-century discourses of moral sentiment, privileging sympathetic entry to the viewpoint of others (a development integral to the European and English novel), were a lubricant for commercial capitalism.[27] In his discussion of sentimental in narratives over time, James Chandler highlights the vehicular trope in Lawrence Sterne's novel *A Sentimental Journey*. Through paronomasia or punning motion is paired with emotion, and physical locomotion with reading as sentimental journey. For Chandler, the vehicular signifies the sentimental, and recurs uncannily in later novels and cinema.[28]

If the sentimental is an undercurrent in *A Fringe of Leaves*, this is complicated by White's meta-fictional treatment of colonial history, exemplified in modernist narrative patterns of spatio-temporal inversion. For example, the direction in which the carriage travels is doubled by the direction of its occupants' dialogue. The carriage travels away from the coast while the occupants engage in retrospective reflection on the encounter they have just had with the Roxburghs aboard the *Bristol Maid*. Amid rich comic dialogue in which the characters speculate about Ellen Roxburgh's future, the narrative effects a metaphoric convergence of their otherwise disparate, diverging vehicles:

> Rocked together and apart by the uneven surface of the street the occupants were at the mercy of the land as seaborne passengers are threatened by the waves (9).

The conflation of carriage with boat thickens space and time. This vehicular trope is repeated and amplified through the next four chapters as boat supersedes carriage and the *Bristol Maid* carries its occupants northwards along the Australian coastline towards its destiny on Queensland's reef. As the boat sails north, the retrospective narration travels south, mapping Ellen's travels from childhood when, as humble Ellen Gluyas of Land's End, Cornwall, she marries above her station, lives with her husband Austin Roxburgh at his estate at Cheltenham, then journeys with him to the novel's uttermost south, Van Diemen's Land where her brother-in-law, Mr Garnet Roxburgh, ravishes her. Van Diemen's Land geographically mirrors and inverts Cornwall's Land's End, as the narrative weaves its doubled, inverted directionality in both space and time, in an 'elaborate cat's cradle'.[29] That is, the narrative's southerly retrospection is hitched to the northerly moving plot of the ship's journey along Australia's eastern coast.

Carriages and boats join other emblems for time's moving containers: for vessels that enigmatically hold or yield the future. These include images of eggs, metonymically associating Ellen's body with birds (her 'plumage' is disarranged in the recollected scene of her seduction, or rape, by Garnet). At dinner with Captain Purdew on board the ship, the yawns that Ellen stifles in her throat are likened to a 'continuum of soft, unlaid eggs in the innards of a slaughtered hen' (156). This grotesque conjunction of unlaid eggs with slaughtered hen confounds birth with death, origin with termination. The knowledge that Ellen is pregnant is withheld from the reader here, though presented through the proleptic image of unlaid eggs; the first time reader awaits the future activity of retrospection.

These contained vessels – duplicates of the boat within which they are nested – are carried in forward motion along the narrative's temporal pathway. The temporality of pregnancy is ruptured by the crisis of shipwreck, when 'suddenly and brutally the sequence of events was wrenched out of control. There was a ramming. And grinding' (167). Bodies and effects are thrown into chaos. The disordering of bodies signals the disordering of plot, shifting and resetting its orientation. Ellen suffers an immediate transformation, as 'Half-fowl half woman', her teeth gash her husband's cheek (167) in an echo of the moment in which Garnet's teeth earlier grazed *her* cheek. Past, present and future events are in this way continually overlain, and spaces impregnated or encrypted with futurity.

The party decants into the longboat where clock-time seems deliriously suspended. The time of Ellen's body overlays the calendar time of events to which she (and the narration itself) is nevertheless captive. Here Ellen's pregnancy transitions to miscarriage, or still-birth. This makes of her body, in a kind of *mis en abyme*, a foundering vessel that replicates the foundering vessels that severally carry her, all becoming waterlogged and merging with the transformative oceanic element:

> On her the waters in the doomed boat reached higher, almost to her waist it seemed, clambering, lapping, sipping the blood out of her flaccid body.
> That was the least part of her. Herself sank. The fringe of her green shawl trailed through depths in which it was often indistinguishable from beaded weed or the veils and streamers of fish drifting and catching on coral hummocks then dissolving free for the simple reason that the whole universe was watered down. (227)

This amplifies an inverted equation drawn even earlier between Ellen's body and the boat. In a conversation with her husband, Ellen becomes the keeper or container of the implied, impending wreck of marriage: 'Her timbers hold the water in rather than keeping it at bay', and '[...] her heart, turning to water, lapped against the timbers of the stays in which she was boarded up' (35). Her husband Austin Roxburgh's fear of sensuality has cued Ellen's state of resigned reservation, a state complicated by the closeting – the boarding up – of her secret self – given she cannot divulge her recent abandonment with his brother, Garnet.

Through these images that join pregnancy to rupture, containment to transformation, Ellen Gluyas Roxburgh emerges as an encrypted, proleptic figure, marked by the past but oriented towards the future. Even her name is laden with significance, encrypted with future event, like eggs. Ellen's unusual Cornish maiden name, Gluyas, appears to be a variant of an Old French word, 'glaive', meaning 'lance' or 'spear'. Her married name, Roxburgh, has its origins in birds ('hroc' or rook) and fortifications (burgh) – and perhaps, also, books.[30] Ellen Gluyas Roxburgh collects, contains and signals a future of which those around her are unaware. She carries, as a vessel, the promise of what lies in the narrative's future, beyond the time of narrated events, into the time of the narration itself – that is, into the time of White and his readers in the (postcolonial) present. White's habitual use of the conditional mood – that which *would have been* had it not been for – signals and produces this doubled narrative temporality. The repeated fraying of boundaries between past, present and future – their overlaying – performs the occupation of Australian space as liminal and speculative.

Michel Foucault's account of heterotopias offers another angle on the play between carriages and chronotopes in White's novel. Unlike Bakhtin whose chronotopes are an element of novelistic discourse, Foucault' heterotopes (or heterochronotopes) designate sites in the world, some of which represent zones of otherness sequestered outside the envelope of the everyday. There is no direct connection between fictive chronotopes and heterotopias in the world, except insofar as they share broad discursive or narrative functions in forging the meanings of space. Even so, Foucault's example of the boat tacking between brothels and colonies offers a resonant point of connection with White's novel:

> [I]f we think, after all, that the boat is a floating piece of space, a place without a place, that exists by itself, that is closed in on itself and at the same time is given over to the infinity of the sea and that, from port to port, from tack to tack, from brothel to brothel, it goes as far as the colonies in search of the most precious treasures they conceal in their gardens, you will understand why the boat has not only been for our civilization, from the sixteenth century until the present, the great instrument of economic development [...], but has been simultaneously the greatest reserve of the imagination. The ship is the heterotopia *par excellence*. In civilizations without boats, dreams dry up, espionage takes the place of adventure, and the police take the place of pirates.[31]

An instrument of economic development and great reserve of the imagination, the boat is both literally and symbolically the vehicle of colonization: the boat fuses the geography of colonies with the literary imagination. It might not be too far-fetched to suggest, then, that White's narrative, with its recurring vehicular metaphors, references itself as a boat, as a heterochronotope. His narrative is an *other* sequestered world that mirrors – and perhaps conveys and secures – the everyday colony. White's novel clearly does not occupy extra-textual space, but in concert with the settler imaginary, his novel is a vector of occupation, of settler possession. This barely admissible knowledge is transported into *A Fringe of Leaves* through the dramatic irony that the novel's occupants (of boats and carriages) are simultaneously colonisers and captives, subject to the powerful colonial system of which they are also agents. That Ellen is a liminal figure, a marginal occupier, captive to the changing social rules of her changing circumstances, does not make her exceptional. Rather, she is exemplary and representative – as most readings of her role in the text suggest. With this in mind I want to think about White's chronotopes as carriages, and to ask how his meta-narrative signals (without fully disclosing) the role of the literary in occupying Australia.

Of chronotopes as carriages

Just as boats and eggs are time's incubators – with their embedded mythological meanings – so, quite evidently, are books. In their aspect as time capsules, books join this series of containers. The narrative reinforces this familiar trope through its self-reflexive, speculative play between historical realism and theatrical sensation. By association books assume vehicular attributes as conveyances for the self-consciousness of White's literary aesthetic. Ellen's failed reproductive body, sensual though it is, finds its parodic counterpart in the asexual sterility of her bookish husband Austin, from whose literary fetishism the narrative elicits much comedy. Austin entertains a fantasy construct of himself as an action hero, an assessment undermined through implied comparison with more hyper-masculine figures (such as his brother Garnet). This ironic presentation climaxes with Austin's indulgence in a feat of bravery when he returns to his inundated cabin to retrieve his waterlogged 'Elzevir', a rare edition of Virgil to which he clings as though it were a life raft. This feat of rescue, he imagines, will furnish him in the future, on return to his comfortable hearth in Cheltenham, with pleasant reminiscences of his heroism. Rather than the conditional mood, we encounter here the mood of future perfect, or of the future anterior, elsewhere ascribed by Elizabeth Povinelli to the anxieties of settler colonial modernity.[32] Austin's idealized masculinity is already bookish, a cultivated narrative. It is located in the anticipation of a future that directs his actions in the present. In other words, he is spurred on towards action by the thought that he *will have been* heroic. But events abort Austin's imagined future, rendering the spectacle of his narcissism both absurd and pitiable.

Austin's heroic interlude extends the irony around his penchant for the pastoral. Indeed White's novel might be described as exercising an anti-pastoral impulse, since the retreat to the country is exposed as fantasy — indeed, as literary conceit. Austin's marriage to the strong farm girl from Cornwall plays out yet also militates against bookish pastoral fantasies. While the narrative punishingly exhibits his foolishness, mocking his feeble efforts to enact derivative ideals of manliness, White's gaze on Austin seems nevertheless tender, moving and implicated. Gradually on the island Austin engages with events, first by manufacturing a poultice to draw the boil on the neck of the doomed Mr Spurgeon and then by springing to the aid of Captain Purdew, only in that moment to be speared himself. At this point, Ellen — subject to the destiny encrypted in her maiden name — becomes both spectator and spectacle: 'Now she too, was interminable, transfixed by time as painfully and mercilessly as by any spear' (239).

Earlier musing on Virgil, Austin had averred that 'death has always appeared to me something of a literary conceit' (35). His brutal mid-narrative death — effected by a spear through the throat — is theatre of the absurd, stripping pretension as well as meta-fictively playing on and rupturing the art–life, representation–reality divide. For Austin's death — as both the moment of transformation and the pivotal event of Ellen's life — is an event that ruptures and reinstates literary conceit. The spear stoppering his querulous voice becomes her point of reference for reordering her own life narrative, which now divides into before and after the spear. Later in the forest clearing with her lover, the convict Jack Chance, Ellen reflects:[33]

> Had it not been for his detachment, she might have re-lived against her will the last moments of what represented her real life. As it was, she only re-enacted them, brightly lit as for a troupe of actors on a stage seen from the depths of a darkened theatre, a woman stepping forward to drag a spear from out of the throat of a man lying wounded upon the sand. (292)

The literary fetishism that reduces death to literary conceit, to mere theatre, is pitted against the cruel theatricality of the scene of exposure as its spectator relives, remembers and re-imagines. Australian space is recast as an agonistic stage for performing the absolute irrelevance of the coloniser.

Impossibly, the space of stage or clearing in *A Fringe of Leaves* marks the site of the vast, absent interior of the continent. On board the boat Ellen longs to explore that other interior, metonymically suggested by the spiky, yellow-tasselled flower she finds while walking with Austin on Sydney's headland. Ellen does not journey 'in' to that vaster space but proceeds along the littoral edge, from boat to beach to forest clearing on the island, followed by coastal forest on the mainland. These are all heterotopias sequestered from the spheres of captivity they otherwise mirror, first among the Aboriginals and then among the colony's better classes. Hovering at the periphery of the narrative, the absent interior is metaphorically returned through the space of church and forest clearing. These contained interiors supplement both the unvisited depth of the continent and the interior self. They function theatrically, bounding and thickening the psychic drama, their spatial stillness ruptured by speed, movement and event. They are sites of divine communion, crisis and transformation of the subject. Ellen's immersion in the cold waters of St Hya's Well anticipates her seduction by Garnet in the forest dell in Van Diemen's Land. It is within a clearing deep in the island's forest that she participates in the rite of cannibalism. In a forest clearing, Ellen is dressed *by* the savages *as* a savage. In terms that anticipate White's most famous image for his own public/literary performance (in the title of his 1981 memoir, *Flaws in the Glass*),[34] she sees that: 'Their faces were her glass, in which she and they were temporarily united, either in mooning fantasy or a mystical relationship' (267). Not unlike Foucault's mirror, Australia's un-penetrated interior – virtualised and refracted in the faces of the savages – is the imagined point through which Ellen's gaze passes to find herself, another concavity. From horse and carriage, to boat, then on foot, her physical locomotion is inversely analogous to the intense psychological crossings – the sentimental journey – that she makes.

Leonie Kramer is neither complimentary nor alone in observing that the figure of Ellen Roxburgh recalls Shaw's *Pygmalion*,[35] and the theatrical connection once again proves salient. Austin Roxburgh at one point fears that his 'wife was the brittle work of art he was creating, the glaze of which might crack were she to become aware of her creator's flaws and transgressions' (202–3). The *Pygmalion* analogy speaks not only to the transformations that 'White's "Eliza"' undergoes in her travels through the English class system and across civilisation-wilderness boundaries.[36] In light of the work of Paul de Man and Peter Brooks, and following Monique Rooney's theorization of melodrama as transformative mode, behind Shaw's play lies Rousseau's *Pygmalion*, the inaugural melodrama of the artist and his sculpture, Galatea. White's theatricality places Ellen Roxburgh as a version of Galatea, a vessel for the self-created and self-mirroring figure of the artist.[37] White's third-person omniscient narration keeps Ellen centre stage. She is not only the figure upon whom our gaze is trained but also through whom events are relayed. In her role she is passive and active, agent and victim, morally courageous and malleable, helpless witness and spectacle. Ellen Roxburgh is correlative with White's literary endeavour at a particular juncture, the protean product of the artist's self-doubting gaze but also perhaps, in her calm endurance and resilience, enacts a forgiveness of that tortured self relayed in White's earlier, more closeted novels.

As the novel draws to a close, a set of crossing structures, generative of literary space, gather around Ellen Roxburgh. In the narrative's culminating sequence, Ellen emerges as a theatrical, statuesque figure who contains the anticipated future effected by White's literary archiving of the Eliza Frazer story. Ellen's return to society retraces and inverts her outward path. Emerging from the wilderness, she arrives naked at the home of the Oakes, a settler family who resemble her original Cornish family. She traverses various echelons of a now more remotely observed and thoroughly de-familiarised colonial world. The object of speculation, she is herself transformed, now fully sensitised to constraint and hypocrisy, to the sufferings of the oppressed. In a reprise of the opening scene, she journeys overland by carriage to Moreton Bay with Miss Scrimshaw, an ambivalent figure finally described as a cryptic eagle whose indeterminate qualities seem to resurrect or reincarnate something of Austin Roxburgh. Thence we follow both on board the *Princess Charlotte* bound for Sydney.

Ellen's confinement to the edge of the continent, an edge retraced through this sequence of narrative returns, belies and incites the novel's cultivation of psychic depths, and perversely figures its literary containment of Australian space. The space of surfaces produces concavities, just as surfaces in White's prose, as I have suggested elsewhere, produce depths in ways analogous to White's literary production of an imagined, collective interiority.[38] These mysterious, auratic depths are both manifested by and encrypted in Ellen's garnet-coloured dress – the 'garnet' externalising the interior self inaugurated by the rupturing encounter with Garnet, a moment linked to and theatrically refracted in preceding and subsequent events. In a final image Ellen embodies time to come. She becomes a spectacle that encrypts the ambivalent literary occupation of Australian space, refulgent in her return to obscurity. At the centre of the narrative optic, in the midst of domestic scenes within the ship, and object of fellow passenger Mr Jevons' admiring gaze, Ellen is ultimately a figure for the (would-be-postcolonial) reader's contemplation: a 'smouldering figure in garnet silk [...] a breathing statuary contained within the same ellipse of light' (404–5).

Notes

1 Patrick White, *A Fringe of Leaves* (London: Jonathan Cape, 1976). All subsequent references to this edition appear in parentheses in the text.
2 Mikhail Bakhtin, *The Dialogic Imagination: Four Essays*, trans. Michael Holquist (Austin: University of Texas Press, 1981), 84.
3 Patrick White, *Riders in the Chariot* (London: Eyre & Spottiswoode, 1961), 514.
4 The account in this paragraph is taken mainly from Marr's biography: David Marr, *Patrick White: A Life* (London: Jonathan Cape, 1991), 378–81, 397, 401, 413, 436, 529, 542–44.
5 Patrick White to David Moore, 15 September 1958, in David Marr, ed., *Patrick White: Letters* (Sydney: Random House Australia, 1994), 148.
6 For my discussion of the relationship between White's writing and his activism, see Brigid Rooney, *Literary Activists: Writer-Intellectuals and Australian Public Life* (St Lucia, Qld: University of Queensland Press, 2009).
7 For example John McLaren begins his review by saying 'Each successive novel of Patrick White comes as a familiar surprise. *A Fringe of Leaves* is no exception': 'Nature and Legend', *Overland* 65 (1976): 71–72 (71).
8 Leonie Kramer, 'A Woman's Life and Love', Review of *A Fringe of Leaves*, *Quadrant* 20 no. 11 (1976): 62–63. See also Suzanne Edgar, 'A Woman's Life and Love: A Reply to Leonie Kramer', *Quadrant* 21 no. 10 (October 1977): 69–71; Leonie Kramer, 'Patrick White's Kind of Woman', letter to editor, *Quadrant* 21 no. 11 (1977): 60; and Veronica Brady, who cites Kramer's earlier criticism of White (Kramer, 'Patrick White's Götterdämmerung', *Quadrant* 7 no. 3 (1973): 8–10) in her essay, '*A Fringe of Leaves*: Civilization by the Skin of Our Own Teeth', *Southerly* 37, no. 2 (1977): 123–40 (123).
9 Laurie Hergenhan borrows this phrase from Thomas Keneally, in Hergenhan, 'The City or the Desert: Patrick White's *A Fringe of Leaves*', *Unnatural Lives: Studies in Australian Fictions about Convicts from James Tucker to Patrick White* (St Lucia, Qld: University of Queensland Press, 1993), 151–66.

10 See for example Brady, 'Civilization' and Dennis Haskell, '"A Lady Only by Adoption" – Civilization in *A Fringe of Leaves*', *Southerly* 47, no. 4 (1987): 433–42.
11 John McLaren, 'Nature', 72; Elizabeth Perkins, 'Varieties of Courage', *LINQ* 5, no. 2 (1976): 91–98 (93).
12 Veronica Brady, 'A Properly Appointed Humanism: Australian Culture and the Aborigines in Patrick White's *A Fringe of Leaves*', *Westerly* 2 (June 1983): 61–68 (62).
13 The High Court of Australia's ruling on Mabo vs. Queensland No. 2 in 1992 overturned the legal fiction of *terra nullius* and found that native title could potentially survive colonization in some circumstances. Postcolonial criticism of White's novel, among others, as a white settler fantasy of indigeneity does extend further back than 1992, as seen in Terry Goldie's *Fear and Temptation: The Image of the Indigene in Canadian, Australian and New Zealand Literatures* (Kingston, Ontario: McGill-Queen's University Press, 1989); a cogent, 'post Mabo' analysis of the 'bankrupt topos' of the white Aboriginal figure in this and other white Australian novels can be found in Russell West Pavlov, '"White Aboriginals": White Australian Literary Responses to the Challenge of Indigenous Histories', in *Imaginary Antipodes: Essays on Contemporary Australian Literature and Culture* (Heidelberg, Germany: Winter Verlag, 2011), 71–86.
14 Brady, 'Properly': 67.
15 Simon During, *Patrick White* (Melbourne, Vic.: Oxford University Press, 1996), 11.
16 Kramer, 'A Woman's Life and Love', 62–63.
17 Guy Davidson, 'Displaying the Monster: Patrick White, Sexuality, Celebrity', *Australian Literary Studies* 25 no. 1 (May 2010): 1–18 (9).
18 Argued in different ways by, for example, Elena Ungari, in 'Patrick White's Sense of History in *A Fringe of Leaves*', *Australian Studies* 2 (2010), accessed 13 January 2013 online: http://www.nla.gov.au/openpublish/index.php/australian-studies/index; and Andrew Elfenbein, 'Narrating Australia: Competing Heroisms in *A Fringe of Leaves*', *Commonwealth Novel in English* 6 (1993): 39–49.
19 The relationship between White's writing and the closet is discussed, although with different overall emphases, by Simon During, *White*, 70–77; and by Guy Davidson, 'Monster'.
20 Andrew McCann, 'The Ethics of Abjection: Patrick White's *Riders in the Chariot*' *Australian Literary Studies* 18, no. 2 (1997): 145–55; West-Pavlov uses the word 'avatar' to describe Ellen Roxburgh (among other characters) as projections of the white settler self, 'White', 73, 86.
21 See Martin Ball, 'The Pleating of History: Weaving the Threads of Nationhood', *Cultural Studies Review* 11, no. 1 (March 2005): 158–73 (168–73).
22 Carolyn Bliss has discussed White's use of the conditional in *Patrick White's Fiction: The Paradox of Fortunate Failure* (London: Macmillan, 1986), 191: 'In every case the conditional puts the reader off balance and renders meaning problematical.'
23 'Metaphor', *Oxford English Dictionary*, accessed 13 January 2013 online: http://www.oed.com/.
24 As discussed by Peter Brooks, *Reading for the Plot: Design and Intention in Narrative* (Cambridge, MA: Harvard University Press, 1984), 3–23.
25 As implicated in notions of sensibility and sentiment in the development of literary systems in the eighteenth century: see John Brewer, 'Sentiment and Sensibility', *Cambridge Histories Online* (Cambridge, MA: Cambridge University Press, 2008), 35, accessed 8 April 2014 online: http://universitypublishingonline.org/cambridge/histories/chapter.jsf?bid=CBO9781139055970&cid=CBO9781139055970A006: 'The poetics

of sensibility depended upon the opening up of the private realm – interior feelings, emotional affect, intimate and familial friendship, the transactions of the home, the business of the closet, parlour, even bedroom – to public view.'
26 Laurie Hergenhan, 'City', 151–66.
27 Terry Eagleton writes of the sentimental as the new badge of an eighteenth-century bourgeoisie 'whose commercial ends seemed best guaranteed by social decorum and political tranquillity': 'The cult of sentiment was the feel-good factor of a successful mercantile nation [...] a social force as well as a state of mind.' Terry Eagleton, *Trouble with Strangers: A Study of Ethics* (Chichester: Wiley-Blackwell, 2009), 18. See also Terry Eagleton, *The Rape of Clarissa: Writing, Sexuality and Class Struggle in Samuel Richardson* (Oxford: Basil Blackwell, 1982).
28 James Chandler, 'The Languages of Sentiment', *Textual Practice* 22, no. 1 (2008): 21–39.
29 I have taken this phrase from 'Down Under', George Steiner's review of *A Fringe of Leaves* in the *New Yorker*, 23 May 1977, 131–32 (132).
30 Gluyas may derive from Old French 'Gleyve' meaning lance or spear, according to http://www.surnamedb.com/Surname/Gluyas, and compare with OED entry for 'glaive'; Roxburgh is a compound of hroc=rook; burgh=manor, and can be associated with book binding via the bibliophilic Roxburghe Club, accessed 8 April 2014 online: http://www.roxburgheclub.org.uk/history/.
31 Michel Foucault, 'Of Other Spaces' ['Des Espaces Autres', 1984], trans. Jay Miskowiec, *Diacritics* 16, no. 1 (Spring 1986): 22–7 (27).
32 Elizabeth A Povinelli, *The Cunning of Recognition* (Durham, NC: Duke University Press, 2002), 33, 178.
33 See Sweeting and Cochunis's discussion of the theatricality of wilderness spaces for emotive spectacle. Adam Sweeting and Thomas C. Cochunis, 'Performing the Wild: Rethinking Wilderness and Theatre Spaces', in *Beyond Nature Writing: Expanding the Boundaries of Ecocriticism*, ed K. Armbruster and K. R. Wallace (London: University Press of Virginia, 2001), 325–40 (326).
34 Patrick White, *Flaws in the Glass: A Self-Portrait* (London: Jonathan Cape, 1981).
35 Kramer, 'A Woman's Life and Love', 63; others who make the *Pygmalion* comparison include Robert McDowell *World Literature Today* 51, no. 2 (Spring 1977): 330–31 (330) and Elfenbein, 'Narrating': 42.
36 Jill Ward uses the phrase 'White's "Eliza"' in her review of the novel in *Critical Quarterly* 19, no. 3 (Autumn 1977): 77–81 (79).
37 See Monique Rooney, 'Voir Venir: The Future of Melodrama' (Keywords Section), *Australian Humanities Review* 54 (May 2013): 81–102 (accessed 8 April 2014 online: http://www.australianhumanitiesreview.org/archive/Issue-May-2013/rooney.html) for an illuminating discussion of melodrama's provenance and significance in light of Rousseau's *Pygmalion*, and also with reference to Peter Brooks, *The Melodramatic Imagination* (1976) and Paul de Man, *Allegories of Reading* (1979).
38 See Brigid Rooney, *Literary Activists: Writer-Intellectuals and Australian Public Life* (St Lucia, Qld: University of Queensland Press, 2009), 51.

Part IV
QUEER WHITE

Chapter 11

KNOCKABOUT WORLD: PATRICK WHITE, KENNETH WILLIAMS AND THE QUEER WORD

Ian Henderson

First Lady:
We're the knockabout girls of the piece!
Young Man:
I thought it was all knockabout.

Patrick White, *The Ham Funeral* (1948/1961)[1]

Hugh Paddick:
Ooh hello! I'm Julian and this is my friend Sandy!
Kenneth Williams:
Ooh hello, Mr Horne, oh lovely! Oh yes, how bona to vada your dolly old family-sized, new-improved eek again! What brings you trolling in here?

'Bona Advertising', *Round the Horne* (1968), BBC Radio[2]

Walked to Foyle's to get *The Living and the Dead* by the much-praised Patrick White. It's like reading something between T. S. Eliot and Henry James with an awful lot of Virginia Woolf thrown in. A rambling messy sort of writing with all the story impetus lost in 'philosophical' musings.

Kenneth Williams, Diary Entry, 1 June 1982[3]

I first read Patrick White in the windowless staffroom of the Greenwood Child Care Centre in North Sydney. It was 1992, White had been dead for almost two years. That hadn't stopped me during my daily rides around Centennial Park pausing outside the house where his partner Manoly Lascaris still lived in

Martin Road. The place retained a fascination for me as an auratic nexus of what Sir Les Paterson (played by Barry Humphries) called the Yartz; Martin Road was the national *salong*. But it was four years since I had dropped out of my Tasmanian undergraduate degree to go find myself in the city – by which I also mean coming out and immersing myself in the Sydney gay 'scene' – and only now was I gearing up for a return to serious study ... and not to any old place but to the University of Sydney. I figured White would somehow ready my soul. Here, by universal repute, was Great Writing, Big Themes, Difficult Art. Green wood indeed, I thought if I could handle that, I could handle anything.

I did know that White was 'homosexual' – he had 'come out' to the public at large with *Flaws in the Glass* (1981)[4] – and that he had lived as one half of Australia's most famous same-sex couple. But it did not occur to me to think of his writing, as I prepared to read it, in terms of his sexuality. Such approaches had been explicitly disavowed in lectures on E. M. Forster back in Hobart, and in the sexual politics of the day it seemed important not to box a writer into such a 'limiting' category. White himself had once expressed a similar attitude in a letter to Ingmar Björkstén in 1973: 'If I wanted to write a novel about homosexuals, I should have written it, but that is a theme which easily becomes sentimental and/or hysterical. It is, anyway, rather worn.'[5] Meanwhile, he represented in my mind the very opposite of the flamboyance I entered into in Sydney: a different way of 'being' homosexual ... serious, full of philosophy and high learning. (I was passé even then.[6]) In my three-hour break from the under twos – I accepted a split shift to facilitate swotting – I wandered up to Stanton Library and grabbed *A Fringe of Leaves* (1976).[7] Lucky chance! If instead I'd selected White's 'grey second novel', I might have been stopped in my tracks.[8] A decade earlier Kenneth Williams, the quintessentially British star of the *Carry On* films, had made just that mistake. Despite voracious reading habits and High Art taste, Williams dismissed *The Living and the Dead* (1941) as a 'rambling messy' amalgam of modernisms past.[9]

White himself might have deplored this novel in terms similar to Williams's. Re-reading it before republication in the last year of his life he concluded it 'should not have been written, and certainly not written when it was'.[10] It was also White's most closeted novel. That its protagonist Elyot Standish was homosexual was 'resolutely disguised from readers', as David Marr writes.[11] 'Had White been able to state Standish's predicament bluntly, the end of *The Living and the Dead* might have been the opening pages of a more profound novel.'[12] It is little wonder that the novel's 'muffled' depiction of homosexuality would not mitigate against Williams's dismissal of its copycat modernism.[13] He was himself in an extraordinary position in terms of his own public persona: celebrated for his portrayal of outrageously camp characters, but tortured by his own homosexuality, able only rarely to engage in sexual acts with another man, and never to experience a serious, long-term sexual relationship.

His loneliness, instead, was turned into writing. Williams, it emerged after his death in 1988, was an obsessive diarist.[14] In turn praising and excoriating his fellow performers, affording brilliant insight into London show business and accounting for the extraordinary range of his reading and his taste for high culture, he also committed his queer sexuality to the page; queer even in relation to the straightforward promiscuity of his friend, Joe Orton. The contrast then is between the outrageous camp of Williams's professional act and the hidden angst and seriousness of his character.[15]

Bringing Williams and White's writings into dialogue presents us with the latter's *oeuvre* as an artistic and life-affirming 'solution' to a historically contingent 'problem' of homosexuality. (I state the latter with the inevitable caveat that any 'solution' for White, as Elizabeth McMahon and Brigitta Olubas remind us, is rather a 'productive irresolution'.)[16] By this I mean the question of how to express artistically – here, in writing – a desiring 'situation' which is at once generative of personal and social insights yet, for many men of Williams and White's generation, personally shaming to admit in print, potentially restricting in terms of one's public appeal and socially precarious (even dangerous) to declare. The choices faced by both Williams and White include deploying coded forms of expression (which both writers enacted to varying degrees and in strikingly different ways), throwing down the gauntlet and 'coming out', or writing seriously – in Williams's case – only to himself. It is difficult not to read the latter as pharmakon: the seeming remedy which becomes a protracted suicide note.

This reading chimes with Marr's description of what *The Twyborn Affair* (1979) offered White:

> The prose of this late masterpiece has the sensuality of a great romantic novel, but it was White's peculiar genius to turn this expectation on its head: purity, not love and happiness, is the goal of Eudoxia Vatatzes, the jackeroo Eddie Twyborn and the brothel keeper Eadith Trist. That quest left White free to explore without self-pity the difficulties of his life as a homosexual: a man who saw himself cursed with unreason and a rebellious body who lived in exile wherever he settled.[17]

That last description captures Williams, also, but the conundrum appears to have carried him off. White by contrast came to acknowledge the centrality of sexuality to his art, but at precisely that moment he also stressed the 'knockabout' quality of his character, and by implication his writing. In a 1980 letter to Geoffrey Dutton, he notes: 'if I am anything of a writer it is through my homosexuality, which has given me additional insights, and through a *very strong vein of vulgarity*.'[18] So if, beyond the grave, Williams the personification of camp was revealed as a tortured diarist with serious intent, White the serious artist here exposes himself as a knockabout girl. Hence with the phrase 'beyond the grave' I want also to underscore how White's Big Themes might be discovered not only in the self-evidently serious intent of much of his writing but also in its comedy, campness, theatricality and vulgarity: in its 'knockabout' quality. Even White's final wish seemed to emphasise this point: graveless his ashes were scattered, as Marr notes, on one of the rubbish-strewn ponds of Centennial Park.[19]

In this way the comparison of White with Britain's campest comedian might be seen to follow through on a last request. And in forging ahead I am indebted to Elizabeth McMahon who sees in *The Twyborn Affair* a final explicit rendering of novelistic 'homographesis', one that, moreover, invites retrospective reassessment of White's entire oeuvre:[20]

> Up until this novel there appears to be a tacit contract between text and reader: the text will not insist on the specific terms of its claims to difference (which may unsettle the reader's homophobia and suggest distinctions within the category of the universal) if the reader agrees to acknowledge the universalist terms of its project (which validate this novel and shore up the validity of those previous). But what if the content and quality of this knowledge are already known? That White was a homosexual? That he has always written as/of the homosexual? That his writing is homographetic?[21]

The threat McMahon identifies in *The Twyborn Affair* is that the 'universal' themes expected of White's writing, and his work's representativeness of nation, attach now to the 'exceptional' character of Eddie Twyborn who 'is explicitly homosexual, a subjectivity that precludes national and representative status'.[22]

> [T]he text's lateness and queerness is doubly and reflexively troubling and the readership is as surely splintered and conflicted as the novel's protagonist. The accepted terms of a shared humanity are rendered unstable, requiring renegotiation of the contract between the text and the reading subject. Furthermore, this newly situated reader cannot return to the previous conception of a proper reader of White's fiction but reads across the oeuvre from this more contested but more vitalized perspective. This 'nonharmonious, nonserene tension' is 'a sort of deliberately unproductive productiveness'.[23]

In this McMahon hazards 'we may now be equipped with the frameworks with which to rise to the critical challenge of calibrating the minority terms of the universalist claims made in and by [White's] fiction'.[24] And so it is from a specific moment of queer encounter – on 1 June 1982 – between White's most closeted novel and Britain's most famous out-but-not-out reader that I would briefly essay one such calibration. Doing so moreover requires me (i) to jump White's critical context out of (Australian) national boundaries, connecting it to a much longer, cosmopolitan history, and (ii) to look beyond high European modernism for an explanation of White's idiosyncratic experimentation with language; to eschew momentarily precisely the comparisons drawn by Williams himself of the trick he turned at Foyles.

White's Language and Williams's Polari

Williams was a near contemporary – born 12 years after White, dying 2 years before him – but in so many ways he was a contrasting figure. His background was working class, and despite pretentions his professional and social life were bounded by English working-class culture and expectations. 'He could have straddled the world,' writes Christopher Stevens, but 'instead, he lived all his adult life in a series of apartments along the Euston and Marylebone Road'.[25] After a stint in the Combined Services Entertainment during the Second World War, he sought a career as a serious actor with not insignificant success before finding fame in revue, radio – *Hancock's Half Hour* (1955–58), *Beyond Our Ken* (1958–64), *Round the Horne* (1965–68) – television, and ultimately in the *Carry On* series of film comedies. His humour was broad, vulgar, packed with innuendo and hilarious: his is still the unmistakable voice of British camp from the mid to the late twentieth century. (Down in Tasmania where it was emulated in school-boy taunts I was deeply ashamed to hear it.)

Williams's diaries – and his colleagues' anecdotes – are filled with accounts of outrageous public behaviour on and off the stage/radio/screen, even if they also record political opinions, erudite references and '"philosophical" musings' of Williams's own.[26] His published diaries surprised readers with the latter. But on occasion Williams's quoting of his own speech reflects his mastery of another equally revealing mode of language, one of the spoken rather than the written word: Polari.[27]

Polari, as Paul Baker writes in a book preoccupied with Williams, is the 'lost language of gay men'.[28] Baker notes 'lexicographer, Eric Partridge, once referred to Polari as a "Cinderella among languages"' but prefers himself to think of it 'as one of the Ugly Sisters: brash, funny and with all the best lines in the show'.[29] Polari's comic potential was exploited by Hugh Paddick and Williams in the enormously popular 'Julian and Sandy' sketches, written by Barry Took and Marty Feldman and broadcast as part of BBC Radio's *Round the Horne* in the latter half of the 1960s.[30] Straight-man Kenneth Horne enters a shop or other place of work ('Bona Books', 'Bona Antiques', 'Bona Law' and so on) to be confronted with 'a pair of camp, out-of-work actors', who proceed to regale him in Polari.³¹ The sketches made Polari famous, recording it also for posterity in its dying days.

Several Polari words are still familiar to today's queer and even wider communities of the former British world: 'camp' (effeminate), 'fruit' (queen), 'bijou' (small but expensive-looking; a jewel), 'hoofer' (dancer), 'mince' (walk in an affected manner), 'trade' (sexual partner), 'zhoosh' (style up). Others are less recognisable – 'bona' (good), 'omi' (man), 'palone' (woman), 'omi-palone' (homosexual), 'lallies' (legs), 'vada' (to see), 'dolly' (nice), 'eek' (face), 'troll' (walk around) – particularly when combined into sentences. This is because, as Baker writes, Polari was the product 'of a number of converging subcultures over many decades'.³² Its roots were in criminal cant, the language of London's Molly houses, Parlyaree (the language of actors, 'circus people' and fairground showmen), 'Lingua Franca' used by sailors in the Mediterranean (a real composite language, not the linguistic term it inspired), Cockney rhyming slang and Romani.³³ It also featured Jewish words and the language of prostitutes with later influences from American Air Force slang and 1960s drug culture.³⁴

I am not arguing White deployed Polari. It was an overwhelmingly working-class phenomenon,³⁵ and if White's own connections to homosexual subculture like Williams's were centred on London, they were made from the opposite end of the town (as David Marr discusses in this book). So although White's voracious consumption of West End theatre and his first artistic success in revue mean he surely heard Polari spoken, he would be unlikely ever to have used it himself.³⁶ Nor would he be likely to identify it in Baker's terms even if he does reveal awareness of Polari habits when discussing the French translation of *The Twyborn Affair*:

> Eudoxia/Eddy would be thinking of himself as a boy while writing the diary. But you know how English homosexuals in talking about one another switch sometimes from masculine to feminine, satirically – I don't know whether you could make use of this habit […].³⁷

Similarly if the tone of speech and the names of White's own pantomime 'Ugly Sisters', Mrs Fauburgus and Mrs Goosgog in *The Ham Funeral* – bag ladies with social pretensions whose dialogue consists of covert attacks on each other's claims to gentility – *sound like* Polari, strictly they are not.³⁸ What I do want to suggest, however, is that the significance of language per se in White's work is illuminated by Polari. Polari after all was glaringly the product of transgressive histories: of itinerant lives and cosmopolitan contact over hundreds of years. Moreover, this comic, accumulative, allusive, contradictory, farcical and self-deprecatory language's heyday is co-extensive with modernism's history.³⁹ If

Polari is literary modernism's mouthy omi-palone sibling, language in White's work is Polari's zhooshy bitch.

White's favouring of characters with cosmopolitan and/or picaresque knockabout histories – real and invented – is well known. But he also celebrates those who, even if their lives are lived in the one place, commune with others through recognition of their own veins of vulgarity. My point is that the literary equivalent of this spirito-corporeal revelation is the incarnation of language per se in something like the form of Polari: as itself always already the bearer of strange patterns of physical human interaction that allude to universal mysteries of interconnectedness. In other words, Polari-esque Whitean language, printed on the page, is made of flesh: it is *the* solid mandala.[40] If White favours readers who can – momentarily – behold it in this way, this is both to provide over-literate elites with an inroad to vulgar insight *and* to forego the necessity of an extensive literary education for an understanding of his art.

Such a communion between reader and text is the true 'secret' of Whitean language, easily misinterpreted as an exclusionary gesture. On the contrary, it is supposed to be conveyed with the facility of one embodied Polari-speaker speaking to another (something more easily effected on the stage, perhaps explaining the greater currency of White's plays in contemporary Australia). Similarly, the occasional disconnect between the literary allusiveness of White's language and the simplicity of a protagonist whose inner lives are being described – something Simon During continues productively to abhor – is surely part of White's point.[41] The character her/himself would see language's corporeal mandala, not its precise meaning (whatever that is) nor its range of apparently high literary references (which are nonetheless another mandala). You do not need to comprehend to see language in this way. You only need to see its birth and life in human bodies.

Look, for example, at the (neglected) words White places at the centre of his 'Great Australian Emptiness': 'in which human teeth fall like autumn leaves, [and] the buttocks of cars grow hourly glassier'.[42] Bums and rotten teeth are also an exit trajectory from a world where 'food means cake and steak', to intercourse and evolution at the moment White's language descends into farcical near-incomprehensibility. So just as many listeners found Julian and Sandy hilarious without understanding a thing – Polari in word and tone becoming innuendo for innuendo per se – so too 'obscure' Whitean language alludes to language's obscurity per se, or rather to language's occulted carnal knowledge, its abject record of bumping bodies, its bearing – like dancing – the collective (divine) experience (wisdom) of our species.

This is in the end to see the verbal as sludge,[43] to render language as abject as a shrunken head, Eirene's 'talisman' in *The Hanging Garden*: a reduction of words to flesh *and* their augmentation to ancient, magical containers of all things.⁴⁴ It is in this way that White's word has belatedly become my own talismanic shrunken head, reaching out from beyond the grave joined – by its life as Polari's stuck-up sibling – to world history and deep time.

That White's second novel failed for Williams, and that White's work as a whole only gradually revealed its connections to homosexuality, can in itself be seen to reflect the quivering course of queer history in the British world. White appeared to reject and then explicitly to rediscover homosexuality as a thing to write 'through', while Polari and Williams's iconic status waned when effeminacy was eschewed by the gay activism of the 1970s, a situation later exacerbated by the AIDS crisis.⁴⁵ 'We shall be persecuted more and more since AIDS came to stay,' wrote White in 1984, *after* his 'vein of vulgarity' letter, 'A lot of screaming queens in [Sydney's] Oxford Street will not help the cause.'⁴⁶ In this moment as I write though it is queer activism and theory which have recovered camp and, for me, a new White, while maturity has enabled me to own Williams's humour and the identities it emboldens. Windowless no more, though the wood be more gnarled than green, I can follow McMahon's gaze, reading revelations from beyond the grave back through White's more youthful work. (No such luck was afforded Williams.)

Coda: Carnal Exegesis

Sure-footed theorists like McMahon and Andrew McCann, among others, have shown how quickly considerations of White's queerness shade into discussions of his social critique (often via abjection), the significance of 'solid' objects in his writing – their *thingness* – and language per se.⁴⁷ In conclusion, I want rather to use the *historical* parallel of Williams's Polari to consider some of the implications for the sacred and Patrick White of 'seeing' his language as so much desiring flesh. It is, in fact, little more than a fleeting queer version of Peter Beatson's starting point in *The Eye in the Mandala* (1976): 'Patrick White's central subject is not the Hidden God but the Incarnation. His novels are an attempt to inject new and urgent meaning into the almost moribund theological doctrine of "the Word made Flesh".'⁴⁸ But if Beatson teases out his interpretation of White's Word in terms of its logical relations to various theologies, I want rather to preserve its negative capability while rendering it a solid object – carnography – with a comic twist: carnography in drag; (in)carnography.

In this I share Lyn McCredden's conclusion that White practises his art of the word through seemingly opposed visions of language: as

> positively *generative*, pointing to, but potentially also embodying the power of the sacred, in its refusal to settle for the known, the fixed or the received and constructing new and restless processes of meaning-making which point to existence beyond signification [.]⁴⁹

However, I lay emphasis on White's 'embodying' the sacred *in* its body-ness whose generation of a beyond is towards a curious phylogenetic history (about which more in a moment). Similarly, Ashcroft's marvellous observation of language's 'horizons' and its relations to White's references to simple, solid objects might be modified for my purposes:

> [L]iterary language, while not limitless, opens up the constant presence of the horizon to the imagination. This means that literary language operates in excess of the boundaries on which ordinary language insists.[50]

Quoting Les Murray ('Everything except language/knows the meaning of existence'), Ashcroft makes the point that it 'is through language that the poet makes us aware of a form of knowledge beyond language', arguing further that this horizon is intimated *in* language 'by locating it in the presence of objects themselves', a quality he refers to as 'luminosity'.[51] Hence:

> One of the reasons tables and chairs will save us is their absolute irreducibility. Irreducibility is not essence, neither is it form – many forms of table exist. Rather it is the irreducibility of the everyday simplicity of its function that offers the horizon of the proximate. This is the paradox of objects: their very irreducibility makes them metaphoric. Their luminosity is the constant promise of something more.[52]

For my purposes, the word in White's novels – language per se – takes on the quality of his tables and chairs, indicative in the 'everyday simplicity of its function' of something beyond.

But this is its queer phylogenetic history; queer because, while pointing to those (as often as not abject) biological chains of existence through which it has developed as so many mother tongues, its production is equally generated through all those non-*pro*creative sexual conjunctions over time (all that 'sodomy' entails). This is Polari's 'secret': and one which is revealed not so much in Polari itself, which remains a language – albeit a joyous one – of the closet, as in a language which tarts up its abject past, lipstick on a decaying mouth, the carnal word in drag.[53]

And from here either faith is matter, something like Émile Durkheim's rendering of the sacred as the accumulation and dissemination of those insights into human life that demand more than a single lifetime's knowledge; or human meat is immanent with God (a matter of faith).[54] And if the former, it is a type of knowledge whose transmission is analogous to queer reproduction: along diagonal lines; *not* from heterosexual parent to child but rather from bad influences the world over. It is an aunt's story. The shadow of this rendering of the word is the blithering of an idiot, words as irreducible objects relayed only for their physical sound; its horizon the material interconnectivity of *all* 'things'.

Notes

1. Patrick White, *The Ham Funeral*, in Patrick White, *Collected Plays Volume One* (Sydney: Currency Press, 1985), 14–74 (42). The play was first written in 1948 but not performed until 1961.
2. Barry Took and Marty Feldman, 'Bona Advertising', *Round the Horne*, Series 4, Episode 13, BBC Radio, 19 May 1968.
3. Russell Davies, ed, *The Kenneth Williams Diaries* (London: HarperCollins, 1994), 655.
4. Patrick White, *Flaws in the Glass: A Self-Portrait* (London: Jonathan Cape, 1981).
5. Patrick White to Ingmar Björkstén, 27 May 1973, in David Marr, ed., *Patrick White Letters* (Sydney: Random House, 1994), 413.
6. Perhaps I was unconsciously influenced by White's notorious disparagement of the Gay and Lesbian Mardi Gras. See Patrick White to Jim Jenkins, 28 December 1984, in Marr, *Letters*, 600.
7. Patrick White, *A Fringe of Leaves* (London: Jonathan Cape, 1976).
8. David Marr refers to the novel as 'grey' in his chapter in this volume.
9. Patrick White, *The Living and the Dead* (London: George Routledge & Sons, 1941); Charles Lock provides a more sympathetic reading of White's debts to other modernists in Charles Lock, 'And Stood Breathing: Patrick White and the Novelistic Discourse of Modernism', *Cercles* 26 (2012), accessed 16 January 2015 online: http://www.cercles.com/n26/lock.pdf. See also Robyn Walton, 'Utopianism in Patrick White's *The Living and the Dead*, *Cercles*, 26 (2012), accessed 22 January 2015 online: http://www.cercles.com/n26/walton.pdf.
10. David Marr, *Patrick White: A Life* (Sydney: Random House, 1992), 639.
11. Marr, *Letters*, 21.
12. Marr, *Life*, 194.
13. Marr refers to Standish's sexuality as 'muffled'; Marr, *Life*, 194.
14. Of the 43 volumes of his diary, only 10–15 per cent has been published. Christopher Stevens claims with some justice that when all the volumes are published Williams will be 'appreciated as a combination of flamboyant diarist and ascetic scribe, part Pepys and part monk – in short, one of England's outstanding writers'. Christopher Stevens, *Born Brilliant: The Life of Kenneth Williams* (London: John Murray, 2010), 338.
15. Of the diaries Stevens writes: 'Nothing he had published [during his lifetime] hinted at their scope or depth; no one would have guessed that they comprised the most exhaustive and meticulous flaying of any recorded human life.' Stevens, *Born*, 335.
16. Elizabeth McMahon and Brigitta Olubas, 'Introduction', *Remembering Patrick White: Contemporary Critical Essays*, ed. Elizabeth McMahon and Brigitta Olubas (Amsterdam: Rodopi, 2010), vii–xv (xi). See also Andrew McCann's chapter in this volume.
17. Marr, *Letters*, 488; Patrick White, *The Twyborn Affair* (New York: Viking Press, 1979).
18. Patrick White to Geoffrey Dutton, 17 September 1980, in Marr, *Letters*, 537. Original emphasis.
19. 'Could it not be one of the beautiful lakes, Manoly had asked? It had to be this: heavy with lilies, with a scurf of plastic and broken glass along the bank.' Marr, *Life*, 644.

20 That is 'the particular writing and reading practices of homosexuality – as these have been identified by the queer-theorists Eve Kosofsky Sedgwick and Lee Edelman'. Elizabeth McMahon, 'The Lateness and Queerness of *The Twyborn Affair*: White's Farewell to the Novel' in McMahon and Olubas, *Remembering*, 77–94 (78).
21 McMahon, 'Lateness', 86–87.
22 McMahon, 'Lateness', 79.
23 McMahon, 'Lateness', 88. McMahon cites Edward Said, *On Late Style: Music and Literature Against the Grain* (New York: Pantheon, 2006), 7.
24 McMahon, 'Lateness', 13.
25 Stevens, *Born*, 1.
26 Referring to Williams's letters, Russell Davies writes: 'Williams possessed a naturally speculative mind which positively relished dealing with abstracts, and deserved far better training than it ever received. No doubt he was proud of mastering the arguments of certain writers, and sometimes quoted them from intent to impress, for he liked to be thought intelligent; but one cannot accuse him of picking out the easy bits. The syntax alone of some passages he cited, from Rilke, or Proust, or Isaiah Berlin, might defeat some readers.' Russell Davies, ed., *The Kenneth William Letters* (London: HarperCollins, 1994), xiii–xiv.
27 See Davies, *Diaries*, 50; and Paul Baker, *Polari: The Lost Language of Gay Men* (London: Routledge, 2002), 3.
28 Baker qualifies both the status of Polari as a 'language' and the category 'gay men' in his text.
29 Baker, *Polari*, 2.
30 *Round the Horne* 'regularly received audiences exceeding 15 million and is still recognised as one of the best-loved and most influential programmes in radio history': see British Broadcasting Corporation, *Round the Horne*, accessed 5 April 2014 online: http://www.bbc.co.uk/comedy/roundthehorne/. Baker claims Julian and Sandy were in turn the most popular of the show's many characters: Baker, *Polari*, 86.
31 Baker, *Polari*, 1.
32 Baker, *Polari*, 19.
33 Baker, *Polari*: cant, 20; Mollies, 22; actors and showmen, 23; Lingua Franca, 28; Cockney, 30; Romani, 31.
34 Baker, *Polari*, 33–35.
35 Baker, *Polari*, 73. That said Baker also writes: 'Personal reflections by Polari speakers reveal a perception that there were two dominant forms of Polari in London: one associated with show business and the West End, and the other with the more insular and stable East End community.' Baker, *Polari*, 70.
36 'Peter Plover's Party' was, as Marr puts it in his chapter, 'a monologue for a flibbertigibbet performed by Cyril Richard', but it worked by mocking 'the pretensions of the London upper middle classes' as Harris and Webby observe in their chapter in this volume, hardly Williams's realm.
37 Patrick White to Jean Lambert, 11 September 1980, in Marr, *Letters*, 535–36.
38 Harris's and Webby's chapter suggests their creation might be dated to White's revisions of the 1947 manuscript before its first production in 1961.
39 Baker gives it as the first seventy years of the twentieth century.
40 Patrick White, *The Solid Mandala: A Novel* (London: Eyre & Spottiswoode, 1966).
41 Simon During, 'Patrick White, Saul Bellow and the Problem of Literary Value', *Australian Literary Studies*, 27, no. 2 (2013): 1–18.

42 Patrick White, 'The Prodigal Son', *Australian Letters* 1, no. 3 (1958): 37–40.
43 'When so few Australian novelists can write prose at all, it is a great pity to see Mr. White, who shows on every page some touch of the born writer, deliberately choose as his medium this pretentious and illiterate verbal sludge.' A. D. Hope, 'The Bunyip Stages a Comeback', *Sydney Morning Herald*, 16 June 1956: 15.
44 Patrick White, *The Hanging Garden* (London: Jonathan Cape, 2012), 134–37, 154.
45 'As a result of new gay rights movements, there was a backlash against a number of established notions of gay identity which had developed over the 1950s and 1960s.' Baker, *Polari*, 115.
46 Patrick White to Jim Jenkins, 28 December 1984, in Marr, *Letters*, 600.
47 See in particular Andrew McCann, 'Decomposing Suburbia: Patrick White's Perversity', *Australian Literary Studies* 18, no. 4 (1998): 56–71.
48 Peter Beatson, *The Eye in the Mandala: Patrick White: A Vision of Man and God* (London: Paul Elek, 1976), 10.
49 Lyn McCredden, '"Splintering and Coalescing": Language and the Sacred in Patrick White's Novel's', in *Patrick White Centenary: The Legacy of a Prodigal Son*, eds Cynthia vanden Driesen and Bill Ashcroft (Cambridge: Cambridge Scholars Press), 43–62 (44).
50 Bill Ashcroft, 'The Horizon of Language', *Southerly* 74, no. 1 (2014): 12–35 (21).
51 Ashcroft, 'Horizon', 22–23.
52 Ashcroft, 'Horizon', 23.
53 See McCann, 'Perversity', 62–65.
54 Émile Durkheim, *The Elementary Forms of Religious Life* (1912), trans. Carol Cosman, ed Mark S. Cladis (Oxford: Oxford University Press, 2001).

Chapter 12

QUEERING SARSAPARILLA: PATRICK WHITE'S DEVIANT MODERNISM

Anouk Lang

Within the body of scholarly work on Patrick White, there is a considerable amount of research which locates him with respect to literary modernism, a relationship as contested as the term 'modernism' in itself. A somewhat smaller but still significant body of scholarship exists which understands him in the light of gender studies and queer theory.[1] It is surprising that these two bodies of work are almost entirely separate, given that within what has been termed 'the new modernist studies' the rise of queer modernisms as one of its emerging sub-fields has been concomitant with a period in which modernist scholars have begun to pay more attention to literary experimentation outside its traditional areas of geographical focus, Europe and the United States. As Heather Love remarks in a 2009 issue of *PMLA*, queer modernism may be simply another name for modernism: '[o]f all the forms of marginal modernism that have surfaced in the past couple of decades, queer modernism seems particularly likely to merge into modernism proper.'[2]

In this chapter, I want to argue the case for connecting these two ways of understanding White's work by seeking to place him within the field of queer modernist studies. This is neither to ignore previous work on White nor to make a claim to supersede it, but rather to situate it in a new frame. Two things are achieved by this move. First, it is a means of bringing White to greater prominence and giving him the visibility he deserves within the global conversations occurring around modernist studies outside Australian literature. Second, it is a way of enriching global modernist studies, whose idealistic proclamations of the need for scholars to expand their geographical horizons do not always match so well with, for example, the largely American and Eurocentric line-up of papers at the annual Modernist Studies Association conference.[3] This strategic approach is, of course, quite apart from the fact that White's work is extraordinarily rich in its inventiveness and its stylistic and syntactic transgressiveness, and therefore worthy of wider dissemination on its own merits as well.

As Laura Doan and Jan Garrity set out in their brief introduction to the field, much of the work on what they term 'modernisms queered' has to date involved a form of creative misreading – in Bonnie Zimmerman's phrase, 'perverse reading' – in order to uncover the latent content of a text.[4] By reading for 'what is not explicitly named but rather potentially inferred', representations of queerness can be extracted that may not be immediately apparent on the surface of the text.[5] Scholars including Brian Glavey, Laura Doyle and Sam See have performed readings of this type on writers who are already familiar names within the modernist canon such as Virginia Woolf, Gertrude Stein, Djuna Barnes, Willa Cather, D. H. Lawrence, Dorothy Richardson and Langston Hughes.[6] In the work of these writers, 'homoerotic desire is often refracted or produced through a specific practice of dissimulation [and] the sign of the queer is almost nowhere figured mimetically'.[7] However, a significant distinction between these authors and White is that he *does* figure queer lives and desires mimetically. His representational interventions and innovations should be seen as all the more remarkable as they do not remain in an indirect and covert mode but – especially in the works written after the late 1970s[8] – bring non-normative sexualities and gender roles into the foreground of the narrative. This is exemplified by *The Twyborn Affair* (1979), as these three descriptions of the same character illustrate:

> Swathed in its translucent cocoon sat the two figures [Eudoxia and Vatatzes], side by side on a stool as austere as the brass lamp, the man's back rigid and admonitory, the woman's form narrower, more sinuous, but no less dedicated, wearing what could have passed for a habit in grey-to-silver luminous silk, the long trailers of sleeves drifting in the wake of the music the two performers were dashing off.[9]

> [Eddie] was walking stiffly, his bearing tentative for a man, holding with Gothic hand against his chest the book he had been, or intended, reading. He was certainly not 'pot-bellied', and his well-covered skull, the hair of a cut to suggest an army officer, should have exempted him from accusations of hairiness by those who supported Marg's theory. (*Twyborn* 135)

> Mauve was [Eadith's] colour when in full panoply. While following a timeless fashion, she dressed with extravagant thought. Strangers stared, barbarians commented aloud, and small boys hooted at her in the street, but those who knew her, patrons and those she patronised, ended by accepting with sentimental affection the more baroque aspects of her self-indulgence: the encrustations of amethysts and diamonds, the swanning plumes, her make-up poetic as opposed to fashionable or naturalistic. (*Twyborn* 310)

Moreover, White's location in Australia – and the effect of his simultaneous alienation from, and fascination with, specifically Australian variants of modernity – means that he has a wider relevance for modernist studies in more dimensions than his queerness. He works over many of the most prominent concerns to have animated work in modernist studies in recent years: in addition to its consistent foregrounding of the manifest inadequacies of language and its fiercely satirical interrogations of social norms and niceties that stand in the way of authentic human contact, White's work is acutely attentive to the currents of transnational energy that pulse through the modern world and to the way these shape the subjectivities of individuals and artists who experience them in postcolonial contexts. As Doan and Garrity point out, more work is needed on the ways that queer modernist writing is inflected by issues around race, nation, imperialism and class, and these are all categories which find expression in White's writing.

At the outset though it is worth setting out what is meant by the term 'queer modernisms' and what it might mean in the context of the argument I am making here. As a critical enterprise, queer studies attends to the erotics of same-sex attraction, but it is also concerned, among other things, with unfixing gender identities from hierarchized relations that are represented as 'natural' and with destabilising the concept of a unitary self. Its connections with modernist studies lie in a shared resistance to fixity, a disregard for boundaries and a fascination with the transgressive, marginal and liminal as well as attentiveness to the experiences of exile and alienation.[10] As Colleen Lamos observes, the concept of a queer modernism itself resists definition against a putative 'straight' counterpart: 'there is not, on the one hand, a "homosexual" modernism and, on the other hand, a "heterosexual" modernism but a single literary corpus that is torn in various ways by the scission between these (supposedly) incongruent longings.'[11] Scholars of queer modernism have pointed to ways in which both form and content can be queered, seeing the textual instabilities of modernist artefacts for instance as representative of the fragmentation of the self and subjectivity.[12] Brian Glavey offers an illustration of this in relation to Djuna Barnes's *Nightwood* (1936) where a refusal of formal unity for fragmentation applies both to the aesthetic form of the novel and to the self represented within it.[13]

An additional zone where modernist aesthetics meet queer aesthetics is the quality of codedness and covertness referred to earlier. As Doan and Garrity point out, the formal techniques of modernism match the 'characteristic circumspection, encodedness and strategic undecidability' of queer identities.[14] This description chimes with White's writing, though as already noted the queer elements in his work become less coded and more overt the further he gets into his oeuvre. One early work in which they are treated at length is *The Aunt's Story* (1948).[15] Here, the fact that the central protagonist – whose very name, Theodora Goodman, suggests gender ambiguity – evades feminine stereotypes, both in her physical appearance and in her narrative trajectory, which is emphatically away from marriage and closure, is a central part of what makes her a visionary character. Reading this novel in the latter decades of the twentieth century, when White began to come to prominence as a writer, a critical reader might initially see this as a text whose primary intertextual interlocutors are feminist writers engaged in interrogating and critiquing the restrictive nature of women's roles as daughters, mothers, wives and carers. Reading it in the first decades of the twenty-first century through the lens of LGBT scholarship, however, a reader might notice the insistence with which the novel's foregrounding of these restrictions is embedded in a critique of heterosexuality and bourgeois social conventions more broadly. This can be seen in the episode early in the novel when Theodora is quizzed by her brother-in-law Frank Parrott about what she intends to do now her mother has died and she has come into some money:

> 'And what are your plans, Theo?' asked Frank.
> 'I shall probably go away.'
> 'Good heavens,' said Fanny, 'where?'
> Freedom was still a blunt weapon. Theodora did not answer, because she did not know.
> 'Anywhere. Or everywhere,' she said at last. 'Except that the world is large.'
> Theodora, blushed Fanny, is quite, quite mad. [...] [Theodora] touched with the ball of the handkerchief the humiliating fringe of her moustache. Perhaps, after all, she would remain the victim of family approval and her upper lip.
> 'Theo is quite right,' she heard the thick voice of Frank [...] 'She may even find a husband,' the voice continued. 'At her age. With her money. In Europe,' it said. (*Aunt* 17–18)

Theodora, interpreted even by her sister as 'quite, quite mad', has her queerness figured in explicitly gendered terms through her moustache, and it is significant that this otherness is linked to geographic distance. While in Australia her eccentricity has left her unmarriageable and marginalized, it is implied that in exotic Europe someone may want this queer fish for a wife, though even then only with the added motivation of her wealth. It is the burden of the novel to show how Theodora's path from rural Australia to the *jardin éxotique* of the Hotel du Midi and finally to the eroded landscape of New Mexico – away from not only the conventions of marriage but also narrative closure – is not the journey of a madwoman who has passed up her final chance of bourgeois respectability, but the more difficult and worthwhile quest of a visionary in pursuit of authentic being. This doubleness of interpretation is an example of the codedness to which Doan and Garrity refer and is attested to by the lack of critical attention to Theodora's gender transgressions.[16]

I turn now to White's representational play with gender roles. In the last several decades, a great deal of attention has been paid by modernist scholars to the study of gender roles and the way they function as one of the axes along which the encounter with modernity can be charted. This is particularly the case with the reconfigurations of women's roles, especially in relation to literary and cultural production.[17] As Douglas Mao and Rebecca Walkowitz put it, 'Integral to modernism's development were phenomena such as women's growing independence and the predominantly female audience for genres legible as 'bad' by middlebrow and modernist alike.'[18] There is, however, much less work on *masculinity* and modernism. This is one of the most obvious areas in which White's work is of interest: his work continually interrogates, often comically, what it means to be a man – as well as a woman – and how to live within the constraints that society and institutions impose on individuals in gendered ways. For White exploring the individual's relation to modernity is closely bound up with interrogating why certain gender identities are the way they are, and what kind of alternatives exist.

Androgyny is one alternative presented, for example, through the character of Arthur Brown in *The Solid Mandala* (1966).[19] Arthur, a kind of holy fool, draws all elements around him into a unity, including the male and female sides of his character, but the world around him – including his brother Waldo whose own gender conflict emerges through the shame he feels for his desire to cross-dress – finds it difficult to accept this:

> [Arthur] liked also to fiddle with the butter and the bread, finally even to make them himself. Dad was disgusted. He said it was nothing for a boy, but Mother approved, as though Arthur's head for figures was not enough; she seemed to be trying to turn the butter-making and bread-baking into some sort of solemn rites.
>
> On occasions when he asked whether he too might squeeze the butter or knead the dough, Waldo was told: 'No. That's something for Arthur. He has a particular gift for it.'
>
> Once Arthur, who was watching the buttermilk gush out from between his fingers, laughed and said: 'It's my vocation, isn't it, Mother?' (*Solid* 35)

Often, a character's queerness emerges from the fluidity of their identities, gendered and otherwise. Arthur Brown slides in and out of male and female personas, while Hurtle Duffield in *The Vivisector* (1970) becomes unmoored from his family identity, and Laura Trevelyan slips between corporeal reality and incorporeal mysticism as she visits Voss in spirit in the desert. All of these figures are in some way visionaries, rejected by society but granted insights denied to others. Those characters that White's novels consign to the lower end of the moral spectrum are, conversely, those who enforce distinctions on others. The Bonners, for whom adherence to the norms of bourgeois heterosexual respectability is a continual preoccupation, are distressed by Laura's oddness and refusal to fit in, while the demonic Mrs Flack and Mrs Jolley in *Riders in the Chariot* (1961) patrol the boundaries of acceptable social behaviour with alacrity. Most explicitly, Don Prowse attacks Eddie Twyborn for being 'a fuckun queen,' in a scene in which the text makes clear that Prowse's rage at, and rape of, Eddie is a displacement of his own internalised homophobia and the threat it poses to his marriage: '"A queen! A queen! A fuckun queen!" Sobbing as though it was his wife Kath walking out on him' (*Twyborn* 284).

This destabilising of gender identity is, I would argue, at the heart of White's attempt to discursively refigure what it means to be modern and to live in the modern world, as so much modernist literature does. While gender performativity is foregrounded through figures such as Eudoxia/Eddie/Eadith Twyborn and Alex Gray in *Memoirs of Many in One* (1986), a more submerged critique of normative gender roles and the institutions that produce them can be found in novels such as *Voss* (1957) which are ostensibly focussed on quite different thematics. Laura Trevelyan, the figure who is perhaps most strongly valorised within the text's moral economy and to whom a measure of transcendence is granted, struggles against the constraints imposed by Victorian mores and manners of Sydney society and the expectations of her family. This novel also showcases and parodies other instances of masculinity in the figures of Turner, Judd and Boyle, offering the more androgynous figures of Palfreyman and Le Mesurier as alternatives. The novel continually foregrounds how normative gender roles are just that – roles – and offers examples of women whose social position has trapped them within these as well: Belle Bonner the virginal *ingénue*, Mrs Bonner the fussy mother. In *The Aunt's Story* – a text whose very title evokes the limited number of roles available to unmarried older women – Theodora Goodman must wait until her mother dies to move beyond the constraints that familial duty and gendered expectations have placed her under, and begin her travels and her construction of what Tim Anderson has described as the creation of a shell against Australian reality.[20] Other critiques of the structures through which gender roles are produced and maintained can be found in *Riders in the Chariot*, through Mary Hare's memories of her painful family history which are figured through the irreversible decay of her house, and the misery of Ruth Godbold's life of drudgery, childbearing and domestic violence. If modernity engenders forces against which individuals find themselves pitted – for

Mordecai Himmelfarb the Holocaust and for Alf Dubbo the racist paternalism of the white Christian minister who takes him from his Aboriginal mother and abuses him – it also represents opportunities for women to become themselves and to evade, to an extent, gendered social expectations. For Eden Standish in *The Living and the Dead* (1941), this occurs in the realm of the political; for Felicity Bannister in 'The Night The Prowler' (1974), the sexual; for Theodora Goodman, the geographical and the imaginative.

Seeing White's characters in these terms also leads us to take a fresh look at the disdain for Australian suburbia and normalcy that his writings exude. If this aspect of his work has in the past been taken as an Anglophilic snobbery for 'the Great Australian Emptiness' we can also perform one of the 'creative misreadings' mentioned earlier, in order to understand it in terms of the critique posed to heteronormativity:

> In all directions stretched the Great Australian Emptiness, in which the mind is the least of possessions, in which the rich man is the important man, in which the schoolmaster and the journalist rule what intellectual roost there is, in which beautiful youths and girls stare at life through blind blue eyes, in which human teeth fall like autumn leaves, the buttocks of cars grow hourly glassier, food means cake and steak, muscles prevail, and the march of material ugliness does not raise a quiver from the average nerves.[21]

It is worth reproducing the wider context of what is probably White's most frequently quoted phrase to draw attention to the gender codes through which it is articulated. The despised professions of journalist and schoolmaster are male ones, as is the role of 'rich man'; the 'beautiful youths' are paired with 'girls' but both are 'blind'; while 'buttocks' and 'muscles' conjure up a masculine semiotic economy. There is, in other words, a gendered dimension to White representing ugliness and beauty in such a way as to paint it as – among its other failings – very heteronormative: the only place for women is where they appear paired with 'beautiful youth'.

This coded queer intervention into suburban stultification speaks to, and extends, critiques of heteronormative structures and conventional gender roles posed by other modernist writers and artists around the globe, such as Jose Garcia Villa whose critique of marriage among working-class Filipinos and its ill effects on both men and women is elaborated by Cruz.[22] Villa's work presents America as the promised land of modernity which offers a range of enticing alternatives to the marriage and the endless cycle of procreation. Work such as this casts White's familiar gesture of contempt for Australian society in a new light. Like Villa with respect to the Philippines, he sees Australia as the locus of stifling and deadening conventions which can be evaded by moving to more cosmopolitan locations: London, Europe and America. This is the *reverse* move to that made by those metropolitan modernists such as D. H. Lawrence who sought aesthetic rejuvenation and symbols of the new in the world beyond Europe and North America's borders. The view of modernism as, in Stephen Slemon's words, a 'wholesale appropriation and refiguration of non-Western artistic and cultural practices by a society utterly committed to the preservation of its traditional prerogatives for gender, race and class privilege' is thus complicated by bringing these so-called marginal modernists into a more central position and seeing the relative valencies of the imperial centre and the so-called periphery shift.[23]

There are, of course, many women writers in Australia writing in the same period as White who offer their own interventions and critiques of women's experiences and the social constraints that structure them, albeit in a realist mode. Where White goes further, I argue, is in linking his gender critique to an extended commentary on suburban normalcy in such a way as to foreground the relationship between heteronormativity and the social and historical co-ordinates of Australian life. His challenge to conventional Australian masculinity can be seen in terms of an intervention into the dominant currents of Australian writing at the time that he was writing: the nationalist and realist tradition. I have argued elsewhere that literary modernism in Australian was shaped by the strenuous efforts of writers and critics to differentiate it from cultural nationalism, and it is a truism within Australian literature that literary expressions of nationalism occurred predominantly in a realist mode.[24] Seen in this light, White's queerness appears not as incidental to his modernism but rather as integral to it, as one of the central ways he articulates his flavour of Australian modernism is through a critique of the kind of normative sexuality and masculinity intrinsic to the representation of the mythic male figures populating narratives of national origin such as the explorer, the jackeroo and the squatter. Moreover, given the way this aspect of his work has troubled critics, who for many years passed over it entirely, it can be seen as a representational innovation that goes further than the experiments in style and syntax being explored by canonical Anglo-American modernists. It is also possible to read an aesthetic of queerness in White's use of symbolism: as Simon During points out White's earlier work operates according to a closeted aesthetic, where transcendental meaning is located in the obscured figuration of symbols and in epiphanies of veiled meaning.[25] If modernist scholarship has only in the last several decades begun to piece together how integral changing gender roles and expectations were to the multiple revolutions of modernity, White deserves a much more prominent place within its canons for getting there a great deal earlier.

What I have sought to show here is that White's exploration and deconstruction of normative gender identities should not be kept in a separate body of scholarship – research into LBGT texts and writers – but needs to be integrated into work that will situate him within broader global currents of literary modernism and thereby bring him into dialogue with other writers who are coming to prominence through attention to what has been termed geomodernism. This term is described by Laura Doyle as denoting a range of innovative aesthetic projects from around the globe that are 'self-consciously "placed" [...] in the modern/colonial network, exactly so as to reconfigure the subjectivities within its geopolitical systems'.[26] If writers in the urban centres of Europe and America gave eloquent expression to the alienating and confounding experience that it was to live in the rapidly modernising world of the early to mid-twentieth century, those at the putative margins of empire not only faced similar ruptures but also underwent the cultural dislocations of being 'out of place', a condition which involved being constantly confronted with the gap between authorized cultural production from elsewhere and the inferiority of home-grown art and culture. Writers who were similarly 'out of place' within the binaries structuring masculine and feminine identities, and/or the conventions of compulsory heterosexuality, had a parallel estrangement from the everyday world of human interaction, where every social transaction is intricately enmeshed with reigning gender norms. White's critique of gender roles, then, can be understood as lying at the heart of his exploration of the travails of modern subjects as they negotiate the perilous terrain of modernity. More than this, however, his recurrent use of the trope of the outsider points to a highly charged aesthetic of alienation, in which cosmopolitanism, geographical mobility, ethnic hybridity and gender fluidity are all figured through each other. Doyle and Winkiel point to this 'outsiderness' as something observable in other geomodernist texts, which evince a powerful self-consciousness about their relationship to other texts, giving 'a sense of speaking from outside or inside or both at once, of orienting toward and away from the metropole, of existing somewhere between belonging and dispersion'.[27] The figure who exemplifies this ambiguity the most clearly is Eudoxia/Eddie/Eadith Twyborn, who moves not only between genders but also between nations – – Greece, the Australian outback and London – though it emerges through other characters such as Himmelfarb and Voss, and there is also an obvious parallel with White's own life and extensive travels.

Guy Davidson has argued that White's relationship to fame 'exhibits contradictions or tensions that are, up to a point, entirely characteristic of the Anglophone literary modernism of which he was a belated proponent'.[28] In his efforts to distance himself from what Davidson terms celebrity, and which I would characterize as middlebrow (and thus degraded) culture, White can be closely aligned with a number of canonical modernist figures, among them Woolf and Joyce. Davidson's argument offers something of a parallel with the case I have sought to build here, given that I have been arguing that White's queerness should put him front and centre of mainstream modernist studies, while Davidson suggests another angle from which to view White as an important figure within a literary movement whose major critics have all but ignored him. These forms of marginality are, as Davidson points out, connected: as White did not have to rely on the income from his writings for a living, he did not come under the same pressures from mass literary tastes as were faced by writers such as Hemingway and Mailer, and therefore did not face the problem of needing to adopt an overtly masculine image as protection against the apparent femininity of the mass literary sphere.[29]

It is ironic that it is White's very marginality – both in terms of sexuality and in terms of national belonging – that makes him a candidate for renewed interest by mainstream modernist studies. Attending to the places where his queer aesthetic reveals cracks in the edifice on which gender hierarchies and the epistemological dichotomies flowing from them are built makes his writing seem even more radical than his mastery of technical innovation. Moreover, the ease with which his dismantling of the categories on which gendered identities are built can be connected to other constituent elements of identity such as national identity, geographical location and ethnicity – of increasing interest to scholars of modernist studies – is further evidence that attention to White in global modernist studies is long overdue. In his fascination with, in Doan and Garrity's phrase, 'the transgressive, marginal, and liminal', White's work points to the importance of attending to the intersection of modernist studies and queer studies. This extends beyond simply a thematic focus on gender and sexuality: to destabilise them as categories is to uncover the ways in which they are discursively constructed. By deconstructing the hierarchical oppositions that structure their relations, White's work challenges our understanding of modernity itself by inviting us to rethink where we draw the line between normative and non-normative, natural and unnatural and dominant and deviant.

Notes

1   For studies which examine White's work in terms of literary modernism, see, for example, Robert Dixon, 'Reading Patrick White's *The Aunt's Story*', *Metaphor* 2 (2013): 5–13 and Simon During, *Patrick White* (Oxford: Oxford University Press, 1996). For studies which discuss him in relation to queer theory and gender studies, see, for example, Valerie Beattie, 'In Other Words: Homosexual Desire in the Novels of Patrick White', PhD, University of Edinburgh, 1996, accessed 12 April 2014 online: https://www.era.lib.ed.ac.uk/handle/1842/7388; Gregory Graham-Smith, 'Against the Androgyne as Humanist He(te)ro: Patrick White's Queering of the Platonic Myth', in *Remembering Patrick White: Contemporary Critical Essays*, ed by Elizabeth McMahon and Brigitta Olubas

(Amsterdam: Rodopi, 2010), 163–79 and Cheryl Stobie, 'Re-Constructing the "Outcast-Initiate" in Patrick White's *The Twyborn Affair*', *Current Writing: Text and Reception in Southern Africa* 25, no. 1 (2013): 52–65, accessed 12 April 2014 online: http://www.tandfonline.com/doi/abs/10.1080/1013929X.2013.795757#.U0t8nVfDWIg. Scholars who do connect these two bodies of work include Andrew McCann, 'Decomposing Suburbia: Patrick White's Perversity', *Australian Literary Studies* 18, no. 4 (1998): 56–71 and Guy Davidson, 'Displaying the Monster: Patrick White, Sexuality, Celebrity', *Australian Literary Studies* 25, no. 1 (2010): 1–18, both of whom remark on the way that critical work on White for a long time passed over the queer dimension to his writing.

2 Heather Love, 'Introduction: Modernisms at Night', *PMLA* 124, no. 3 (2009): 744–48 (744).
3 As an example of how the structural forces shaping scholarship at a global level mitigate against the inclusion of Antipodean scholars and therefore material, the first Modernist Studies Association conference ever planned for a location outside Europe or North America – New Zealand in 2009 – had to be relocated back to North America when it became clear that the cost of the airfare would preclude the attendance of most of the delegates who were coming from the United States.
4 Laura Doan and Jan Garrity, 'Modernism Queered' in *A Companion to Modernist Literature and Culture*, ed David Bradshaw and Kevin J. H. Dettmar (Oxford: Blackwell, 2007), 542–50; Bonnie Zimmerman, 'Seeing, Reading, Knowing: The Lesbian Appropriation of Literature' in *(En)Gendering Knowledge: Feminists in Academe*, ed Joan E. Hartman and Ellen Messer-Davidow (Knoxville: University of Tennessee Press, 1991), 85–99.
5 Doan and Garrity, 'Modernism'.
6 Brian Glavey, 'Dazzling Estrangement: Modernism, Queer Ekphrasis, and the Spatial Form of Nightwood', *PMLA* 124, no. 3 (2009): 749–63; Laura Doyle, 'Transnational History at Our Backs: A Long View of Larsen, Woolf, and Queer Racial Subjectivity in Atlantic Modernism', *Modernism/Modernity* 13, no. 3 (2006): 531–59; and Sam See 'The Comedy of Nature: Darwinian Feminism in Virginia Woolf's Between the Acts', *Modernism/Modernity* 17, no. 3 (2010): 639–67.
7 Doan and Garrity, 'Modernism'.
8 Prior to the publication of *Twyborn*, White had not publicly acknowledged his homosexuality though his sexual orientation and long-term relationship with Manoly Lascaris had been an open secret for many years. See Davidson, 'Displaying', 4–5.
9 Patrick White, *The Twyborn Affair* (London: Jonathan Cape, 1979), 17. Subsequent references to this edition will be included in parentheses in the text.
10 Doan and Garrity, 'Modernism'.
11 Colleen Lamos, 'Queer Conjunctions in Modernism', in *Gender in Modernism: New Geographies, Complex Intersections*, ed Bonnie Kime Scott (Urbana: University of Illinois Press, 2007), 336–43 (336–37).
12 See Cassandra L. Langer, 'Reframing Romaine Brooks' Heroic Queer Modernism', *Journal of Lesbian Studies* 14, no. 2 (2010): 140–53.
13 Glavey, 'Dazzling', 254.
14 Doan and Garrity, 'Modernism'.
15 Patrick White, *The Aunt's Story* (London: Vintage, 1994). Subsequent references to this edition will be included in parentheses in the text.
16 As Elizabeth McMahon observes, one of the effects of the explicit treatment of homosexual identity in *The Twyborn Affair* is that it alerts us to the closeted writing practices of White's earlier novels. McMahon, 'The Lateness and Queerness of *The Twyborn Affair*: White's Farewell to the Novel', in McMahon and Olubas, eds, *Remembering*, 77–91 (86).

17 See, for example, Shari Benstock, *Women of the Left Bank: Paris, 1900–1940* (London: Virago, 1987) and Bonnie Kime Scott, ed., *The Gender of Modernism* (Bloomington: Indiana University Press, 1990); and in the Australian context Maryanne Dever, *Wallflowers and Witches: Women and Culture in Australia, 1910–1945* (St. Lucia, QLD: University of Queensland Press, 1994); Drusilla Modjeska, *Exiles at Home: Australian Women Writers 1925–1945* (Sydney: Angus & Robertson, 1981) and Angela Woollacott, *To Try Her Fortune in London: Australian Women, Colonialism, and Modernity* (Oxford: Oxford University Press, 2001). For a discussion of how and why modernist studies has moved away from aesthetic features as a defining feature of modernist literature towards the engagement with modernity, see Susan Stanford Friedman, 'Planetarity: Musing Modernist Studies', *Modernism/Modernity* 17, no. 3 (2010): 471–99.
18 Douglas Mao and Rebecca L. Walkowitz, 'Introduction: Modernisms Bad and New' in *Bad Modernisms*, eds, Douglas Mao and Rebecca L. Walkowitz (Durham, NC: Duke University Press, 2006), 1–17 (8).
19 Patrick White, *The Solid Mandala* (London: Eyre & Spottiswoode, 1966). Subsequent references to this edition will be included in parentheses in the text.
20 Tim Armstrong, 'Patrick White: Modernist Impact, Critical Futures', IEC Conference, King's College London and the Institute of English Studies, University of London, 23–25 June 2010.
21 Patrick White, 'The Prodigal Son', *Australian Letters* 1, no. 3 (1958): 37–40.
22 Denise Cruz, 'Jose Garcia Villa's Collection of "Others": Irreconcilabilities of a Queer Transpacific Modernism', *Modern Fiction Studies* 55, no. 1 (2009): 11–41.
23 Stephen Slemon, 'Modernism's Last Post', *ARIEL: A Review of International English Literature* 20, no. 4 (1989): 3–17 (3).
24 Anouk Lang, 'Modernity in Practice: A Comparative View of the Cultural Dynamics of Modernist Literary Production in Australia and Canada', *Canadian Literature* 209 (2011): 48–65.
25 During, *White*, 73–4, quoted in Davidson, 'Displaying', 5.
26 Doyle, 'Transnational', 556.
27 Laura Doyle and Laura Winkiel, 'Introduction: The Global Horizons of Modernism' in *Geomodernisms: Race, Modernism, Modernity*, eds, Laura Doyle and Laura Winkiel (Bloomington: Indiana University Press, 2005), 1–14 (4).
28 Davidson, 'Displaying', 1.
29 Davidson, 'Displaying', 3.

CONTRIBUTORS

Margaret Harris is Challis Professor of English Literature Emerita at the University of Sydney. With Elizabeth Webby she led the Australian Research Council Discovery Project 'Patrick White in the Twenty-First Century'. She is a leading expert on the work of modernists Christina Stead and Patrick White as well as on the life and work of George Eliot.

Ian Henderson is the Director of the Menzies Centre for Australian Studies, King's College London and lectures in the College's Department of English Language and Literature. He has published widely on nineteenth- and twentieth-century Australian literature and has particular interests in Australian modernism, representations of Aboriginality in Australian colonial and Victorian writing and the history of reading.

Ivor Indyk is founding editor and publisher of HEAT magazine and the award-winning Giramondo book imprint, and Whitlam Professor in the Writing and Society Research Centre at the University of Western Sydney. A critic, essayist and reviewer, he has written a monograph on David Malouf for Oxford University Press, and essays on many aspects of Australian literature, art, architecture and literary publishing. His current research projects include the history of Australian literary publishing and the expression of emotion in Australian literature, with a particular interest in Patrick White, and such concepts as awkwardness, shyness, embarrassment and wonder.

Gail Jones is Professor in Writing in the Writing and Society Research Centre at the University of Western Sydney. Acclaimed both as a cultural theorist and as a novelist/short-story writer, she is the author of two short-story collections, and the novels *Black Mirror*, *Sixty Lights*, *Dreams of Speaking*, *Sorry*, and *Five Bells*. Shortlisted three times for the Miles Franklin Award, her prizes include the WA Premier's Award for Fiction, the Nita B. Kibble Award, the Steele Rudd Award, the Age Book of the Year Award, the Adelaide Festival Award for Fiction and the ASAL Gold Medal. She has also been shortlisted for international awards, including the IMPAC and the Prix Femina. Her fiction has been translated into nine languages. Before coming to UWS, she worked in the Department of English at the University of Western Australia.

Anouk Lang is a Lecturer in Digital Humanities at the University of Edinburgh. She works on twentieth- and twenty-first-century literatures, Anglophone modernist writing, postcolonial studies and digital humanities. She is the editor of *From Codex to Hypertext: Reading at the Turn of the Twenty-First Century* (2012).

Georgina Loveridge is a PhD candidate in the Department of English at the University of Sydney. Her thesis, '"A Landscape Without Figures": Patrick White's Poetics of Space', examines White's construction of space, both real and imagined, within the domestic, national and transnational frames.

David Marr is one of Australia's best-known writers and also one of the country's most respected journalists. He is the author of *Patrick White: A Life* (1991) which won the Age Book of the Year and the NSW Premier's Literary Award for Non-Fiction. It remains one of the most cited texts in other studies of Patrick White. He also edited *Patrick White Letters* (1994). He is also the author of *Dark Victory* (2004), *Power Trip: The Political Journey of Kevin Rudd* (2010) and a number of high-impact *Quarterly Essays* on Australia culture and politics.

Andrew McCann is an Associate Professor of English at Dartmouth College. He is the author of *Popular Literature, Authorship and the Occult in Late Victorian Britain* (2014), *Marcus Clarke's Bohemia: Literature and Modernity in Colonial Melbourne* (2004) and *Cultural Politics in the 1790s: Literature, Radicalism and the Public Sphere* (1999). His book on Christos Tsiolkas, *Christos Tsiolkas and the Fiction of Critique: Politics, Obscenity, Celebrity*, is due in 2015.

Mark McKenna is a Senior Research Fellow in History at the University of Sydney. From 2000 till 2005, he was an ARC QEII Fellow in History at the Australian National University. He is the author of *An Eye for Eternity, The Life of Manning Clark* (2011), winner of the 2012 Prime Minister's Prize for Non Fiction, the Douglas Stewart Prize for Non-Fiction (2012 NSW Premier's Literary Award), the Nettie Palmer Prize for Non-Fiction (2011 Victorian Premier's Literary Awards), the 2011 Queensland Premier's Literary Awards Prize for Non-Fiction and the 2011 South Australian Premier's Award for Non-Fiction.

Angus Nicholls holds a joint appointment as Senior Lecturer in the Departments of German and Comparative Literature, and is Chair of the Department of Comparative Literature, at Queen Mary University of London. He is the author of *Goethe's Concept of the Daemonic* (2006) and *Myth and the Human Sciences: Hans Blumenberg's Theory of Myth* (2015). He co-edits the journals *History of the Human Sciences* and *Publications of the English Goethe Society*.

Brigid Rooney is a Senior Lecturer in the Australian Literature Program in the Department of English at the University of Sydney. Her book, *Literary Activists: Writer-Intellectuals and Australian Public Life* (University of Queensland Press, 2009) includes Patrick White among its case studies. She is the author of numerous journal articles and scholarly book chapters on twentieth-century and contemporary Australian fictional works and is co-editor with Robert Dixon of *Scenes of Reading: Is Australian Literature a World Literature?* (Australian Scholarly Press, 2013).

Elizabeth Webby is an Emeritus Professor at the University of Sydney, where she held the Chair of Australian Literature from 1990 to 2007. One of the first scholars to publish on White's drama, she is a specialist in colonial literary culture and Australian women's writing. With Margaret Harris, she led the Australian Research Council Discovery Project 'Patrick White in the Twenty-First Century'.

Aruna Wittmann is completing her doctorate in psychoanalysis and postcolonial studies at King's College London. She works as a freelance contributor to the *TLS*, and teaches on the Literature and Psychoanalysis course at King's.

INDEX

Aboriginal peoples and cultures 3, 7, 9, 42, 44, 49, 50–51, 82, 87, 118, 128n8, 164–66, 173, 176n13, 199
Adelaide Festival 4, 6, 18
Adorno, Theodor 9, 119, 126–27, 155, 157–58, 160
allegory 82, 119, 121–27, 140n2, 157, 163–64, 165
Armfield, Neil 4–5
Astley, Thea 73

Bakhtin, Mikhail 163, 167, 170
Beaton, Cecil 24
Bellow, Saul 1, 152
Benjamin, Walter 9, 125, 127, 140n2, 157–60, 161–62n22
Blake, William 83, 109–11
'Bolaro' (sheep station in New South Wales) 110
Boyd, Arthur 81, 82–85
Bunce, Daniel 36–37, 40–41, 45, 47–48

Campbell, David 86
Centennial Park (Sydney) 5, 77, 86, 91–92, 94, 120, 122, 181, 184; *see also* Martin Road
Cervantes, Miguel de 20
Chaucer, Geoffrey 20
Chekhov, Anton 159
Chisholm, Alec 29, 44–49
Christesen, Clem 82
Clark, Manning 8, 78, 81–98
Clark, T. J. 9, 156–57, 158, 160
Coombs, Nugget 90

Dark, Eleanor 87
Dobell, William 87

'Dogwoods' (house in Castle Hill) 24, 110
Dostoevsky, Fyodor 22, 86, 89, 159
Durkheim, Émile 189
During, Simon 1–4, 9, 10n1, 25, 106, 117–18, 152, 166, 187, 200
Dutton, Geoffrey 68, 71, 76, 78, 88, 95, 183

Eliot, T. S. 2, 124, 133, 181
epiphany 6, 98, 122, 127, 133, 143, 200
'Everage, Dame Edna' 125
expressionists, German 70, 132
Eyre & Spottiswoode 77

Faulkner, William 139
Foucault, Michel 170–71, 173
Freud, Sigmund 142, 150, 152

Gandhi, Mahatma 20
Goethe, Johann Wolfgang von 41, 46, 51, 53, 56–57, 93, 95, 97
Golding, William 95

Harris, Max 82
homosexuality 3–4, 6, 7, 71, 93, 107, 149–51, 182–89, 195, 203–4n16; *see also* queerness
Hope, A. D. 86–87, 91, 114n21
Huebsch, Ben 47, 72–73, 77
Humphries, Barry 84–85, 88–89, 125, 182; *see also* 'Everage, Dame Edna'

Indigenous peoples and cultures 43; *see also* Aboriginal peoples and cultures

James, Henry 159, 181
Jonathan Cape 77–78
Joyce, James 72, 124, 139, 201
Jung, Carl 3, 50, 93–94, 100n27, 107

Labor party and government, Australian 3, 87–91, 105; *see also* Whitlam, Gough
Lascaris, Manoly 5, 19, 23–24, 31, 74–77, 79, 91, 97–98, 114n29, 181
Lawler, Ray 27
Lawrence, D. H. 20, 83, 87, 194, 200
Leichhardt, Ludwig 29, 35–57, 81
letters: *see* White, Patrick: letters
Liberal party and government, Australian 90
'Lulworth' (house in Sydney) 110–11

Malouf, David 17, 19, 32, 88, 94–95, 127n4
Mansfield, Katherine 20
Martin Road (Sydney) 24, 86–87, 95, 97–98, 110, 181–82
Marr, David 5, 7, 17–18, 19, 24, 30–31, 48–49, 67–79, 102, 164, 182–84, 186; biography of White by 2, 24, 29, 32, 69, 79, 107; edition of White's letters 2–3, 21, 23–24
McAuley, James 81, 87
McQueen, Humphrey 93–95
Meale, Richard 19
Milton, John 109–11
Mobbs, Barbara 5, 17, 24, 30–31
modernism and modernist aesthetics 3, 8–10, 32, 42, 52, 70–71, 112, 113n16, 124–25, 127, 132–33, 136, 141, 151–52, 155–60, 167, 168, 182, 185, 186–87, 190n9, 193–95, 197–202; *see also names of specific authors*
Murdoch, Iris 95
Murray, Les 189

Nietzsche, Friedrich 41, 51–52, 56–57
Nolan, Sidney 8, 19, 81–87, 92, 95, 97–98, 164

Palmer, Vance 82
Paterson, A. B. ('Banjo') 46, 110–11
Polari 9–10, 185–89, 191n35
Politzer, L. L. 36–37, **39**, 45, 52, 54–56
postcolonial theory/approaches 3, 4, 8–9, 117–19, 128n8, 156, 164–65, 170, 175, 176n13, 195

queerness 4, 6–7, 9–10, 119, 181–90, 193–202, 202–3n1; *see also* homosexuality

Racine, Jean 70
republic, movement for an Australian 3, 89–90, 93, 107

Sarsaparilla 4, 67, 75, 77, 85
Schreber, Paul 9, 141–52
Sharman, Jim 19
Stephensen, P. R. 82
Stow, Randolph 23
Strindberg, August 70, 93
symbols and symbolism 8, 107, 108–9, 111, 121, 123–27, 146, 159–60, 171, 200

Tucker, Albert 82, 156

Wedekind, Frank 70
White, Patrick: activism 2, 5, 21, 92–93, 165; biography of: *see under* Marr, David; bodies in 1, 4, 8, 28, 69, 104, 118, 134, 135–36, 145–46, 157, 158–59, 169–70, 172, 183, 187, 189; diary 19–22, 33n12; expressionism in 8–9, 131–40; gender identities in 26, 122, 124, 151, 172, 186, 193–202; *see also* homosexuality *and* queerness; imagism in 156, 158–59; letters, published *see under* Marr, David; letters, unpublished 23, 35, 67–69, 74, 76, 77–78; mysticism in 48–51, 61n50, 91–92, 107, 112, 122–23, 156–57, 159, 160, 167, 173, 198; Nobel prize, award of 67, 89, 97, 105, 165; notebooks 7, 18–29, 35–36, **37**, **38**, 39–40, 45, 48–49, 51–53, **54**, 55–57, 69; sacred, and the 1–8, 117–27, 188–89; suburbia, treatment of 3, 4, 85, 89, 120–21, 125, 158, 199–200; time, treatment of 9, 112, 117–18, 121, 132, 139, 157, 159–60, 163–75, 188
works: *Aunt's Story, The* 9, 18, 20, 22, 25, 30, 70, 74, 81, 104, 141, 143–47, 148, 151–52, 155–60, 196–97, 198; *Big Toys* 4, 20; *Cheery Soul, A* 4; *Cockatoos, The* 25; see also White, Patrick: "Night the Prowler, The"; *Eye of the Storm, The* (film) 6, 18; *Eye of the Storm, The* (novel) 5, 20, 24, 29, 77, 89, 106, 110, 131–40; *Flaws in the Glass* 2, 8, 21, 23, 25, 48, 73, 95, 101–12, 173, 182; *Fringe of Leaves, A* 9, 20,

23, 29, 57n3, 61n50, 119, 163–75, 182; *Ham Funeral, The* 4, 6, 18, 20, 26–28, 70, 75–76, 164–65, 181, 186; *Hanging Garden, The* 6, 18, 29–31, 187; *Happy Valley* 18, 20, 31–32, 71–72; *Living and the Dead, The* 9, 20, 70, 73, 77, 181–82, 199; *Memoirs of Many in One* 2, 8, 19, 20, 23, 25, 30, 32, 107, 120–27, 198; *Netherwood* 20, 23; *Night on Bald Mountain* 76; "Night the Prowler, The" 121–22, 199; *Peter Plover's Party* 26, 70, 191n36; plays and dramatic writing 2, 4–5, 7, 11n19, 12–13n36, 18–20, 23, 25–28, 32, 69–70, 72, 187; *see also under names of specific plays*; "Prodigal Son, The" 22, 67, 103, 114n18; *Riders in the Chariot* 3–4, 20, 27, 29, 57n3, 61n50, 77, 85, 89, 106–7, 119, 132, 134, 163–64, 198–99; *Season at Sarsaparilla, The* 4, 18, 76; *Shepherd on the Rocks* 23, 70; short stories 20, 23–24; *see also Cockatoos, The*; *Signal Driver* 23; *Solid Mandala, The* 20, 89, 106, 110, 137, 152, 197; *Tree of Man, The* 27, 75, 77, 81, 83–85, 91, 110, 114n21, 119, 122; *Twyborn Affair, The* 2, 6, 20, 30, 68, 73–74, 77–78, 107, 110, 119, 120, 132, 138, 183–84, 186, 194, 198, 201; *Vivisector, The* 6, 18, 20, 23, 28–29, 78, 89, 107, 134, 197; *Voss* (novel) 3, 7, 18–19, 20, 22, 24, 29, 32, 35–57, 74–75, 81–82, 83, 85–87, 110, 119, 127, 132, 134, 165, 197–98, 201; *Voss* (opera) 19

Whitlam, Gough 87–88, 89–91, 105, 165
Williams, Kenneth 9, 181, 182–86, 188, 190n14, 191n26
Woolf, Virginia 181, 194, 201
Wright, Judith 127n4

Yeats, William Butler 133, 157, 159

www.ingramcontent.com/pod-product-compliance
Lightning Source LLC
Chambersburg PA
CBHW021827300426
44114CB00009BA/355